Louis H. Gunnemann

EXPANDED BY

Charles Shelby Rooks

The Shaping of the United Church of Christ

An essay in

the History of

American

Christianity

United Church Press

Cleveland, Ohio

United Church Press, Cleveland, Ohio 44115
Copyright © 1977 by United Church Press
Foreword and chapter 9 copyright © 1999 by United Church Press

All rights reserved. Published 1999

Printed in the United States of America on acid-free paper

04 03 02 01   5 4 3 2

ISBN 0-8298-1345-4

CONTENTS

FOREWORD

Louis Gunnemann produced two notable books that contribute greatly to accumulated knowledge about the formation of the United Church of Christ in 1957 and its ecclesial existence since then. *The Shaping of the United Church of Christ* identifies the circumstances leading to the merger of the Congregational and Christian Churches and the Evangelical and Reformed Church, and analyzes the first twenty years of the union. *United and Uniting: The Meaning of an Ecclesial Journey* views the merger through the lens of the ecumenical vision that created the UCC. This shaping image is carried forward to 1987. Gunnemann's books should be read together. They then become extraordinary handbooks for comprehending the complex history of an ecumenical pioneer.

When the existing store of copies of *The Shaping of the United Church of Christ* was depleted a couple of years ago, grave concern was expressed by some in the church about the loss of virtually the only available text for educating seminary students, confirmation and membership classes, and UCC members generally about their denomination. Further, no similar document exists that enables far-flung ecumenical comrades and the secular world to comprehend UCC intricacies. In agreeing to reprint the book, United Church Press concluded that its value might be enhanced by adding a chapter bringing the UCC story to the forty-year mark. My varied and widespread volunteer and staff involvements in UCC national activities during its first thirty-five years led to the request that I provide the update.

The added chapter, chapter 9, is very different from the rest of the book. Gunnemann gave *Shaping* the subtitle "An Essay in the History of American Christianity." It covers the first two decades of the story comprehensively and with skill. Because the book could not be greatly enlarged, the challenge I faced was to decide what to include from a lifetime of memories, anecdotes, and relationships. In the end, chapter 9 contains my subjective reflections on five themes of what I am convinced is a wonderfully melodious and hopeful song the UCC has sung enthusiastically throughout its life, and especially between 1977 and 1998. If others hear that music also, my purpose is well served.

7

Faithful to the rest of the book, the addition focuses entirely upon the national setting of the United Church of Christ, and especially the General Synods. Obviously, there is much to record about other scenes of the United Church of Christ and even about national entities besides the General Synod. That auspicious task is better suited to other circumstances, however. One final word: readers should be aware that the notes to chapter 9 have unusual importance. In fact, they are an index to significant documentation which could not be included in the text. Those who wish to expand their knowledge about the UCC should find them very helpful.

I became acquainted with Professor Gunnemann only during the last decade of his life. I wish I had known that privilege and joy much sooner. Louis Gunnemann was an impressively warm, sensitive, and perceptive human being, and an excellent scholar. I count it an exceptionally high honor to be associated, even in this small way, with his important historical resources about the United Church of Christ.

CHARLES SHELBY ROOKS

PREFACE

In this book I have examined the historical development of the United Church of Christ to show *why* it came into being and *what* it means as a denominational organization. The shaping of this denomination belongs to the general reconfiguration of American church life that took place in the middle decades of the twentieth century. Concern about Christian unity was widespread even as denominations increased in size and adopted more secular models of organization. New polity issues emerged as the churches sought to devise institutional structures expressive of a new sense of mission in the world.

A study of the shaping of the United Church of Christ becomes, therefore, a study of the major formative influences in American denominational development in this period. It is of special interest, however, for the United Church itself since this young denomination's leadership is beginning to pass to second-generation members. Within the next decade the original vision of the architects of the union will have receded almost completely from the view of those who must carry the responsibility for the church's work and life. In this respect the church's history has a crucial role: to inform coming generations of the intentions and concerns of their spiritual forebears in the formation of this denomination.

My research in this enterprise was stimulated by two circumstances. In the first place, as a seminary teacher responsible for classes in United Church history and polity, I was acutely aware of the difficulty of directing students to source materials. In the second place, my own reading brought me to Hanns Peter Keiling's *Die Entstehung der "United Church of Christ" (USA)*, a doctoral dissertation published in 1969 by Lettner-Verlag of Berlin. This book, bearing the subtitle *Fallstudie einer Kirchenunion unter Berücksichtigung des Problems der Ortsgemeinde*, raised questions for me which could be answered only by tracing the historical development of the United Church within the context of the American religious and social milieu in that period.

I am indebted to Dr. Keiling for even more than the stimulation provided by his thesis. Through his detailed bibliography I learned of the location of many primary source materials which otherwise would have involved a longer and tedious process. *The Formation of the United Church of Christ (U.S.A.): A*

9

Bibliography by Hanns Peter Keiling has been published by the Clifford E. Barbour Library at Pittsburgh Theological Seminary. His American advisor, Prof. Ford Lewis Battles, directed me to the library of the World Council of Churches in Geneva, Switzerland, where Dr. Keiling had deposited a carefully cataloged collection of materials.

Historical research, however, is much like detective work. One clue led to another, and I found myself driven to examine sources that turned up in surprising places. The references for chapters 1 through 4 give indication of the range. For later chapters I relied chiefly upon secondary sources since a vast body of research has been done in that subject area.

For the sake of readers I want to comment on the plan of the book. At the very beginning of my research I had decided to spend minimal time on the lengthy period of negotiations, controversy, and debate that led to the union. It quickly became clear, however, that it is impossible to understand the United Church apart from the critical years between 1937 and 1957, preceding the union. The plan of the book then emerged as follows: a descriptive account of the birth of the idea and its eventual fulfillment in the union, followed by an analysis of the formative years from 1957 to 1975, and finally an examination of the forces leading to the union as exhibited in the uniting communions. Some readers may wish to begin, after reading the Introduction, by turning to chapter 5 first. Then chapters 1 through 4 take on a significance that can be enhanced by reading chapters 6 through 8.

Through the years of research and writing I have felt "surrounded by a great cloud of witnesses." Since my own years in the ministry encompass the story of the United Church to this date, I have known or had contact with hundreds of men and women who were deeply involved in the formation of this church. So many of them contributed so much! Each one deserved to be named. I had finally to make the hard decision not to fill the pages with names. Omitting them has been a burden for me, but I trust that readers will give thanks to God for the unnamed dedicated people whose works are written on every page. Some names were needed, of course.

An enterprise of this kind places the writer in unlimited indebtedness to many people. I do hope that all who have helped me, whether named or not, will feel some ownership in this book. It could not have been written without the help given by United Church congregations and individuals in the Indiana-Kentucky Conference, especially Immanuel Church of Lafayette where I served as pastor, and by individuals in Wisconsin, Minnesota, and Iowa. Dayton Hultgren, president of United Theological Seminary, and Harry Bredeweg, minister of the Indiana-Kentucky Conference, tapped the interest and dedication of those people to provide the necessary funds for research.

Four colleagues in teaching and ministry have given invaluable assistance: Thomas C. Campbell, Sheldon E. Mackey, and William M. Thompson have read the manuscript with great care and have provided most helpful comments. Paul L. Hammer has assisted me with some especially difficult German translation. Other colleagues, particularly those who have served with me on the faculty of United Theological Seminary of the Twin Cities, have done more than they will ever know by their genuine and encouraging friendship.

The courtesies and assistance given so freely by library staff people provokes within me not only gratitude but genuine admiration and respect for their professional competence. I have benefited immeasurably from the services given by the staff members of the libraries and archives at United Theological Seminary, New Brighton, Minnesota; the World Council of Churches in Geneva, Switzerland; Eden Theological Seminary of Webster Groves, Missouri; The Congregational Library in Boston, Massachusetts; Lancaster Theological Seminary, Lancaster, Pennsylvania; and the George Arents Research Library at Syracuse University, Syracuse, New York. In addition, I am indebted to Howard E. Spragg and Wesley A. Hotchkiss of the United Church Board for Homeland Ministries for their help in locating materials of the American Missionary Association and of the late Truman B. Douglass; to conference ministers throughout the country who sent interpretive materials from their offices; to David Colwell for materials relating to the work of the Commission on Christian Unity and Ecumenical Study and Service; and to Myra Vaughn, of Elk Mound, Wisconsin, for her resources in Wisconsin Congregational history. From this vast amount of material I learned much even though I could not directly use all items.

Conversations with Joseph H. Evans, J. Martin Bailey, Charles H. Lockyear, David M. Stowe, Reuben A. Sheares, Everett C. Parker, and William K. Newman, all officers in the denomination's organization, led me to sources of invaluable information and gave me much needed insights. James E. Wagner and Ben M. Herbster helped me find focus in some confusing areas.

The encouragement and assistance given by the staff of the United Church Press account for the completion of the project, a project that I hope will be of value to all who are interested in the ongoing institutional formation of the church.

To my wife, Johanna Menke Gunnemann, who has been both companion and coworker in the entire effort, I shall forever be happily in debt. Not only did she assist in the research, type and retype the manuscript, and correct many stylistic infelicities, but with perception and insight she listened patiently to my interminable discourses on the many issues and fascinating discoveries we made. Her love has been, as always, sustaining.

Louis H. Gunnemann
United Theological Seminary of the Twin Cities
New Brighton, Minnesota

INTRODUCTION

Christian unity, if it is to have meaning for those who affirm it, requires symbolic expression in events and institutions that are recognizable in the wider Christian community. The birth of the United Church of Christ, celebrated June 25, 1957, provided both the event and the institution for members of the Congregational Christian Churches and the Evangelical and Reformed Church who for nearly twenty years had labored to be responsible to the vision of unity that is shared by all who confess Christ as Lord. When the delegates comprising the Uniting General Synod gathered in the Cleveland Music Hall to formalize and implement the covenant of union adopted by the merging communions eight years earlier, they were joined by fraternal representatives of Christian bodies from around the world as a demonstration of the place this church union had in the growing movement of Christian unity.[1] They interpreted the event as "a special witness in this day, . . . and of dedication to the broadening and deepening of God's Kingdom in and among all men."[2]

Other observers assessed the meaning of the event from different perspectives. Looking ahead, Reinhold Niebuhr claimed the formation of the United Church of Christ would be "a landmark in American Religious history." In words that were prophetic he affirmed that the union "offers a particularly vivid example of the kind of mutual invigoration which is proceeding in the whole range of American Protestant pluralism, and it offers some hope of order out of what is chaotic in that pluralism."[3]

Less prophetically, but with a sense of the distinctiveness of the event, *The Christian Century,* an independent ecumenical journal, editorialized:

We believe the emergence of the United Church of Christ will stand as a milestone in our spiritual history when occurrences far more sensational have been forgotten. . . . The radical significance of the event in Cleveland was that in it American Protestantism turned a corner. A trend that had run in one direction for 300 years was reversed.[4]

Many other church leaders in America, as well as in Europe and Asia, took notice in a like refrain of the formation of the United Church of Christ. While it is possible to dismiss the rhetoric and hyperbole used to signal religious developments in the 1950s as meaningless, it is clear that this union produced rather high expectations in many segments of the Protestant community. The account in the following pages is an attempt to assess developments in succeeding years in relation to those interpretations and expectations. The perspectives employed in this writing, however, are radically different from those used by observers twenty years ago, for in the 1950s few church leaders and religious thinkers could anticipate the wrenching developments that lay just over the horizon in the 1960s.

Church life in the period following World War II and the Korean War exhibited little or no awareness of the upheavals ahead. Church expansion, often parallel to the increase of the population and frequently exceeding it in growth rate, entered a boom period both in membership and in church-building. A "religious revival" seemed evident not only in churches filled with worshipers but also in the favorable nods given by public officials and secular organizations to religious practices generally. The voluntary support of religious institutions was considered a responsibility not only of adherents to particular religious faiths but of the society as well. The decade of the Fifties ended with 69 percent of the nation's people listed as church-affiliated, up from 43 percent in 1910 and at a level not reached again. In 1957 Evangelist Billy Graham's New York Crusade yielded $2,500,000 income and 56,767 decisions for Christ. Religion in general was good business.

Church union in such circumstances seemed to be guaranteed a successful future. In a time of resurgent religious interest the merging of smaller denominational units into larger organizations was seen as a reasonable way to increase denominational effectiveness. It is probably fair to say that the concern for *Christian unity,* which received so much attention in the three previous decades, was subtly transformed into a concern for *church unity* in response to the organizational opportunities offered to denominations by burgeoning religious activity. Commitment to Christian unity in the Fifties provided the religious language by which church unity as a goal could transcend the mundane objectives of denominational development. In other words, the institutional response of religious denominations to the opportunities presented by widespread religious interest in a time of increasing population arose from mixed motives. That response was couched in somewhat traditional religious terms, but it was also significantly energized by a pervasive self-confidence in organizational capability. The new United Church of Christ came to birth in such a time; but who could have comprehended in 1957 that this new denomination was to "inherit a moral and social revolution" in the Sixties?

Discomfiting signs of a very different future received minimal attention as the delegates to the uniting synod went about their business of sealing the union and designing procedures to implement it. Religious language, the "in-house" vocabulary of the church, was quite expectedly dominant. And quite properly it was used to interpret the meaning of the occasion within the ongoing stream of the church's life in a Christian era. Exceptions to this prevailing tone showed themselves in two brief addresses at the synod. Ray Gibbons, speaking for Christian social action, described the "new frontier" of the church as "moral and social," identifying the critical points in the family, the community, education, the economy, mass communication, political life, race relations, international affairs, and in the issue of freedom.[5] Truman B. Douglass, on the same occasion, declared: "I have said that a major peril that the Church faces in its mission in America is that its conspicuous successes will obscure the view of its failures." He went on to say that a major failure of the church had to do with those outside the church who are concerned about the meaning of life, who want to be taken seriously as persons; "this unsatisfied need to be taken seriously is one of the most terrifying signs of what has been called the annihilation of man."[6]

In 1957 there were portents of the turbulent Sixties that did penetrate slowly into the consciousness of Americans who were filling the churches in those days. To what extent this contributed to an uneasiness for which church activity was a compensation will always be a matter of speculation. The religious activity of an affluent society tends toward a false optimism and a general disregard of irritating concerns. No one in the nation, however, could escape the anxieties produced by the growing fury of the Cold War as it moved inexorably toward the critical point in the Cuban Missile Crisis. Further, in communities all through the South the implications of the Supreme Court's desegregation order of 1954 were being weighed and resistance was developing. When this came to a head in an event at Central High School in Little Rock, Arkansas, as school opened in the autumn of 1957, the nation knew that the long-unresolved issue of racial inequity would require continuous public attention. Nevertheless, at that point neither the architects of the new denomination nor the supporting constituencies had any intimation of the radical impact the issues behind these developments were to have on church life in the ensuing decades.

Social and religious upheavals had a multifaceted effect upon all the denominations of the nation in the years following the optimistic Fifties, but in a distinctive way for the new United Church of Christ. The ink was barely dry upon the new constitution and bylaws, drafted in the last biennium of the decade and adopted in 1960, before the denomination was plunged into a time that tested the vision and commitment of all who had "dreamed dreams and seen visions" of what the new church organization might be. As a result, the United Church of Christ was shaped in ways that no one could have foreseen when the denomination was brought to birth. Conceived as a new form of church organization to overcome the inhibiting elements of traditional polities, the United Church had little time to refine and tune its organization before dealing with issues that tested every aspect of its institutional structure. As a consequence, the first two decades of the life of the United Church provide a

15

revealing case study of the reconfiguration of American church life produced, on the one hand, by social circumstance and, on the other hand, by distinctive internal spiritual forces characteristic of Christian churches in the midtwentieth century.

These internal spiritual forces of particular church bodies bring to every new stage of development the determinative characteristics of their histories, which are woven together within the whole fabric of Christendom. At the same time they show the conditioning influence of societal circumstance. The histories of the Congregational Christian Churches and the Evangelical and Reformed Church exhibit these elements in denominational formation on the scene of American Christianity. Three of these factors are of special importance for understanding the United Church in relation to the ongoing religious life of the nation.

The first derives from the impact of the concern for Christian unity upon denominational structures in American church life. That concern, which gained remarkable momentum in the first half of the twentieth century, resulted in many proposals for union between 1910 and 1960. Fifteen of these eventuated in actual denominational mergers.[7] One of them brought the Evangelical and Reformed Church together with the Congregational Christian Churches to form the United Church of Christ. Within the movement for Christian unity this union created widespread interest because of the different strands of theology and church polity represented in the uniting bodies. Calvinian, Lutheran, Wesleyan, Zwinglian, and left-wing theological perspectives are not only indicated in the historical development of these bodies but are clearly identifiable in the congregations of the United Church today. Congregational and presbyterial ways of organizing church life, frequently in conflict in American churches, were sufficiently modified so as to settle comfortably with each other as new perceptions of church organization developed. The concern for and commitment to unity, particularly prominent in the first half of the twentieth century, has important rootage in the two bodies that came together.

The second shaping element in American church life exhibited in the uniting bodies is the revolution in religious organizations in the early and midtwentieth century.[8] Marked by increasing bureaucratization and secularization, church organizations tended to lose touch with their faith bases. Theological orientation and organizational principles were separated as religious denominations sought to meet an expanding population, an increasingly complex society, and a growing urbanization. Traditional principles of church organization had been based upon theological premises. A church's polity, or form of government, usually expressed a particular perspective on the doctrine of the church. The organizational revolution in American social structures led denominations to subordinate church government to organizational development considered essential to the viability of the church as a voluntary association. The de-emphasis of such polity

16

considerations was characteristic of most denominations in that period as a matter of default, and in the formation of the United Church this tendency had important repercussions on American church life. As the denominational structure evolved the implications of this choice became increasingly clear, especially in the decade of the Sixties.

A third shaping element in American church life that can be identified in the merging groups which formed the United Church of Christ was a shifting accent in cultural and religious pluralism. Ecumenism was heightening the realities of religious pluralism even as economic developments sharpened the realities of cultural pluralism. From early days in the settlement of the country, ethnic and national groupings had been reflected in denominational differentiation. As the melting pot worked, however, ethnic/religious differences lost their meaning for the maintenance of denominational distinctions and made church bodies more receptive to ecumenical responsibilities. This is reflected in the United Church of Christ, which combines the Germanic-background Evangelical and Reformed Church with the predominantly Anglo-Saxon Congregational Christian Churches. Moreover, the increasing secularity of the culture tended to call denominational "distinctions" into question.

Closely related to the pluralism of national origins is that of racial pluralism. An ever-increasing Black population, combined with growing numbers of Orientals, had made the reality of pluralism more visible. Generally, white denominations—even those with diverse ethnic groups from Europe—had not concerned themselves before the 1950s with those of a different color of skin. In that decade nonwhites began to assume a more prominent place in main line churches; this was largely due to the Civil Rights Movement and the rise of Black Power consciousness. All nonwhites received benefit from the efforts of the Blacks. In the very early beginnings of the United Church of Christ the issue of racial pluralism was joined by a vigorous involvement in the Civil Rights Movement. Although the number of Black churches in the denomination was small, white congregations in the larger cities had begun to acquire racially mixed membership.

Religious, ethnic, and racial pluralism, once expressed and sustained by separate denominational structures, became important new realities for churches to address in the ecumenical movement. A major commitment of ecumenism was to overcome what H. Richard Niebuhr called the "evil of denominationalism." His words bear quotation:

The evil of denominationalism lies in the conditions which makes the rise of sects desirable and necessary: in the failure of the churches to transcend the social conditions which fashion them into caste-organizations, to sublimate their loyalties to standards and institutions only remotely relevant if not contrary to the Christian ideal, to resist the temptation of making their own self-preservation and extension the primary object of their endeavor.[9]

17

Could the burden or evil of denominationalism be overcome in the formation and development of the United Church of Christ? This hope was expressed in a variety of ways by the architects of the union, who, in their Evangelical and Reformed or Congregational Christian experience, had either intuitively or rationally concluded the need to address the changing situation of American church life. Such idealistic motives should not be discounted, even though a study of the development of the new denomination shows a complex of forces working toward union. There is discernible in all the records of union negotiations, of organizational development, and of institutional policy the discipline exercised by the Protestant principle that commands continual renewal and reform as God's people shape the institutions of God's mission in the world.

CHAPTER 1

TOWARD UNION: BEGINNINGS

It is generally agreed by historians of American Christianity that tracing its rootage in European soil is the most productive way of understanding its development in this nation. Since the forebears of those who formed the United Church of Christ in 1957 had deep roots in the Continent and in England this approach seems logical.

Many aspects of its brief history, however, suggest a different beginning point. The European heritage is in no way denied when attention is given first to the events and their immediate American context that brought the new denomination to birth and shaped its development. For the United Church of Christ is a denomination belonging to that style of church organization which is most at home in America, the voluntary association. Whatever particular characteristics it may retain from its European heritage have been transmuted within the religious atmosphere that elevates freedom of choice and freedom of dissent above all authoritarian dictums. Moreover, the occasion of its birth at a point in American religious history that is receiving special attention—the Fifties and Sixties—is of critical significance in understanding the dilemmas of denominationalism, which are reflected repeatedly in its development.

A STORY OF BEGINNINGS

Beginning events have an importance of their own. When James E. Wagner, president of the Evangelical and Reformed Church, and Fred E. Hoskins, minister and secretary of the General Council of the Congregational Christian Churches, joined hands on the stage of the Music Hall in Cleveland, Ohio the evening of June 25, 1957, delegates of the uniting bodies declared with them:

We do now, as the regularly constituted representatives of the Evangelical and Reformed Church and of the General Council of the Congregational Christian Churches, declare ourselves to be one body and our union consummated in this act establishing the United Church of Christ, in the name of the Father, and of the Son, and of the Holy Spirit. Amen.[1]

That long-awaited declaration had been preceded by the adoption of a joint resolution officially authorizing the use of the *Basis of Union with Interpretations* as the document for regulating the affairs of the United Church until a constitution could be prepared and approved.[2] The bare facts of the record give no hint, however, of the intense discussion, negotiation, debate, and conflict that had occupied the attention of the uniting bodies for nearly twenty years prior to the event of union.

Those years—1937 to 1957—are an integral part of the history of the United Church of Christ. They also represent, because of the nature of the debates, a time of critical importance to all American Christianity. At the heart of the debate was the nature of denominationalism and its viability as a form of organized church life in a secularized, democratic, and technocratic society. Both of the uniting bodies had developed through the formative years of denominationalism in America. Each one exhibited aspects of the crucial problems of denominational life.

The exact beginning of the movement leading to union may never be established. Church unions were much in vogue during the first half of the century. Moreover, the great ecumenical conferences that led finally to the formation of the World Council of Churches in 1948 had involved leaders from both groups, most notably Douglas Horton, Truman B. Douglass, George W. Richards, Samuel D. Press, and Louis W. Goebel. They were well acquainted with one another and shared the ecumenical visions of the time. In addition, several church-union proposals of wider scope had given occasion for communication among these church leaders. In 1918 the Conference on Organic Union was held in Philadelphia. From it came what is known as the "Philadelphia Plan," which proposed a union of eighteen groups including at that time the Congregational Churches, the Reformed Church in the United States, and the Evangelical Synod. This plan, suggesting the name "United Churches of Christ in America," came to naught. In December 1949 a Conference on Church Union at Greenwich, Connecticut developed what came to be known as the "Greenwich Plan."

Shared theological concerns had also established a significant relationship between leaders. In 1928 Douglas Horton, at that time minister of Hyde Park Church in Chicago, translated Karl Barth's *The Word of God and the Word of Man.* This was followed by a translation of Barth and Eduard Thurneysen, *Come Holy Spirit,* by George W. Richards, Elmer Homrighausen, and Karl Ernst, all of the Reformed Church in the United States. All four of these translators of Barth were in close communication as they had a hand in introducing what was known as Neoorthodoxy into the American theological milieu.

Of greater significance, perhaps, is the concern for unity and commitment to its accomplishment that shows repeatedly in the attitudes and activities of the uniting denominations. In a study done under the auspices of the Institute for Social and Religious Research in 1933-34, H. Paul Douglass showed that in "attitudes favorable toward practicable union," the Reformed Church in the United States, the Congregational Christian Churches, and the Evangelical Synod of North America ranked one, two, and four respectively among twenty denominations.[3]

If any single event is to be indicated as the beginning of the movement

20

leading to the formation of the United Church of Christ, the honor very likely belongs to the formation of a study group of ministers, in St. Louis in 1937, in which Congregational Christian and Evangelical and Reformed clergy were involved. Prompted by the shared interests of Truman B. Douglass, then pastor of Pilgrim Congregational Church, and Samuel D. Press, president of Eden Theological Seminary in nearby Webster Groves, the meetings of this study group led to the recognition of common bonds and responsibilities. Writing about it later Dr. Douglass confirmed the role of this group in laying at least some of the groundwork for the union:

> After some months of this regular thinking together about the fundamentals of our faith and the nature of our task as ministers, the members of our comradeship came to have a high regard for one another and to feel a strong unity of mind and heart around the primary things of importance. The awareness of this community of thought and purpose led one of us to remark quite casually that what we had discovered in our small company might be taken as an indication that the two denominational fellowships which we represented could come together in unity.[4]

Dr. Press, then a member of the Committee on Closer Relations with Other Churches of the Evangelical and Reformed Church, was moved by his experience in the St. Louis group to send a telegram in June 1938 to Truman Douglass and George Gibson, at a meeting of the General Council of Congregational Christian Churches in Beloit, Wisconsin, with the query: "What about a rapprochement between our communions looking toward union?"[5] As a result of that telegram, Douglas Horton, as minister of the General Council, and Dr. Press held an informal meeting in Chicago. Louis W. Goebel, who later succeeded George W. Richards as president of the Evangelical and Reformed Church, suggested that Dr. Horton send an official overture to Dr. Richards proposing conversations between the two denominations. In succeeding months communications began to flow between the two agencies officially responsible for such discussions: the Commission on Interchurch Relations and Christian Unity of the Congregational Christian Churches, and the Committee on Closer Relations with Other Churches of the Evangelical and Reformed Church.[6] It was not until mid-1942 that the proposed conversations toward union became public. In June of that year the Evangelical and Reformed General Synod and the Congregational Christian General Council gave official endorsement to union negotiation.* In the same year the Joint Committee on

---

*The words General Council refer to two different bodies. In the Evangelical and Reformed Church the General Council was the General Synod ad interim and consisted of the officers of the denomination with sixteen elected clergy and laity. In the Congregational Christian Churches the General Council was the national assembly of delegates, meeting biennially. It was comparable, therefore, to the Evangelical and Reformed General Synod, also a national body.

21

Union began its work, preparing altogether ten drafts of a Basis of Union issued between 1943 and 1949.[7]

The drafting of agreements toward union between church bodies requires intimate knowledge of their traditions, histories, and practices. Each denomination brought to the drafting of union agreements those understandings of themselves and the larger Christian community that had been molded by many years of experience. Moreover, both were the results of earlier unions and thus had experience to draw upon: the Congregational with the Christian Churches in 1931, and the Evangelical Synod with the Reformed Church in 1934. At the same time, the circumstances of this proposed union, both internally and externally, were significantly different.

Internal differences reflected demographic and social distinctions related to the historical development of the two groups. Congregational Churches were rooted in some of the earliest colonial establishments of England on American shores. Their expansion westward was confined almost exclusively to Anglo-Saxon peoples until the late nineteenth century. The heritage of the Evangelical and Reformed Church, on the other hand, was German and Swiss, with the earliest settlements of Reformed people in Pennsylvania and the Carolinas occurring nearly one hundred years after Plymouth Colony had been established. A nineteenth-century immigration of German Evangelical people and more German Reformed people placed the center of that church's life in the midwestern states. The consequent geographical distribution of the two church bodies appeared to be happily complementary, giving the proposed united church a more favorable national character.

Social and cultural differences appeared to some to be quite pronounced. There were many persons in the two denominations, both pro-union and anti-union, who saw these differences as chief obstacles to the formation of a new church body. Although the divergencies were in part due to different national origins, they had been produced also by the circumstances of history. In a nation formed originally by a population with an Anglo-Saxon majority, the Congregational Churches were very much "inside" the establishment. The intimate relationship between the "congregational way" and American democracy has been of greatest interest to students of the nation's history.[8] Congregationalist contributions to the nation's culture and civil life have left an indelible stamp upon American life.

On a comparative basis the Evangelical and Reformed Church had far more modest contributions to offer, partly because of historical circumstance (smaller numbers at a later period in the nation's history) and partly due to a different religious ethos. The focus of concern for Evangelical and Reformed people was generally the church rather than the culture and the nation. In consequence, educational institutions, hospitals, and other eleemosynary organizations, established and maintained for and by the institutional church, seemed to have less of an impact upon the general culture. This dissimilarity in outlook about the

22

church's responsibility to society, while a highly complex matter, can be identified at many points in the union negotiations and in the formative years of the new denomination.

In an analysis made in 1944 Thomas A. Tripp compared Evangelical and Reformed Church statistics with those of the Congregational Christian Churches and found that in total membership the new united church would be among the four largest Protestant church bodies in the nation.[9] Using 1942 statistics, Tripp pointed to the differences between the two denominations. At that time both groups were losing parishes but gaining in total membership. Evangelical and Reformed Church parishes averaged 232 members, while those of the Congregational Christian Churches averaged 181 members. Rural-urban distribution of the two bodies showed more Congregational Christian parishes in rural areas but with fewer members, whereas Evangelical and Reformed parishes in rural areas were fewer in number but greater in membership. Also, as of that date, Evangelical and Reformed churches had a higher per capita giving rate, a larger proportion of male membership, and more young people but a lower membership growth rate. In themselves these statistical differences have limited significance. When correlated with historical and cultural circumstances, they take on greater importance for understanding the long period of negotiation before union was accomplished.

Differences in theological traditions and religious styles are somewhat less easy to define because of the religious homogenization so characteristic of American Protestantism. Sociologists generally placed the labels of "liberal" on the Congregational Christian Churches and "conservative" on the Evangelical and Reformed Church. Because of their varied connotations such labels tended to render a disservice to those seeking to understand these churches. Liberal and conservative trends do not follow precisely denominational lines. A more helpful characterization of the theological climate in these churches was given by Reinhold Niebuhr, who claimed that the Evangelical and Reformed Church "was informed by a theological tradition which might best be defined as a *liberal evangelicalism*," while the Congregational Christian Churches expressed a *"modern liberalism* shading off to Unitarianism." Niebuhr then went on to say: "There were, in short, differences in the theological climate of the two churches, but there were no insuperable obstacles in these differences; and the theological accommodation between the two bodies conformed, on the whole, to the accommodation which has been taking place in the whole ecumenical movement."[10]

There were divergencies in religious styles that reflected both cultural and historical circumstances. Congregational Christian Churches accentuated the *preaching role* of the minister; many of the most prominent preachers in the nation were in Congregational Christian pulpits. In the Evangelical and Reformed Church the *pastoral role* of the minister took precedence; congregations emphasized family nurture, education, and pastoral service.[11]

23

To outside observers the most striking dissimilarity was in church polity. The differences between congregational polity and presbyterial polity were rooted deeply in American religious history. Those differences could not be minimized. The Congregational Christian Churches were more polity-conscious than were Evangelical and Reformed people. The complexity of the polity matter revealed itself at later stages in the negotiations. At the same time, rapprochement was not a fantasy, for in practice both polities had undergone important modifications that permitted some hope for a workable accommodation in union.

UNION-PLANNING

The Joint Committee's task of designing a structure of union between these two polities was one not theretofore undertaken in American church history. New ground was to be broken, and in that process unanticipated discoveries were made about both groups. In retrospect those discoveries proved decisive for the formation of the new united church. No one, either in the Joint Committee or in the executive and administrative committees at that time, could have anticipated that seventeen years and three months would pass before the hoped-for union could be accomplished. In that prolonged period of discussion, debate, and negotiation, vast changes in both the church and the society would have bearing upon the final outcome.

The twenty-year period, from the incubation of the idea in 1937 to its full birth in 1957, saw the United States move from an isolationist stance to that of total involvement as a great power in the affairs of the whole world. Church life and activity reflected that shift. Editorials, feature articles, and letters-to-the-editor in both *Advance* and *The Messenger* carried the debate over isolationism and pacifism.* Concurrently they carried increasingly disturbing news about the church situation under the National Socialists in Germany. Word of Pastor Martin Niemoeller's incarceration in a Nazi concentration camp (March 4, 1938) impressed even the doubters that the threat to the church was exceedingly grave.

Concern about persecution of the Jews in Germany occasioned a joint Christmas Eve message in 1938 to the Germans from both Catholics and Protestants in America, including Congregational Christian and Evangelical and Reformed leaders. The Jewish question became a matter of conscience for American Christians.

The outbreak of World War II in September of 1939 added to the dilemma of the isolationists who found themselves profiting from increased industrial output for the allied war machine. No matter how strong the isolationist sentiment, the improved economic circumstances cast a heavy vote on the side of some involvement in the European conflict. Neither were the churches oblivious to the war dangers in Asia. *The Messenger* carried warnings of rising anti-

Advance was the Congregational Christian monthly journal; *The Messenger* was a weekly paper serving Evangelical and Reformed people.

24

American feeling in Japan in April 1941 and in May discussed the likelihood of war with Japan. America's entry into the war in December 1941 put an end to the isolationist-interventionist debate within the churches. Attention was shifted to meeting the nation's wartime needs and caring for people whose lives were disrupted.

Although the nation was at war the Joint Committee on Union was not sidetracked from its work. The ten drafts of the Basis of Union produced between 1942 and 1948 reflected the concern to find a way to bridge the differences that were considered by some to be insurmountable obstacles to union. Moreover, leaders in both denominations took official steps to make the union movement public. Fraternal delegates were exchanged in 1942. George W. Richards, president of the Evangelical and Reformed Church, spoke on "Ecumenicity" at the General Council of the Congregational Christian Churches assembled in June of that year. In the same month Truman B. Douglass and A.E. Randall represented the latter group at the Evangelical and Reformed General Synod.* The first public draft of the proposed Basis of Union appeared in *The Messenger,* May 18, 1943, and was distributed for information to the regional synods of the Evangelical and Reformed Church. Earlier, however, *The Messenger* gave the proposed union considerable prominence throughout the Evangelical and Reformed Church by a lead editorial indicating a growing sentiment for union and proposing get-acquainted activities.[12] Union momentum was developing.

At this stage in union-planning and growing sentiment in the churches, the vision of Christian unity continued to inform and inspire those who had to deal with the complex issues posed by the different traditions. That vision had given the Western Christian world a "shot in the arm" when it was interpreted at the Oxford Faith and Order Conference in 1937 as the delegates considered the critical issues of church, community, and state. Amos N. Wilder commented on the awareness among the delegates at Oxford that "denominational self-sufficiency in so far as it has existed has been humbled by the menace of pagan developments."[13] Unity was, therefore, not simply a dream but considered an answer to the rising forces of paganism. It was a vision that called for abandonment of the archaisms of organizational life, denominational and sectarian division, and the pietistic moralism inherited from nineteenth-century church expansion. Hence, the feeling of being under a mandate from the Christian world was a prominent element in early union efforts.

*The chronology of official actions taken by the two groups to forward the union effort is given in the appendixes. However, greater detail is available only in the Minutes of the Commission on Interchurch Relations and Christian Unity, as far back as September 27, 1939; the Advance Reports and the Minutes of the General Council of 1940; the Minutes of the Committee on Closer Relations with Other Churches, 1939-41; Minutes of the Evangelical and Reformed General Council, 1940-42; and the Acts and Proceedings of the General Synod, 1942.

Circulation of revised drafts of the Basis of Union and periodic reports of the Joint Committee to the parent bodies began in 1943 to highlight points of debate that were to become critical as time went on. Between March 1943 and September 1944 four drafts of the Basis of Union were prepared. An early, yet somewhat minor, debate over the proposed name, "The United Church in America," was carried in the pages of *Advance*. Although later modified to "United Church of Christ," the proposed name was an important affirmation of a principle expressed in every draft of the Basis of Union:

> We, the regularly constituted representatives of the Congregational Christian Churches and of the Evangelical and Reformed Church, . . . believing that denominations exist not for themselves but as parts of that Church, within which each denomination is to live and labor and, if need be, die; and confronting the divisions and hostilities of our world, and hearing with a deepened sense of responsibility the prayer of our Lord "that they all may be one"; do now declare ourselves to be one body; and do set forth the following articles of agreement as the basis of our life, fellowship, witness, and proclamation of the Gospel to all nations.[14]

In January of 1944 an informal meeting of Evangelical and Reformed synod presidents and conference superintendents of the Congregational Christian Churches gave attention to differences and similarities in organizational style. Initiated by Dr. Horton and Dr. Richards, the meeting served to advance the cause of union among regional leaders in both groups. That effort was followed shortly thereafter by a proposed schedule for the consummation of the union, as drawn up by the Joint Committee. This included a proposed vote by the Congregational Christian General Council in June 1944, to be followed by a two-year period of getting acquainted on local, regional, and national levels, a joint meeting of the national assemblies in 1946, and then final steps by each denomination for consummation of the union in 1947.

Attention to the proposed union required a major block of time in the 1944 General Council of the Congregational Christian Churches and the Evangelical and Reformed General Synod that summer. Prominent leaders voiced special concerns about the implications for time-honored traditions in both groups. Denominational self-consciousness was exhibited in both positive and negative statements. Nevertheless, both national assemblies approved the next steps as proposed. The goal of union by 1947 seemed assured, yet those delegates at Grand Rapids who listened closely to the discussion at the 1944 Congregational Christian General Council could see the storm warnings ahead. In that council it became clear that the proposed union with the Evangelical and Reformed Church was bringing to the surface some fundamental questions and unresolved issues within the Congregational Christian Churches. For the Evangelical and Reformed Church there was to be a time of waiting and wondering, during which union ardor diminished and critical questioners gathered support.

Up to 1944 the efforts of Congregational Christian leaders were devoted to union negotiations. From June 1944 on, as a result of issues identified at the Grand Rapids General Council, the focus of attention within those negotiations was on seeking a common mind about the nature of Congregationalism and its place in relation to the growing denominational organizations of other Christians in the United States. The ensuing debate exposed questions about denominational organization for all church bodies. While it resulted in considerable distress for many individuals and was disruptive of church life in many segments of the Congregational Christian group, from the perspective of history the debate may be judged to have been salutary and constructive.

The official committees charged with guiding the two denominations into union exhibited from the beginning a "will to unite" that was to prove characteristic of most of the church leaders throughout the negotiating period. George W. Richards, chairman of the Evangelical and Reformed committee, reported that "after examination of the forms of government, statements of faith, modes of worship, and methods of work, the members of the committee were convinced that, if there is a will to unite on the part of the ministers and the members, union can be effected in due time."[15]

A similar perception of this mood about union was reflected in the words of Congregational Christian leaders as well, both in correspondence and in official reports. At a meeting arranged in January 1947 by the Joint Committee, conference superintendents (Congregational Christian), and synod presidents (Evangelical and Reformed), recognition of the differences in organizational structure and procedure led to the conclusion that "there is quite a difference in the conceptions of the Church." At the same time the "will to unite" was held up as the means of overcoming differences and accomplishing union.[16] Douglas Horton made a point of the flexibility and adaptability of Congregationalism as assurance that dissimilarities could be overcome without difficulty.

During this period there seemed to be a tendency in both merging groups to obscure the fundamental differences for the sake of harmonious steps toward union. Evangelical and Reformed members did not at first understand the nature of the issues that created growing concern among their Congregational Christian friends. The process of defining Congregationalism, so critically important to the possibility of union, caused increasing tensions in negotiations between the two church bodies. Differences in the theory and practice of church organization were assumed from the beginning to be negotiable matters, subject to reconciliation. As time went on, however, it became more and more apparent that this was not to be the case. An early euphoria about the process of union gave way to moods of discouragement as one effort after another was frustrated. Evangelical and Reformed people gradually realized that their previous experience with the uniting of two church bodies (1934-39, when the Evangelical Synod of North America and the Reformed Church in the United States merged) would not be repeated easily in this new effort. Whatever disappointment they experienced in the protracted negotiations, however, was offset by

27

their preoccupation with the organizational implementation of the constitution they had adopted in 1939 and put in force in 1941. Nevertheless, their negotiators on the Joint Committee had to face the realities that were the responsibility of their Congregational Christian counterparts. They came to the union effort buoyed by a successful experience in organic union. Their Congregational Christian colleagues had no such experience, even though several groups had been brought into the fellowship of Congregational Christian Churches on a national level in 1892, 1925, and 1931.* The term organic union, widely employed in ecumenical circles, had not been absorbed into American Congregational thinking about the church.

An indication of the different mind-sets among the members of the Joint Committee on Union is given by tracing the changes made in successive drafts of the Basis of Union between 1943 and 1947. The first draft, published early in 1943, reflected very strongly the attitudes and expectations of Evangelical and Reformed members concerning the union and the way it could be achieved. Its chief emphases showed the characteristic concern for a form of church organization that would express the unity of the church in its national structure. As a consequence, the authority, power, and functions of the General Synod, defined as a representative body, were laid out in some detail. In succeeding draft revisions the central place given to the General Synod was gradually reduced and taken by procedural stipulations, which made that body but one among several organizational units with strict limits attached to its authority and power. This trend reflected the realities of the Congregational Christian situation in which organizational units beyond the local church had limited authority. It also demonstrated clearly that the Congregational Christian Churches were not a denomination in the same sense that the Evangelical and Reformed Church was a denomination.† In the effort to sort out that distinction the Congregational Christian fellowship entered a time of severe crisis.

---

*Following the establishment of the National Council in 1871, three other groups of churches were welcomed into the council: the Congregational Methodists in 1892; the Evangelical Protestant Church in 1925; and the General Convention of the Christian Churches in 1931. In every case, the action of the council had no bearing upon the relationship of local churches except as they sought standing within Congregational associations. In each national-level affiliation there was afforded opportunity for participation in common concerns and for identity in a larger fellowship.

†These differences are discussed in chapter 3. However, it is important to note here that the crucial accent of Congregationalism upon *the local church as the Church* and national organizations as agencies of fellowship and mission produced a denominational sense quite different from the Evangelical and Reformed accent upon *the Synods and General Synod as the Church.* In the first instance "denomination" denoted primarily a style of church life exemplified in fellowship; in the second instance "denomination" always referred to the larger (national and sometimes regional) organization.

A CRISIS IN NEGOTIATIONS

The dimensions of that crisis were comprehended slowly by the two groups. Although some critical discussion appeared in *Advance* as early as 1946, raising the issue of the possible loss of cherished Congregational traditions, some important differences began to show in the flow of communications between executives of the two groups as strategies were developed for implementing the Basis of Union when completed. An exchange of letters between Douglas Horton and Louis W. Goebel in mid-1946 over Horton's informal suggestion that preliminary work begin on a constitution for the new church demonstrated not only the differences in the way the two organizational systems worked but also the difficulty each group had in understanding the other. In Horton's view such informal efforts would advance the union. In Goebel's view informal activity of that kind would be illegitimate, since there had been agreement to prepare a constitution only after the union had been effected on the Basis of Union. Horton was proceeding within the tradition of a fellowship where such informal preparation was the appropriate preliminary step to general agreement. Goebel, working out of the constitutional framework of synodical procedure, could not concur in any action not permitted by the constitution or explicitly confirmed by the responsible bodies.

This fundamental difference in political style was illustrated again in 1946 when Truman B. Douglass, executive vice-president of the Board for Home Missions (CC), proposed a meeting of agency and board executives from both bodies to consider "whether the general plan of board organization (for the new church) shall be that now found in the Evangelical and Reformed Church or that of the Congregational Christian Churches, or something different from either." To this Dr. Goebel replied that the Evangelical and Reformed Church "would not readily agree that the representatives of the boards and agencies outline the general pattern of board organization prior to the appointment of a committee of the General Synod of the United Church for a careful study of this problem."[17] Both executives were acting in harmony with the established organizational protocol in their respective groups. Those contrasting procedures with corresponding political styles were to be illustrated again and again before the union was consummated. In this instance Dr. Douglass acknowledged Dr. Goebel's point and backed away from his proposal. Nevertheless, the pattern of board and agency organization was in fact established before the Basis of Union was adopted.

This issue precipitated a minor crisis when the Executive Committee of the General Council (CC), heeding the concerns being expressed by many agency people, voted to prepare a supplement to the Basis of Union for purposes of clarification.[18] The pro-merger group protested, fearing this would cause Evangelical and Reformed leaders to back away. The result was such confusion that many came away from the midwinter meetings of early 1946 convinced

29

that the union effort had come to naught. The Executive Committee concluded that a proposal for a joint meeting of the General Council (CC) and the General Synod (E&R) be abandoned. Nevertheless, the General Council, meeting in Grinnell, Iowa in June, reaffirmed commitment to the union effort and gave the Executive Committee authority to call a special session of the council if that seemed necessary. Additional encouragement was given to facilitate working out financial arrangements and organizational relationships for the boards and agencies of the two groups.

In July of 1947 the final draft of the Basis of Union was adopted by the General Synod of the Evangelical and Reformed Church by a vote of 281 to 23. This vote referred the document to the thirty-four synods for consideration and a ratifying vote at their spring meetings in 1948. In the meantime opposition to the union became more vocal and public within the Congregational Christian fellowship. Two groups published dissenting arguments: the League to Uphold Congregational Principles and the Evanston Meeting. The latter, called in November 1947, resulted in the formation of what was known as the Committee for the Continuation of Congregational Christian Churches.

The Evanston Meeting, consisting of about 190 clergy and laity from twenty-seven states, set off an intensive effort by pro-union leaders in the Executive Committee and the Committee on Interchurch Relations to find ways to reconcile the differences generated within Congregational Christian Churches by the proposed Basis of Union. Four points of issue were identified by the Evanston group: the idea of a national constitution embracing all congregations, the autonomy of the local church, uncertainty about equity in the pension funds, and the regularizing of relationships between ministers and churches. Opponents believed the Basis of Union abandoned traditional Congregational practices in respect to these points and asked again for some form of federative union. As a result of official efforts to meet these charges, a set of "Comments" or "Interpretations" concerning the Basis of Union was developed early in 1948. In the long run this effort seemed to add to the controversy, although some opponents were at first mollified.

In their efforts to win over anti-union people to their position, members of the Executive Committee (CC) began to generate concern among Evangelical and Reformed leaders as well as in their general constituency. There was fear that the synod voting would be affected by the "Interpretations." As a consequence, the General Council (E&R) sent a communication to the thirty-four synods:

The General Council, taking note of written statements being circulated by individuals and groups as interpretations of the Basis of Union, declares that no such interpretive material is binding. The General Council calls attention to the fact that the Basis of Union, approved by the General Synod, is the only document before the synods for consideration and action. It reaffirms its conviction that the United Church of Christ can be established according to

30

the provisions of the Basis of Union, and is confident that our two denominations, so united, will become a more effective instrument for the advancement of the Kingdom of God.[19]

As the intensity of disagreement increased within the Congregational Christian fellowship throughout the first months of 1948, there was growing awareness in the Executive Committee (CC) that a schism was very possible. A much publicized statement from representatives of the Evanston group hinted that churches voting affirmatively on the union proposal would be, in effect, leaving the fellowship of the Congregational Christian Churches. It is unclear whether the voting was influenced by such statements. By April the voting returns seemed to be short of the expected 75 percent approval. It was at this point that the Executive Committee concluded that a vote on the Basis of Union should not be taken at the upcoming General Council in June at Oberlin. In addition to the strongly voiced opposition of a relatively small number of ministers and laypeople, there was the discomfiting realization that the actual number of members participating in the voting of most churches was unimpressive. At the same time proponents of the union were actively seeking a way to generate support.

DISCOURAGEMENT AND HOPE

In all respects the year 1948 was the most crucial in the entire union effort. The threat of schism within the Congregational Christian fellowship cast a shadow over both communions. Every effort to build bridges of understanding between pro- and anti-union forces seemed to create new problems. Nevertheless, the actions of the General Council (CC) at Oberlin in June did appear to achieve a degree of unity. The key to that achievement was the adoption of the Basis of Union *with Interpretations* and resubmission of the same to the churches for voting. The use of a set of interpretations to satisfy the arguments of anti-union people and to win greater support throughout the Congregational Christian constituency was a result of some earlier efforts to meet major objections in late 1947 and early 1948 by developing interpretive *Comments* in the Committee on Interchurch Relations and the Executive Committee of the General Council. The significantly favorable vote on this by the General Council—1,000 to 11—seemed to indicate a successful compromise. When the Evanston Meeting group thereupon voted to disband, there was a general feeling of optimism. But even more critical days were to come.

The Evangelical and Reformed General Council, as indicated above, had reminded the synods that their voting had no relationship to any kind of comments or interpretations of the Basis of Union being circulated in Congregational Christian circles. Moreover, Louis W. Goebel was present at Oberlin and, when asked to comment on the significance of the *Interpretations*, made it clear that if these were added to the original document, they would have to be submitted for

31

new voting by both the General Synod and the thirty-four synods of the Evangelical and Reformed Church. Thus the action at Oberlin had considerably changed the situation for that group by introducing a concept that had been generally unacceptable. Paragraph (a) of the *Interpretations* reads: "The Basis of Union calls for a union of the General Council of Congregational Christian Churches *and the General Synod* of the Evangelical and Reformed Church to form the General Synod of the United Church of Christ."* This was not consistent with the Evangelical and Reformed understanding of organic union. It was essentially a foreign concept to that communion's belief in the nature of the church.†

Subparagraph (4) of the second major *Interpretation* introduced still another concept: "[The constitution of the United Church of Christ] will define and regulate as regards the General Synod but describe the free and voluntary relationships which the churches, associations, and conferences shall sustain with the General Synod and with each other." Traditional Evangelical and Reformed practice saw the constitution as the guarantor of orderliness, justice, and freedom in all organizational relationships, and therefore binding for all. The concept of a descriptive constitution had not been considered in that group.

A time of disillusionment set in. What had begun as a high venture in Christian idealism was now foundering on the rocks of organizational and political realities. Adjustment to these realities caused difficulty for persons in both communions for whom the vision of union had continually informed and strengthened the will to unite. The realization that Congregational *churches* could not by their very nature act together as *church* came slowly to the Evangelical and Reformed constituency. As the General Council (E&R) considered the *Interpretations* at a September 1948 meeting, an effort was made to reintroduce the idealist spirit by proposing the insertion of a sentence into paragraph (b) (4) as follows:

> We hope that the Constitution of the United Church may, through the guidance of the Holy Spirit and the experience of the new church, not merely develop a compromise of the two former polities *but may bring a new polity and plan of organization to the United Church.*[20]

It was obvious, however, that the sentence could not be included in the *Interpretations*, which the General Council at Oberlin had already adopted and sent to

---

*Italics added.
†On February 2, 1948, when apprised by Douglas Horton that some "interpretations" had been devised to meet anti-union objections to the Basis of Union, Dr. Goebel wrote a very strong letter of protest that such a procedure would "wreck the union." Nevertheless, Congregational Christian leaders felt bound to prevent a schism by attaching "assurances" of Congregational polity to the union agreement. Louis W. Goebel files 55 (1), Folder 48-6, Eden Seminary archives.

the churches. Consequently, the action was rescinded at a special meeting on November 10, 1948.

The sentence is, nevertheless, of great importance for understanding not only the differences between the two church bodies but also the turmoil induced in both by the union effort. At one of the first joint meetings for planning the union, George W. Richards, then president of the Evangelical and Reformed Church, had expressed the hope that the new united church would develop a new polity. James E. Wagner, then a member of the General Council (E&R), had written in 1945:

There was general concern that the merger, if it is to be effected, must not be simply a superficial paper organization, a merger in form, but rather a union of mind and spirit on the part of two religious bodies which will have pushed beyond their divergent historic traditions and their present differences in organization and thought and found a higher level of oneness in devotion to Christ and His Church.[21]

This concern prevailed among Evangelical and Reformed people both as a result of their experience and of a basic faith conviction that institutional form must always be regarded in organismic terms. An organism is a live body that adapts to the environment. The church as an organism must always devise new ways of living in the different societies of the world, but at the same time it remains distinctive because of its head, Jesus Christ. This concept prevailed in the union of the Evangelical Synod with the Reformed Church in the United States, resulting in a form of church organization that could not be characterized fairly in terms of any traditional polity. Church order was for the sake of God's work in the world.[22]

Whatever hope Congregational Christian pro-union leaders had for a new form of church organization was never given an opportunity to develop because of the defensive position they were forced to take by opponents of the union. A fundamental issue in Congregationalism was the exercise of power, but the nature of the issue was often misunderstood. Anti-union leaders frequently cited the Evangelical and Reformed system of government as a threat to freedom because of the authority expressed in its constitutional provisions. Within the Congregational Christian Churches, however, the absence of agreement about authority tended to make suspect every action of the Executive Committee and the General Council itself. In the end that issue took the opposing parties to the civil courts.

Here again, historical circumstances and the distinctive religious and cultural heritages of the two uniting church bodies may be seen in the different understandings of the uses of authority and power. The dissimilarities can be defined in an oversimplified way by saying that, in general, Congregational Christian people feared authority but respected power in organizational procedures, while Evangelical and Reformed people were inclined to respect authority and to fear

33

the use of unauthorized power. Congregational self-understanding as a principle of church organization had been hammered out in the fires of resistance to arbitrary ecclesiastical and political authority in the sixteenth and seventeenth centuries. Discovery of the uses of the power generated by consent of the group introduced a dynamic element into New England church life at the same time it became the key to new concepts of civil government in the American colonies. Congregationalists shared in the Anglo-Saxon struggle for freedom that transformed civil and religious life in the Western world. The Evangelical and Reformed experience had been much different; while concerned about freedom, the people had experienced the abuse of unrestrained ecclesiastical and political power and had learned the importance of order to protect freedom. Constitutional limitation of power as the basis of freedom, according to the classical Reformed meaning, was the focal point of their concern. Continental European piety informed that concept with the claim of corporate responsibility as a first principle of faith.[23]

The events of the last six months of 1948, following what some called "the Peace at Oberlin," are confusing but nevertheless instructive for understanding the United Church of Christ. What really had taken place at Oberlin? In both Congregational Christian and Evangelical and Reformed circles there was vigorous debate over the question: Should the *Interpretations* be considered an "amendment" to the Basis of Union, or were they intended to serve simply as "clarification"? In other words, had the contract for union been amended when the *Interpretations* were added?

Evangelical and Reformed leaders initially saw the *Interpretations* as clarifications and therefore not binding upon the two parties entering the union. Some Congregational Christians understood them the same way.[24] When the General Council (E&R) met in September 1948, a resolution was adopted stating:

The General Council of the Evangelical and Reformed Church recognizes the right and privilege of the General Council of the Congregational Christian Churches to interpret the Basis of Union according to its own understanding. The Evangelical and Reformed Church, however, interprets the adoption of these interpretations *as not binding* it or the United Church to any traditional polity for the present or for the future.[25]

In a letter to Douglas Horton, conveying word of the General Council's action to the Executive Committee (CC), Dr. Goebel continued to express the hope of Evangelical and Reformed leaders that the new united church would develop a new form of church organization. He wrote:

I hope that the statement makes it sufficiently clear that the General Council of the Evangelical and Reformed Church, speaking for the Church, still is vitally interested in the union. . . . Some members of the General Council, as well as a portion of the membership of the Church, believed that the "Interpretations" could be construed as binding us in advance . . . to a Congregational polity. It is, of course, obvious that if this construction is put upon the "Interpretations," the two communions would not go forward to a union, but the Evangelical and Reformed Church would simply be absorbed by the Congregational Christian Churches. . . . Our statement, therefore, has no other purpose than to protect the freedom of the United Church to evolve its own polity. I think you can readily understand that the spirit of freedom in the Evangelical and Reformed Church is such that it cannot permit itself to be tied to the past by purely historical, traditional or sentimental considerations. We would not be true to the genius of our Church if we thus permitted our freedom to be circumscribed.[26]

This letter is quoted at some length because, along with the full text of the resolution adopted by the General Council in September, it represents the last vigorous attempt of the Evangelical and Reformed group to make the point that the union was envisioned as an opportunity to move denominational organization beyond the inhibiting elements of traditional polity. The weakness of that hope and vision was that it was never given sufficient substance to make it a viable alternative for Congregational Christian people to consider. George W. Richards, who was probably the chief theoretician of church organization in the Evangelical and Reformed Church and who had extensive ecumenical experience, had been a long-time exponent of organic union. Although he argued that "it is possible the time may come when churches will unite with a form of government which will preserve the rights of the congregation, the presbytery, and the constitutional episcopacy,"[27] he and other Evangelical and Reformed leaders did not want to propose in advance a specific type of church organization.

Congregational Christian leaders, while often sharing that vision, had to deal directly with those who sincerely believed that Congregational polity must be guaranteed. Anti-union forces had repeatedly sought assurance on that point, and the addition of Interpretations to the Basis of Union was an effort to meet that request. As a result, the Evangelical and Reformed commitment to the union was put to its severest test up to that time. While many felt that too many concessions had already been made in the direction of Congregational polity, Dr. Goebel's letter and the accompanying action of the General Council (E&R) represented the hope that the principle of a new polity for a new united church would still prevail.

The clear question for both groups, then, was: What price must and can be paid for union? Was it schism in the Congregational Christian fellowship, or in the Evangelical and Reformed Church the abandonment of commitment to a new kind of unity in denominational organization? This clear dilemma obviously had to be faced together. The crucial time was a meeting of representatives of the two bodies on November 10, 1948 in Cleveland, Ohio.

The joint statement adopted at that meeting was made possible by a special

35

action of the General Council (E&R) rescinding its action of September 30. It declared the two groups in "agreement that these interpretations do not present any fundamental variance from the Basis of Union," and that the "Congregational Christian Churches will come into the union on the Basis of Union and the interpretations." At the same time the General Council (E&R) agreed to call a special meeting of the General Synod to vote on the *Basis of Union with Interpretations* upon being informed that the Congregational Christian Churches were "ready to unite pursuant to the action at Oberlin."[28]

Two important consequences flowed from this joint statement. First, the Congregational Christian leaders were committed to securing a favorable vote from the churches on the *Basis of Union with Interpretations* so that the General Synod (E&R) could act on them. This necessity heightened the tensions between pro- and anti-union forces. Second, Evangelical and Reformed leaders faced the task of interpreting the new situation to a constituency that was showing some uneasiness.

Opposition to the union in Congregational Christian circles grew rapidly and became better organized. Although the Evanston Meeting group had voted to disband at the close of the Oberlin General Council, many supporters continued their efforts to generate concern in the churches. A National Anti-merger Fellowship was organized. The much-feared division in the Congregational Christian Churches, which pro-union forces had so assiduously sought to prevent, was becoming a reality. By the time the special meeting of the General Council, authorized at Oberlin, had convened in Cleveland on February 4, 1949, the features of the rift were apparent. Before the special session the January issue of *Advance* carried an editorial concluding that it was clear "nothing short of complete abandonment of the [union] proposal" would satisfy the anti-union group.[29]

At Cleveland the Committee of Fifteen reported that 72.8 percent of the churches voting had approved the proposal and recommended that the union be consummated upon evidence that the Evangelical and Reformed General Synod and synods had voted favorably on the *Basis of Union with Interpretations.** When the authorizing resolution reached a vote after vigorous debate, the General Council approved 757 to 172. While the majority vote was clear, it was also evident that the delegates had been affected by the debate, for the 172 negative votes represented the largest number at any of the several General Council votes on the union.

Of greater importance was the clear indication in the floor debates that a vote

*The 72.8 percent vote was slightly below the 75 percent recommended by the Committee on Interchurch Relations and Christian Unity to the General Council's Executive Committee, January 22, 1947, as the Minutes of the latter body show. However, neither the Executive Committee nor the General Council itself ever officially adopted the 75 percent goal.

of approval would mean division and legal struggles. Subsequent statements from the National Anti-merger Fellowship, which became the Committee for Continuation of Congregational Christian Churches of the United States, declared that affirmative-voting churches would be leaving the Congregational Christian fellowship to join the Evangelical and Reformed Church. Accompanying that was a clear warning that unresolved issues would be taken to the civil courts.

With that rift in the ranks of the Congregational Christian Churches, the move toward union and the subsequent shaping of the proposed United Church of Christ acquired a new significance in the reconfiguration of American denominational organization. The hope of organic union for adequate organizational implementation was sidetracked while Congregationalism undertook the task of defining itself as a denomination.

CHAPTER 2

TOWARD UNION: FACING THE ISSUES

The denominational development of the Congregational Christian fellowship covers a period of nearly one hundred years, but it was only toward the end of that period that the most critical issues were faced and decisive actions taken.[1] When legal proceedings were undertaken in the civil courts early in 1949 by those who opposed the union, sharp differences in Congregationalism's self-understanding were clearly delineated. The arguments presented in court (the court of original jurisdiction and also the appeals court) by both parties were finally more important in the formation of the United Church of Christ than the court's decision. Those arguments defined Congregationalism in ways that had never been clearly articulated in the early negotiations with the Evangelical and Reformed Church.

DEFINING CONGREGATIONALISM

In the course of the legal proceedings that began in April of 1949 and ended with a reversal of the lower court's finding on behalf of the opponents to the union in 1953, there was a full development of some concepts concerning Congregational organization that had appeared originally in the *Interpretations* added to the Basis of Union by the General Council at Oberlin in 1948. They had to do with the autonomy and power of the General Council. Witnesses from among the General Council's leadership responded to the court's queries by affirming that the General Council was "like unto the local congregation" in its autonomy and power. The General Council was held to be accountable only to itself as a "gathering of Christians under the Lordship of Christ." But plaintiffs argued that the General Council was a "representative body" accountable to the churches from whom the delegates were drawn.[2]

Those opposing the union contended that the General Council was simply a national "agency of fellowship," deriving its existence from the will of the churches. Its actions, therefore, insofar as they affected the existence of the local churches, required their approval. This position was grounded in various actions, dating back to 1907, by which the denominational organization was gradually developed. In 1913 the National Council (later renamed the General Council), acting on a 1907 Report of the Committee on Polity, adopted a plan of national organization that provided "lines of representative order." The effect of that action was "representative administration of all our interests," in effect giving control of all agencies of fellowship and mission to the churches.[3] In arguing thus from the history of national development, the anti-union churches were also making a case for their contention that in the event of the consummation of the union with the Evangelical and Reformed Church, those Congregational Christian churches choosing not to become part of the United Church of Christ would have rightful claim to the assets of the various missionary and pension funds.

Several prominent leaders of the pro-union movement gave testimony before the court that had far-reaching effects upon the shaping of the United Church of Christ. In his testimony Truman B. Douglass claimed that the two basic principles of Congregational polity—autonomy and fellowship—were derived from the theological principle of the "Headship of Christ in the Church." This, in turn, was derived from the Reformation doctrine of the "priesthood of all believers," according to Dr. Douglass. The polity of Congregational Churches placed maximum responsibility on all members of the church. In consequence, the agencies of fellowship, such as the General Council, stood under the "Headship of Christ" and could take immediate responsibility for the agencies' decisions, without instruction from the churches.

In his court testimony Douglas Horton took a similar position but developed it more fully in his address as Minister of the General Council at the opening of its meeting in June 1950.[4] A year later Dr. Horton expanded his thesis in lectures given at Mansfield College, Oxford, England. Those lectures, subsequently published under the title *Congregationalism: A Study in Church Polity*, drew upon seventeenth- and eighteenth-century Congregational theorists to support his view that the "council is a kind of congregation." He wrote:

Here is an illustration . . . which runs through my whole thesis. If a council is a congregation in respect of its holy covenant, shall we not do well consciously to make it as much a congregation in this regard as we possibly can? It has been found to be a means of grace in the General Council in the United States to apply an ancestral practice to a new situation: before the communion service on the first day of the council meeting, the entire company rises and repeats together the oldest of the American covenants, that of Salem of 1629. . . . In its formal dimension the Council does not differ from the ordinary Church.[5]

Although like a congregation, therefore a church, the council was distinct from the local church, and neither was subordinate to the other since both were under Christ. Thus the General Council, consistent with early Congregational theory, had the legal right to rule itself, and, by the same token, could not be ruled by others.[6]

In presenting this theory of the council as church, Dr. Horton was addressing not only those of his own communion who were seeking substantial grounds for the union, but also the Evangelical and Reformed Church. That body, committed to organic union, had found the *Interpretations* difficult to accept since they emphasized the union of the national representative bodies of the two communions rather than a union of the churches. Whether the Horton thesis actually influenced Evangelical and Reformed people is impossible to ascertain, of course. Of greater importance is the fact that the *Interpretations* were officially accepted by both the General Synod and the regional synods of that church body, and seemed thereafter to present no particular obstacles in the union effort.

The official response of the Evangelical and Reformed Church to the court decision, through its General Council and then at the 1950 General Synod, exhibited again the commitment to union. In characteristic fashion President Louis W. Goebel declared: "So long as they continue to extend to us the hand of friendship and fellowship, it would seem to us that we, who are members of a church committed to the principles of the reunion of Christ's Church, are bound to continue our willingness to accept that . . . hand." That spirit seems to account for the fact that the General Synod itself was not inclined to assess the situation critically. If anything, a "second-mile" attitude prevailed, leading to authorization for the General Council to participate, if necessary, in a redrafting of the Basis of Union and in the preparation of a constitution for the United Church. This authorization suggests that the delegates were either not sufficiently informed of or did not comprehend the actual situation. For the action was inconsistent with early concerns that no constitution be prepared until the union had been effected.[7]

This attitude of the Evangelical and Reformed Church was undoubtedly encouraging to pro-union Congregational Christian people. Moreover, since the burden of dealing with union issues remained within the latter fellowship, an assurance of commitment by the union partner provided incentive for continuing the effort to work through polity issues. Following the original court decision in favor of the opponents to the union, the Executive Committee of the General Council took steps to appeal it.[8] At the same time, efforts were redoubled to reconcile opposing views. Upon an authorization voted in 1950, a twenty-one-member Committee on Free Church Polity and Unity was established to undertake a study of "the principles and polity of Congregationalism," with "particular reference to the spiritual and legal methods for the participation of the free autonomous fellowships in the ecumenical movement."[9] Representatives of both viewpoints concerning the union were included in the committee.

When completed, the Report of the Committee on Free Church Polity and Unity was submitted to the 1954 General Council in New Haven. That body, in turn, sent it to the churches for their information, giving neither official approval

41

nor disapproval. At the same time, the churches received from the General Council's legal counsel an opinion about the report. Two factors apparently reduced the report's impact and frustrated efforts at reconciliation. First, on December 3, 1953, the New York Court of Appeals rejected the plea of union opponents to overturn the decision of the Appellate Division, thus confirming the position of the General Council concerning the union.[10] With the last legal obstacle removed, the union effort could be undertaken again without restraint. Second, the content of the report was itself ambiguous and indefinite, failing to remove the uncertainties about free-church polity that had opened so much debate. Lacking an authoritative word for the issues faced, the work of the committee received minimal consideration.

The single issue of greatest importance not definitively treated in the report had to do with the authority and power of autonomous units within the Congregational system of polity. Lack of clarity about this matter had been the major point of contention all along. Although the report drew upon wide-ranging opinion within the Congregational Christian fellowship and upon historical materials, it tended to reflect the anti-union position that the wider bodies of fellowship—associations, conferences, General Council, and boards—were *agents of the local churches and under their control.* The fact that the courts had ruled such a claim as without legal foundation did not resolve the issue for many on both sides of the union question.

Much of the confusion throughout the debate within the Congregational Christian fellowship was rooted in the failure to distinguish between authority and power with respect to the principle of autonomy. To speak about freedom and autonomy without recognition of the distinctive characteristics of authority and power is to misconstrue the principle of autonomy in social organization. Autonomy as a principle of social organization has to do first of all with the delineation of the boundaries of authority.[11] *Authority* is the right to exercise power—a right claimed or given by law or tradition. An autonomous organization, such as a local church, claims freedom from external authority and, in consequence thereof, sets the limits of its own authority in all other relationships. In so doing, the autonomous organization also limits its power, for *power* is the ability to determine the actions of others and the autonomous unit, by limiting its authority, cannot do to others what it will not permit to be done to it.

Historically, Congregational principles of church órganization arose as a protest against what were considered to be arbitrary claims of ecclesiastical authority and the consequent abuse of power. The claim to be free from such authority was based upon the faith affirmation of the supremacy of Christ's authority in the church. This claim led initially to a theonomous rather than the autonomous concept of church organization. However, as the voluntary principle of social organization developed in New England and all through the colonies, church organization was transformed from a theonomous to an autonomous model.

42

That transformation produced ambiguities for Congregationalism as population expanded and society became more complex. Eventually it required the development of a larger and more inclusive organization that by its very nature and function circumscribed the autonomy of the churches and produced tensions between units of power whose authority (the right to exercise power) was based chiefly on tradition or expediency and not upon a fully developed constitutional structure. Hence, the issue exposed in the union process was the right (or authority) of the several units of organization within the Congregational Christian fellowship to exercise power affecting one another.

In all organizations both formal and informal power play significant roles. Formal power, based upon legally established authority, is easily recognized. Informal power is more difficult to identify because it is not authorized. This inevitably complicated the debates relating to the roles of the wider agencies of fellowship, in particular the General Council's leadership. In a system that does not utilize constitutionally established procedures, centers of informal power become critically important for the functioning of a fellowship comprised of autonomous units. Maintenance of ministerial standing, for example, was rooted in local ordination but of necessity belonged to the wider fellowship rather than to the local church as population expanded and the number of churches grew. Inevitably, the handling of that function in the associations transferred a certain amount of power to those whose expertise and skill in the transmission of information and the regularizing of procedures made them of considerable importance for a stabilized and qualified ministry for the churches.

A parallel example on the national level of the denomination's organization may be seen in the office and role of the secretary of the General Council.[12] Until Douglas Horton assumed that position in 1938, the office of secretary was in many respects subordinate to that of the moderator. The title of Minister of the General Council, added to that of secretary, at Horton's suggestion, reflected the growing influence of the office. Horton's style of leadership and his deep involvement in ecumenical affairs gave that position a large measure of informal power. This was of considerable consequence, on the one hand, adding to the denomination's voice in the nation and, on the other hand, deepening the tensions between local churches and national offices.

A common assumption that all power, and therefore all authority, lay within the local church was being challenged thereby on practical or functional rather than theoretical grounds as Congregational churches developed their denominational structure.[13] There were purposes and functions of fellowship that required for the agencies the same autonomy enjoyed by the local church. Tension in some measure between these bodies would be unavoidable. Local churches, lacking authority over an autonomous agency, were not, however, without power. Two kinds of power were traditionally exercised: negative power, exercised through withdrawal and noncooperation, and consensus

43

power—constructive involvement with other local churches in the development of a common mind among delegates concerning issues under consideration. In the same way agencies of the wider fellowship could exercise power, usually of an informal character, over the local churches.

THE TIME OF UNCERTAINTY

While the Congregational Christian Churches were clarifying ambiguities within their denominational tradition in a process that placed exceptional strain on their fellowship, the Evangelical and Reformed Church was engaged in the consolidation of the union it had established in 1934. In many respects the most critical years in the latter union had been faced between 1934 and 1938 while the constitution was being drafted. Carl E. Schneider, church historian, called it a "reconstruction period" in which "with new insights of the Spirit, denominational traditions succumbed to the transcending ecumenical witness of the kingdom so that the concept of church *merger* was supplanted by that of an organic union."[14] Although such a characterization of the formative years of the new Evangelical and Reformed Church obscures the difficulties and issues that had to be faced, it is important as an indicator of the prevailing mood of that group as it looked forward to the United Church of Christ. Intensive debates over polity and doctrine produced understanding if not agreement. Coupled with commitment, this understanding enhanced the trust factor, which had been so prominent throughout the period of the union effort.

As an example of denominational formation through union, the Evangelical and Reformed Church experience stands in sharp contrast to that of the United Church of Christ in ways that will be discussed in succeeding chapters. However, for the purpose of perceiving the shifting dynamics of its relation to the Congregational Christian Churches in the "waiting period" between 1950 and 1954, attention must be given to the major features of its denominational development.[15] Several may be noted. First, denominational self-identity and unity were enhanced by common tasks related to the circumstances of World War II. The cries of war-distressed peoples led the first General Synod, under the newly adopted constitution, to establish the War Emergency Relief Commission in 1940. This and other human needs lifted up by the war awakened a generous response of concern that gave focus to all segments of the denomination. Second, the development of the national levels of organization, in which both of the union partners had relatively short experience, was influenced by the national character of war-related needs. Third, in the postwar period the emphasis moved to the strengthening of regional or state-level organization. By 1953 the General Synod had authorized full-time synod presidencies for the improvement of synod programs.* Finally, the new denomination had experienced

*In Evangelical and Reformed structures the term synod was employed on both national and regional levels. Regional synod boundaries, however, were not always related to state boundaries.

44

healthy growth, thus further enhancing self-identity and perhaps a subtle sense of self-sufficiency as a truly American denomination. That is to say that two small, German-background denominations, with only ethnic and confessional distinctions, had moved, from 1934 to 1954, into the mainstream of American denominational life.

In consequence of these developments the relationship between Evangelical and Reformed leaders and their Congregational Christian counterparts underwent subtle changes in the early 1950s. Events and developments between 1952 and 1954 show the critical nature of the changes. When the General Council (CC) met in June of 1952 at Claremont, California, the concern for reconciliation of opposing viewpoints was under the cloud of an announcement that the reversal of the lower court's decision by the Appellate Division of the New York courts would be appealed by the anti-union forces. Notwithstanding that cloud, the Claremont General Council did pass resolutions intended to pave the way for reconciliation. The primary incentive came from a resolution prepared by the Massachusetts Conference, calling for the initiation of a "constitution-drafting process." In a near-unanimous vote the General Council did authorize the suggested process, contingent upon approval of the Executive Committee (CC) and the General Council (E&R).[16]

As in the case of some earlier reconciling efforts, this one was ineffectual because of its ambiguities. In the first place, it was clear that a "constitution-drafting process" still depended upon the concurrence of the two executive groups. Second, the resolution called for "a draft of a proposed constitution for the General Synod of the united fellowship," a concept with little support in the Evangelical and Reformed Church, as shown in the General Synod (E&R) authorization below. Third, since the Basis of Union was still the implementing document for union, the initiation of a constitution draft would be tantamount to the substitution of a new basis of union. This possibility may have persuaded some anti-union people to support the resolution, since they felt the Basis of Union to be unacceptable. What new factors led to the proposal which had theretofore been considered impossible? Did the inconsistent action of the 1950 General Synod (E&R) give encouragement to the idea? That Synod authorized the General Council (E&R):

(1) To agree on behalf of the General Synod to a re-drafting of the Basis of Union and interpretations, if in the studied judgment of the General Council such becomes expedient. This power shall not be interpreted as authorizing the General Council to agree to any provision inconsistent or at variance with the Basis of Union and its interpretations. The re-drafted Basis of Union, if such is prepared, shall be submitted to the Synods for approval or rejection.

(2) To select persons to serve on a committee for the preparation of a proposed Constitution and By-laws for the United Church, if in its judgment such becomes expedient.[17]

45

It is clear that both the General Synod (E&R), in its 1950 action, and the Executive Committee (CC), in its support of the Massachusetts-inspired resolution at Claremont, were seeking every possible means of winning the anti-union movement to the side of union. At the same time, such efforts clearly were responsible for increased confusion and resistance because they seemed to be offering procedures that were not realistic. Intentions were misunderstood and words were misread. Many at Claremont probably viewed the resolution as did L. Wendell Fifield—a way of securing "a new document which would profit by what had been learned during our unfortunate controversy."[18] However, neither logic nor experience could support the expectation. The Evangelical and Reformed Church, having insisted on principle that the drafting of the constitution must await a living-together of the two communions, could not logically agree to a constitution before union. Further, the experience of the Congregational Christian fellowship, through years of intensive debate, was one of failure to bridge the gap between two understandings of Congregational polity. What amounted to parliamentary maneuvering was not likely to produce a miracle of harmony.

When the Cadman vs. Kenyon case was adjudged in favor of the union opponents February 20, 1950, the court issued a permanent injunction against any collaboration or joint activity between the two denominations. While the immediate effect was hardly disastrous, simply requiring cessation of a variety of cooperative efforts, the more serious results were evident in the period between 1952 and 1954. Not until December of 1953 was this restraint removed by the higher court's action. By that time the growth and development of the denominational life of the Evangelical and Reformed Church had added to the distance from the Congregational Christian fellowship.

Of equal, if not greater, importance was a change in executive leadership in the Evangelical and Reformed Church.* Louis W. Goebel had served as president for fifteen years, leading the denomination into greater unity and to greater ecumenical responsibility. In all of the union negotiations he had served as a statesman whose word and spirit maintained respect and trust on both sides. Both he and Douglas Horton had provided continuity throughout the course of the negotiations for their respective communions. At the 1953 General Synod (E&R) James E. Wagner was chosen to succeed Dr. Goebel. Wagner had served in numerous posts in the denomination, especially in the General Council, and consequently was intimately acquainted with all that had gone on in union efforts. He brought to this new position not only broad experience but a leadership style that inevitably proved to be salutary at a time

*Congregational Christian leadership underwent a parallel change two years later when Douglas Horton resigned (1955) to become dean of the Divinity School at Harvard University. He had served as Minister of the General Council since 1938 and was succeeded by Fred Hoskins in 1955.

when relationships between the two bodies required realistic reassessment and the bridging of a widening gulf.

Two events presaged the changes. In December 1953, shortly after the New York Court of Appeals ruled against the opponents to the union, Dr. Wagner wrote:

Many questions have been raised among us, further, as to just what is meant by a "constitution for the General Synod of the united fellowship." The fact that the words "General Synod" and "the united fellowship" appear to have been placed, not in opposition, but in complementary relation to each other, has suggested that what the Claremont action contemplated was only a unification of top-level administration of the work being carried on by our two fellowships. The reply made many times to that possibility has been that the Evangelical and Reformed Church is interested only in merger in the fullest, most real, organic sense—in precisely the sense in which we experienced it ourselves a score of years ago. We want to be "one body," not just "one head" with whomever we join heart and hand.[19]

This was an obvious response to the 1952 resolution of the General Council (CC) and an indication that some concern had been raised in Evangelical and Reformed circles. The fact that no attention had been given to the matter at the 1953 General Synod (E&R) suggests reluctance to deal with the matter as long as legal restraints were in force.

A second event two months later exhibited the width of the gulf that had grown between the proposed union partners. On February 9, 1954 a joint meeting of the Administrative Committee of the Evangelical and Reformed Church and the Advisory Committee of the Executive Committee of the General Council (CC) was held in Cleveland to consider next steps following the removal of legal restraints on the union as of December 3, 1953. President Wagner gave an appraisal of the problems facing the Evangelical and Reformed Church, citing the letdown of interest resulting from the long delay, the denomination's internal program development, resistance to the idea of drafting a constitution before the union was consummated, a shift in the denomination's self-understanding to a more presbyterian concept of the church, and the fear that the major arguments on behalf of the General Council (CC) before the courts had made organic union impossible.[20]

These comments had an unintended negative effect, which spread through the Congregational Christian fellowship. L. Wendell Fifield, who had attended the February 9 meeting, wrote a report for the Committee on Free Church Polity and Unity, indicating his judgment that the Evangelical and Reformed Church had closed the door "to any further negotiations looking toward union." He interpreted the growing Evangelical and Reformed self-consciousness and shift toward presbyterial polity as indication of a tacit rejection of the *Basis of Union and the Interpretations*.[21]

47

As a result of the uncertainties growing out of the February 9 meeting, the planned joint session of the General Council (E&R) and the Executive Committee (CC) on April 26 was postponed to October 12-13, 1954. In the interval several developments led to a more hopeful prospect. Most important in many respects was the statement issued by the Evangelical and Reformed General Council at its regular meeting, February 16-18, just one week after the meeting with the Advisory Committee (CC).[22] The statement was constructive and reassuring concerning the union, expressing in an irenic spirit the major concerns of the Evangelical and Reformed Church. In all respects it was consistent with the stance maintained throughout the union negotiations, and it reflected nothing of what some felt to be the negativism of the earlier joint meeting. At the same time, the statement, following so soon after that meeting, undoubtedly indicated that in the resumption of union negotiations new considerations required attention. In no way, however, did these indicate any waning of the commitment to the Basis of Union.

Of noteworthy significance also was the restrained action of the New Haven General Council (CC), June 23-30, 1954, reaffirming its desire for union as expressed in the Claremont resolutions of 1952 and "renewing its instructions as previously given to the Executive Committee . . . , so far as they are still applicable."[23] This action was, in effect, acknowledgment of the need to resume union negotiations within the context of an altered situation: On the Congregational Christian side this was the result of the long legal struggle, which had substantiated the General Council's position, and on the Evangelical and Reformed side a new denominational self-consciousness. Although the court decisions did not end the struggle within the Congregational Christian Churches, the altered context of the union negotiations was obvious. But the dimensions and full implications of the altered context would become clear only as the negotiations were resumed.

When placed side by side the statements of the General Council (E&R) and the General Council (CC) exemplified the chasm yet to be bridged. In the one case the Basis of Union was reaffirmed; in the other case what amounted to a substitute procedure was being promoted. How widely the differences were perceived is a matter of speculation, of course. Nevertheless, the respective statements did provide ground rules for new efforts toward union. Both parties to the union effort had constructed their statements so as to provide flexibility and reconciliation of viewpoints. These were decisive in relation to the outcome. In the Evangelical and Reformed statement the prefatory paragraph reiterated the position that "the faith and polity of any church must always be under the judgment and guidance of God's Holy Spirit." This affirmed reliance upon the guidance of the Spirit had kept the door open to union at many critical points. In the Congregational Christian statement the phrase "so far as they are still applicable" referred to the possibility that the Claremont position was probably not inflexible.

48

A JOURNEY TO SHARED UNDERSTANDINGS

The final stage of union negotiations opened in October 1954 with a joint meeting of the Congregational Christian Executive Committee and the Evangelical and Reformed General Council. In prepared statements both Wagner and Horton set forth their respective assessments of the issues to be faced, each concluding with affirmations of commitment that set the mood for continued effort. Fred S. Buschmeyer, serving as recording secretary, observed:

It was suggested that the joint meeting would do well to determine, at the outset, a frame of reference against which, or within which, decisions would be made. It was suggested that such a frame of reference might be found in this kind of statement: "It is our mutual aim to do those things which will make us a better witnessing church for the God and Father of our Lord Jesus Christ, at this particular time in history." It was pointed out that unless such a frame of reference were kept in mind we might easily become bogged down in purely personal preferences, fears, or differences of opinion. For the record it need only be stated that the discussion . . . was full, frank, and free; with wide participation, with virtually every fear or question ever heard by either denominational group placed clearly before the joint meeting, and with mutual readiness to provide the most accurate and honest answers possible.[24]

In an interesting way Wagner's and Horton's conclusions about a possible ground for hope converged on the Basis of Union. Although he laid out in detail the several obstacles to union that had become of paramount concern in his denomination, Wagner focused attention on resistance to the "top-level administrative merger" which the Claremont resolution seemed to imply. Added to that, in his judgment, were the implied binding explanations of the meaning of the Basis of Union offered by legal counsel in court on behalf of the General Council (CC). In both instances the implication of Wagner's comments was that such moves were not in accord with the *Basis of Union with Interpretations* to which the Evangelical and Reformed Church had agreed in overwhelming votes.[25]

Horton, sensitive to the reconciling intention of the Claremont resolution calling for work on a "constitution," felt nevertheless compelled to remind the group:

If it is decided to appoint a joint committee to consider what kind of a constitution should be adopted by the proposed United Church, let me say from the side of the Congregational Christian Churches that it would be desirable *not* to attempt to substitute another instrument for the Basis of Union and the Interpretations . . . , to dispense with them would be to dispense with the sole set of papers on the foundation of which the State has told us that we may erect our structure without jeopardy to any of the civil rights for which some of our people feared.[26]

It should be noted in passing that many supporters of the Claremont resolution

49

had not understood the implication that a "by-pass" of the controversial Basis of Union would make the General Council again vulnerable to legal attack. Horton was, therefore, carefully narrowing the arena of further negotiation.

Subsequent developments in the joint meeting demonstrated the wisdom of the two statements, particularly in the first paragraph of a public statement issued at its conclusion:

In accordance with actions of the General Council of the Congregational Christian Churches and the General Synod of the Evangelical and Reformed Church, we *reassert the validity of the Basis of Union with Interpretations as the basis for this merger.* We feel that the matter of the drafting of a constitution is adequately provided for in this instrument.[27]

This return to the "starting-point" gave the joint meeting much needed direction for steps leading to the consummation of the union. It enabled the group to set the convening General Synod for 1957 and to authorize a series of cooperative efforts designed to enhance acquaintance and fellowship between the two communions. In every respect a meeting that initially seemed to promise little became decisively significant for the hopes of those who had committed themselves to union.

Recorded minutes seldom convey the real spirit and atmosphere of a meeting. Raymond Walker, chairman of the Executive Committee (CC), sought in a later report to interpret what had transpired:

Here our spirits reached an ultimate low. Twelve years of effort appeared to be ending in futility. And then something happened! Earnestly we had prayed for Divine guidance—for a revelation of the will of God. It came! The Spirit of a new Pentecost fell upon the baffled company.[28]

Notwithstanding the successful rapprochement between the two church bodies reached at Cleveland, controversy seemed to be exacerbated by the reports from that meeting. Critics of the Executive Committee's role in union negotiations found new cause for concern, charging in particular that the Claremont and New Haven resolutions had been disregarded. The inevitability of such protests had been foreseen by many supporters of the resolutions, whose concerns for reconciliation had led them at least to make an effort to satisfy the anti-union people. Now with legal hurdles cleared such efforts at reconciliation would no longer take the form of compromise. The union, so long desired and supported by the denominational leadership and in the overwhelming votes of the General Council, must go forward. As in other instances, the determination to move ahead in the union effort was expressed not only in implementing resolutions but in the symbolic language of the faith. Both the minutes of the October 12-13 joint meeting and the report issued by it provide examples of the power of symbolic language when employed in relation to specific visions and goals.

Although of great significance to those seeking to forward the union, such language was neither acknowledged nor employed by the organized opposition in their publications.[29] That fact suggests that the gulf between the pro- and anti-union elements of the Congregational Christian fellowship is illustrative of a more fundamental division in organized American church life—between the church understood primarily as a people gathered by Christ the Lord and the church understood as a voluntary religious organization. The concept and practice of the voluntary religious organization in a democratic society are vulnerable to the same erosion of Christ's authority in the church as in an authoritarian and hierarchical society. In the voluntary religious organization, however, the democratic principle of the consent of the governed tends to elevate the will of the people above that of Christ.[30] This tendency is present in all American church life but often goes unrecognized. Symbolic religious language, although in itself ambiguous, often provides a necessary counterforce to such tendencies. The tension between these tendencies showed in American Congregationalism over the issue of the formation of the United Church. At the same time it is important to acknowledge that among those opposing the union were persons whose concerns stemmed from convictions about the nature of the church rather than democratic procedure. Howard J. Conn, a consistent opponent of the union, sought to base his opposition on the concepts of "fellowship and freedom" and argued therefrom that ecclesiastical organization beyond the local church tended always to preempt Christ's place as Head. Organized opponents to the union, however, chose to ignore such theological arguments generally in their published material.

The period between the 1954 joint meeting and the Uniting General Synod in June 1957 was marked by intensive activity in both denominations. Early in 1955 President Wagner prepared a statement for all ministers and lay delegates to the spring meetings of the thirty-four Evangelical and Reformed synods.[31] His interpretation of the prospect of the United Church was directed toward two major concerns: first, to help Evangelical and Reformed people see positive potential in the Basis of Union with Interpretations and, second, to help them claim the union effort as a responsibility laid upon them by their church tradition. Wagner supported the positive construction he was placing on the Basis of Union by drawing attention to parallel practices and trends in contemporary Congregationalism. He saw these as evidence that denominational practice in that fellowship would make possible the preparation of a constitution meeting the needs of both church bodies. While the concept of a constitution being definitive for the General Synod but descriptive of the relationships among churches, associations, and conferences was different in principle from Evangelical and Reformed understandings, it was, he contended, not so different in practice.

The Executive Committee of the General Council (CC) undertook a similar effort of interpretation in a Letter Missive sent to all Congregational Christian

51

churches in February 1955. Emphasis was placed upon reassurance concerning the rights of local churches under the Basis of Union and upon the mandate given by the General Council to work with the Evangelical and Reformed Church toward union. The *Letter* announced also the cooperative steps being arranged to enhance the acquaintance of each church with the other.

Perhaps the most significant step in getting acquainted was the formation, by joint agreement, of a committee for the study of basic Christian doctrine. Sixteen theologians, drawn in equal numbers from the two church bodies, were assigned the task of exploring theological presuppositions and doctrinal positions held within the two communions. This work became a preparatory step in the development of the Statement of Faith for the United Church.

Each denomination held national meetings in 1956. The General Council (CC) met in Omaha in June to take actions enabling the denomination to participate in the 1957 Uniting General Synod. An unexpected, but in every way a salutary, feature of the Omaha General Council was an all-night session to hear the reading of the Minutes of the Executive Committee for the period from June 30, 1954 through April 6, 1956. This effort was a response to a repeated charge that the Executive Committee had made secret commitments to the Evangelical and Reformed General Council. The salutary effect of that extraordinary parliamentary proceeding was to enhance the delegates' trust in the Executive Committee and to solidify support for the union. The final vote on the motion authorizing the 1957 Uniting General Synod was 1,310 to 179, with eleven abstentions. By that action the General Council took the final decisive step in the formation of the United Church of Christ.

Breaking tradition, the General Synod of the Evangelical and Reformed Church met at the end of the summer of 1956 instead of the usual June date. It was then able to respond to the favorable action at Omaha and to authorize its own involvement in the Uniting Synod in 1957. A spirit of anticipation and thankfulness marked the synod, even while some uneasiness was expressed about the precise character of organizational relationships in the new united church structure. In its report to the synod the General Council lifted up an issue that became a focus of later debate in the Constitution Commission: the relation of autonomous boards to the new General Synod. It had been an issue in the developing national organization of the Congregational Christian fellowship, and it was to continue to be a matter of debate in the new united church. Evangelical and Reformed Church concern, of course, grew out of its own tradition of holding all national agencies accountable to the General Synod.

In many respects the 1956 national meetings of the uniting churches marked the beginning of a new phase of union development. Decisive actions had been taken from which there was no turning back. Nevertheless, most of the issues were unresolved. From this point on, however, the issues became the common concern of the two communions; they were no longer confined to debate within the Congregational Christian fellowship. By the 1956 actions of the General

Council (CC) and the General Synod (E&R), the new stage of union development had its focus upon the effort to build a new structure of denominational church organization upon the principles of the Basis of Union. In that process the real significance of the long-debated issues in Congregationalism would be exhibited. Both national bodies adopted parallel "structures resolutions" providing for continuation of the current organizational structures of the merging bodies until the new United Church constitution and bylaws were approved and implemented.[32]

The mood of the delegates in both national meetings in 1956 reflected an awareness of the implications of their decisions to move ahead. Each body communicated its action to the other in words that expressed both a profound sense of accomplishment and a sense of deepened responsibilities. In its message to the Evangelical and Reformed Church, the General Council (CC) conveyed this mood:

We are heartened . . . that the delay has not diminished your willingness to accept us as equals in the bond we have covenanted together nor lessened your eagerness to walk with us as companions along the new way which God has graciously opened to us. We have known tribulations in our efforts toward union. We ask you to believe that the severity of our travail is also the measure of our desire that this union should come to pass and of the resoluteness of our purpose to accomplish it. These years of hope deferred have been difficult for us, as for you. Yet, by God's mercy, some good things have been wrought during the time of waiting. . . . The written covenant we have made—the Basis of Union with Interpretations—has been subjected to rigorous testing and is declared to suffice. . . . We desire to proceed with the union in accordance with this covenant.[33]

A similar spirit and resoluteness was evident in the message sent to the Executive Committee of the General Council of Congregational Churches by the General Synod (E&R):

We lay this act before you as a pledge of our continued faith in the wisdom and the rightness of this undertaking. We are more fully committed than ever to the covenant we have made with you in the Basis of Union with Interpretations, and we look forward with high anticipation to the consummation of this union. . . . We look upon this venture not as an end in itself, and even as we join with you in this union we devoutly pray for the unity of the whole Church of Christ and pledge to labor toward that end. . . . In drawing closer to you in bonds of unity, we have found ourselves drawn closer to our common Lord.[34]

UNION ACHIEVED

Although the interval between the 1956 meetings and the Uniting General Synod of June 25-27, 1957 was marked by continued criticism and another effort through the civil courts to forestall the union,[35] the new mood of determination did not fade. It was reflected primarily in careful planning for the upcoming uniting synod, with appropriate emphasis upon celebration and upon the implementing actions required by the Basis of Union. A Joint Planning Committee had been authorized by the two executive bodies in June 1955. This group, comprised of ten persons from each uniting communion, became the Business Committee for the uniting synod and was responsible for guiding the assembly in consideration of all necessary organizational steps.

Louis W. Goebel, former president of the Evangelical and Reformed Church, and George B. Hastings, a Congregational Christian layman, were elected co-moderators. In accordance with the provisions of the Basis of Union, Fred Hoskins and James E. Wagner were elected co-presidents of the new United Church. Co-secretaries named were Fred S. Buschmeyer and Sheldon E. Mackey. The selection of a treasurer was left to the Executive Council.* The latter body was formed by twenty-four persons chosen on an equal representation basis from the Executive Committee (CC) and the General Council (E&R). Implementing actions requisite for organizational continuity and merging, prepared in advance by the Joint Planning Committee and submitted to the synod for approval, included those that had been stipulated by the Basis of Union: the merging of the American Board of Commissioners for Foreign Missions with the Board for International Missions (later to be called the United Church Board for World Ministries); the Board for Home Missions (CC) and the Board of National Missions (E&R), along with other Congregational Christian and Evangelical and Reformed agencies serving homeland church concerns, into what later was named the Board for Homeland Ministries; and the social action agencies.

Three new ad hoc bodies were also formed: the Commission to Prepare a Constitution, the Commission to Prepare a Statement of Faith, and a Committee on Methods of Solicitation, Collection and Disbursement of Missionary, Benevolent, and Administrative Funds of the United Church of Christ. Membership of all agencies was drawn in equal numbers from the constituent bodies.

The Uniting General Synod was the first presentation of the "public face" of the new United Church of Christ. After fifteen years of official negotiations, the United Church of Christ had become visible in a public gathering of delegates. The importance of the uniting synod was chiefly symbolic. No critical debates and no crucial decisions were possible under the carefully designed agenda, framed within the provisions of the Basis of Union. The synod was simply a public representation of the reality of the union. For the delegates assembled, however, it was an occasion for celebration. Gratitude for an achievement which at one time seemed only a dream was spontaneous and joyful. In the spirit of their spiritual forebears of New Testament times, they were able "to thank God and take courage."

*F.A. Keck, treasurer of the Evangelical and Reformed Church, was chosen to serve. He was succeeded in April 1960 by Charles H. Lockyear.

54

Two clouds of uncertainty cast shadows upon the festive occasion: further civil litigation and the question of the number of Congregational Christian churches that could be counted as belonging to the United Church. The latter issue had been raised by union opponents before the uniting synod met. Local Evangelical and Reformed churches were in the United Church by vote of their regional synods. When the Basis of Union had been submitted to the Congregational Christian churches, 72.5 percent of *those voting* favored the union. But many had never voted at all. How did the local church (CC) become part of or remain apart from the United Church of Christ?

The question had important implications on two levels: the basis for computing the number of delegates for the second General Synod of the United Church and the issue of ministerial standing. The first part of the question led the Uniting General Synod to authorize the use of the last published membership figures "available six months before the next General Synod is to be convened, with the clear understanding that this action has no bearing on the question of the adherence of particular churches to the United Church of Christ."[36] This action represented the determination of pro-union people to avoid any move that would violate the free decision of any local church concerning its relation to the United Church. At the same time, by provision of the Basis of Union, Articles VI and VII, both ministerial standing and membership were inclusive of all in both communions.

The practical result of this was to shift the burden of a decision about participation in the United Church on local churches, individual members, and individual clergy. Where the local church and its minister were relatively indifferent about denominational relationships, membership in the United Church was nominal insofar as denominational officers were concerned. Also, local churches and ministers could simply participate without making any decision, since standing in the association was assumed. A final possibility was a vote by the local church to determine its relationship to the United Church. In those churches the result was often unfortunate division, with the formation of splinter groups affiliating either with the United Church or with the National Association of Congregational Christian Churches and, in a few cases, with the conservative Congregational Christian Churches.

Thus the gap between the enactment and the consummation of the union was filled with tension and concern. Pro-union people, committed to finding ways to express the wholeness and unity of the Body of Christ, could not be comfortable with the accomplishment of a union that did not include the total membership of the uniting bodies; anti-union leaders felt that many local churches were caught in an impossible situation where continued involvement in the association and conference would be counted as involvement in the United Church, while withdrawal seemed to be forfeiture of any claim on the national agencies to which they were accustomed to give support.

The Uniting General Synod marked the end of fifteen years of formal union effort. In the succeeding decade the consummation of the union would require equally great effort with new goals in new circumstances. Bishop Stephen C. Neill once wrote: "There is a general impression that, once the covenant of union has been signed, uniting churches live happily ever after. . . . In reality, just the fact of coming together makes tensions more severely felt than they were in separation."[37] That reality became increasingly clear to all as the uniting synod adjourned and steps were undertaken to build the organizational structure of the United Church.

CHAPTER 3

CONSUMMATION AND FORMATION

The critically formative years of the United Church of Christ lie between the Uniting General Synod of 1957 and the Synod of 1969. Embracing the decade of the turbulent Sixties, these years of "actualizing a church union," to employ a phrase of Prof. James M. Gustafson,[1] were fraught with tensions arising not only from organizational unification but also from the dramatically different circumstances of a society in radical transition. While the preparation and approval of the Constitution and By-Laws, thus consummating the union, did take place between 1957 and 1961, before the nation's trauma began, their implementation was accomplished in the context of radical challenge to religious institutions. The dimensions of that challenge would be measured by succeeding generations, but Sydney Ahlstrom's characterization is appropriate for understanding its implications for the new church:

> The decade *did* experience a fundamental shift in American moral and religious attitudes. The decade of the sixties was a time, in short, when the old foundations of national confidence, patriotic idealism, moral traditionalism, and even of historic Judaeo-Christian theism, were awash.[2]

Interaction between these two kinds of tensions—those from the internal process of institutional formation and those from external circumstance—is difficult to assess. At the same time particular instances of radical social change can be identified as points of pressure in the organizational development of the new denomination. Examples are the racial crisis and the issues of freedom and welfare, which surfaced at the 1963 General Synod and continued to command attention throughout the decade.

As the designers and builders of the institutional structure of the United Church set about their tasks following the Uniting General Synod, they were soon to discover

> that church unity at the institutional level requires processes of negotiation, ordering of resources and personnel, and development of patterns of administration and work that are in many respects as complex as doctrinal definitions of the unity of the Church in Jesus Christ. Thus the oneness that is affirmed by a uniting Synod is not institutionally actualized until many other factors are explored and adjusted.[3]

Exploration and adjustment did indeed claim the attention and energies of ever larger numbers of people as the union was actualized. In the long period of union discussions that preceded the 1957 uniting synod, acquaintance and mutual understanding tended to be limited to persons in posts of national leadership from both denominations. Over the years they had learned to know one another well. The formation of the new denomination's organizational structure, however, broadened the involvement of people from both groups and from other levels of institutional life. As they entered upon their new tasks of constitution-making, the preparation of a statement of faith, and the design for financial support, many of them were for the first time able to understand their own traditions in relation to others. Long hours of intensive discussion and debate led to a mutuality of understanding that blurred denominational distinctions. Mary D. Fiebiger, a member of the Commission to Prepare a Constitution, wrote:

Naturally, many questions arose in commission meetings and there was not always unanimous agreement on each issue. Compromises were made. It is significant, however, that not once in the past two years was any vote taken in the commission that resulted in a division along denominational lines.[4]

The positive aspect of the period under consideration in this chapter was the deepening and often exhilarating discovery of the reality of the United Church. Inevitably, the practices, habits, and loyalties of former denominational ties demonstrated their tenacity and influence. At the same time constitution-making and organization-building produced new perspectives about the church and resulted in new loyalties. For many of those engaged in these tasks the unresolved issues of the protracted debates before the act of union in 1957 were still important. After 1957, however, those issues were cast into a new framework of religious, social, and historical considerations. As a result the *consummation* of the union of the Evangelical and Reformed Church with the Congregational Christian Churches can be said to have taken place between 1957 and 1961 as the constitution and bylaws were developed and approved. In that period an increasingly important self-consciousness about the United Church began to demonstrate itself. That, in turn, was to prove a steadying factor in the period between 1961 and 1969 in the *formation* of the United Church as the organizational structure was developed and tested under the growing pressures of radical social change.

GROWING TOGETHER

Statistics and events concerning both denominations provide important data for understanding the context of church life within which the consummation of the union took place.

The closing years of the Fifties mark the final spurt of church membership growth in relation to the national population. Between 1956 and 1960—years coinciding almost precisely with the period of the consummation of the union—the percentage of the population affiliated with churches in the United States increased seven points, bringing the total to the all-time high of 69 percent. Statistics of the two segments of the new United Church parallel but do not correlate exactly with these.[5]

	Evangelical and Reformed 1956	1960	Change
Churches	2,736	2,718	−18
Members	784,270	817,951	+33,681
Ordained clergy	2,602	2,837	+235
Pastors	1,885	1,933	+48

	Congregational Christian 1956	1960	Change
Churches	5,549	5,402	−147
Members	1,379,394	1,436,884	+57,490
Ordained clergy	6,014	6,287	+273
Pastors	3,409	3,670	+261

When compared with church affiliation totals for the nation, both the Evangelical and Reformed Church and the Congregational Christian Churches showed somewhat smaller increases in membership. When the national gain was 11.5 percent, these bodies in the same period showed 4.29 percent and 4.09 percent respectively. The percentage of increase corresponds with the prevailing rate in both churches in the period from 1940 to 1956, except for a sharp upward change in 1945-46. The decreased numbers of churches reflect the general trend toward fewer but somewhat larger congregations. It is important to note, however, that the two uniting bodies were not well represented in those regions of the country showing the greatest population growth, the South and Southwest.

The obvious conclusion to be drawn is that during the time of the consummation of the union both churches maintained rates of growth exhibiting high spirit and morale. Concerns about the new United Church constitution and the eventual form of organization on national and regional levels did not interfere with the ongoing life and mission of the local churches and their agencies.

From another perspective the period of the consummation of the union is noteworthy for the events in which there were clear signs of growing together. The first of these—the birth of the *United Church Herald*—was not only of symbolic importance but also proved to have immeasurable influence in giving the United Church a sense of unity and identity.[6] In its first issue, dated October 9, 1958, the objectives and editorial policies of the *Herald* were clearly aimed toward expressing the reality of the United Church.[7] The editors agreed that the "united journal must provide concrete, visible evidence that the United Church of Christ is in process of becoming a reality."[8] To that end they sought to balance news items from the two church groups, while at the same time introducing feature articles of value to church people everywhere. A four-page spread of brief items under the heading "News Within the United Church of Christ" was followed by a section entitled "News of the World-wide Church," thus expressing the strong sense of ecumenical involvement to which the new denomination was committed.

Of equal, if not greater, importance in forming the identity of the United Church was the *Herald*'s role in giving voice to a theological perspective that was generally accepted although never explicitly affirmed in an official way. The *Herald*'s first editorial set a tone and adopted a stance that was never challenged:

The basic editorial emphasis of the journal of the United Church of Christ will be upon God's redemptive purpose for mankind as revealed in Jesus Christ, our Lord, and *made known* by the Holy Spirit *to those who within the Christian church seek the development and constant renewal of human character and culture through the proclamation of God's Word.*[9]

Although obviously not intended by the editors to be a statement for the United Church, it did have the effect of turning the church's public face toward a theology of human improvement without completely offending those who hold to more conservative views. Its ambiguous thrust was hardly consonant with Roger Hazelton's characterization of the "theological temper of the United Church" as "middle of the road," flexible, inquiring, and serious about tradition.[10] More important than the statement itself was an editorial policy that was open to divergent views and controversial issues.

Letters to the editor tended to offer enthusiastic endorsement of the new journal of the United Church. Acceptance of the Evangelical and Reformed constituency was strengthened by that denomination's tradition of heavy support by means of congregationwide subscription policies. Although Congregational Christian readers were fewer in number, their endorsement of the *Herald* was equally favorable.[11]

Other "growing together" events between 1957 and 1961 that provided elements of reality to the union were reported from time to time in the *Herald*. Joint planning for a 1962 merger of the Pilgrim Fellowship (CC) and the Youth Fellowship (E&R) began late in 1958, with intermediate steps laid out for both groups. A new church school curriculum, intended to replace the Church and Home Series (E&R) and the Pilgrim Series (CC), was announced in October 1959. Planning for this curriculum had begun in 1952. In anticipation of a merging of women's and men's organizations, as indicated in the proposed constitution of the United Church, there were joint meetings of the Women's

Fellowship (CC) and the Women's Guild (E&R) in the summer of 1959, followed in the autumn by joint meetings of the Laymen's Fellowship (CC) and the Churchmen's Brotherhood (E&R).

An in-depth experience of mutual discovery resulted from participation of Evangelical and Reformed synod presidents, Christian educators, and members of various joint committees in the 1960 Missions Council (CC) Midwinter Meetings held in February at Buck Hill Falls, Pennsylvania. This traditional Congregational Christian gathering had a role in the decision-making process of that denomination's various agencies that had been difficult for Evangelical and Reformed people to understand. The 1960 meetings did much to dispel the "mystery" of that process of informal sharing and coordination.

The merging of Mission House Theological Seminary (E&R) and the School of Theology of Yankton College (CC) in September of 1960 gave institutional expression to the basic ecumenical intention of the United Church. This seminary merger resulted in the creation of a new school, United Theological Seminary of the Twin Cities, with the announced purpose of providing a center for ecumenical theological education in the upper midwest region of the country. The seminary opened its doors on a new campus in New Brighton, Minnesota, a suburb of Minneapolis-St. Paul, in September 1962.

As on the national level so in the local scene, the United Church of Christ gained increasing visibility in the four years of consummating the union. In 1961 Co-president James E. Wagner reported that since the Uniting General Synod there had been eleven mergers of local churches involving the two constituent bodies. During the same period the Board for Home Missions (CC) and the Board of National Missions (E&R) had cooperated in establishing twenty-nine new mission congregations.

By 1959, when the Commission to Prepare a Constitution was to make its report to the Second General Synod, many delegates were self-consciously "United Church" as a result of two years of growing together. By 1961, when voting on the constitution was completed, that self-consciousness had removed many inhibitions of old habits, whether Congregational Christian or Evangelical and Reformed.

PRODUCING A CONSTITUTION

As the United Church of Christ looked forward to its second General Synod in 1959, the focus of attention was on the report of the Commission to Prepare a Constitution. On the one hand, interest in the constitution represented an awareness of the important role such a document would have in the formation of the denomination; on the other, it reflected the point of greatest anxiety, since divergent views about a constitution had, in various degrees, separated the uniting bodies and also some segments of the Congregational Christian fellowship from the national leadership.

Deferment of the preparation of a constitution until the act of union was formally and publicly declared had been an Evangelical and Reformed position from the beginning of the union effort. Since support of that position by the national leadership of the Congregational Christian Churches had been a chief cause of dissension within that fellowship, there were many who saw the issue as a remaining roadblock that could forestall full consummation of the union. It is clear, in view of subsequent developments, that preparation of the constitution *following* the act of union contributed significantly to its uniqueness and eventual acceptability.

Anxieties about the proposed constitution were evident in the careful plans laid out by the commission, with the full approval of the Executive Council, concerning the procedure for adoption of the proposed Constitution and By-laws. With its draft of the document the commission submitted a schedule at the 1959 Second General Synod calling for: (1) submission of a draft (following the synod) by November 1959 to conferences, synods, local churches, and agencies *for study*; (2) revision by February 1, 1961 for submission to the Third General Synod in 1961; (3) submission to the synods and churches for voting so that the Constitution and By-Laws could be declared in force by the Fourth General Synod in 1963.

This proposal of the commission and the Executive Council appeared to many of the delegates at the 1959 General Synod as a way of avoiding debate about the document at those sessions. Moreover, many delegates expressed fear that enthusiasm about the United Church might wane rapidly in an extensive period of organizational design and implementation. As a consequence the synod resolved itself into a Committee of the Whole for three lengthy periods of discussion of the proposed draft of the Constitution and By-Laws. From this vigorous involvement of the delegates in consideration of what should be included in the document came a substitute proposal concerning procedures and a timetable for its adoption. It called for submission of the draft, with a covering letter from the synod, to conferences, synods, churches, and agencies for study *and suggestions* by December 1, 1959; revision of the draft on the basis of suggestions by February 20, 1960; resubmission of the document to the whole church again; and consideration of the same at an adjourned meeting of the Second General Synod to be held in the summer of 1960, with the understanding that the Constitution and By-Laws could then be declared in force by the Third General Synod of 1961, if ratified by two thirds of the Congregational Christian churches voting and two thirds of the Evangelical and Reformed synods.[12]

The effect of this new timetable was to shorten the process of consummation of the union by two years and at the same time allow for more discussion. More importantly, it affected the mood and spirit of the church in a positive way, giving to the delegates a sense of ownership of the document and giving assurance to the churches that issues could be resolved constructively. Only the most skeptical could doubt the wisdom of the decision when viewed from the perspective of the adjourned sessions of the Second General Synod in the summer of 1960. Robert W. Spike probably spoke for many when he wrote after the 1960 sessions:

It is honest to say that a year ago there were real strains in respect to the union. Differences in historic practice and the tension of creating new agencies like unto none that existed made many people fearful that a serious roadblock had been reached. It is just as honest to say that a whole year of negotiation bore fruit in Cleveland. A carefully deliberating and thoughtful General Synod put its stamp on a charter, *wrought not out of least common denominators but out of reconciliation.*[13]

Dr. Spike's use of the word reconciliation deserves serious reflection in any effort to understand the developing spirit of the United Church of Christ. Reconciliation was in fact confirmed in many ways, but most notably by the response of the church as a whole in voting approval of the Constitution and By-Laws and thereby consummating the union in the Third General Synod in 1961. This is not to say that sharp disagreements disappeared and all controversy was eliminated. Conflict, however, tended to be absorbed constructively into stronger commitment. Reconciliation of divergent viewpoints came with mutual understanding. Obviously, delegate sensitivity varied with respect to the mood and spirit reflected in the deliberations of the 1959 synod. For some the points of conflict were alarming. Others felt these to be counterbalanced by the exhilaration that accompanied the adoption of the new "Statement of Faith" and the "Call to Christian Action in Society."

The significance of a manifest sense of reconciliation in the experience of the Second General Synod (both in 1959 and the adjourned session of 1960) is shown by the handling of a major point of contention—the structure of the major boards and their relationship to the General Synod. Although the matter was not resolved to the satisfaction of all parties, the conclusion of it in the final form adopted in the new constitution marked important shifts of understanding and sentiment in the uniting constituencies.

Behind the point of contention, of course, was an area of confusion and anxiety—the nature and use of a constitution. Co-president Fred Hoskins, in his message to the adjourned session of the synod in 1960, addressed the matter directly and with helpful clarity. Alluding to the "remarkable admixture of assumptions of what adopting a constitution would mean," he noted that some people "shudder" at the word, fearing undue restraint and rigid authority, while others see a constitution as a "mystical, self-authenticating," problem-solving device. Arguing that "we now have a built-in necessity to strive for *ways to protect the individual, his freedom and his church,*" Dr. Hoskins stated: "When the time is appropriate I am prepared to insist that the document we shall have before us is a superb contribution to the achievement of responsible freedom under God."[14] Clearly the new denomination was faced with the necessity to come to a reconsidered and vital view of the use of a constitution. Neither unreasonable fears nor presumptuous expectations could provide a foundation for a dynamic form of organizational structure. "The mythology that one denomination may have built up about the other has to be swept away in the course of preparation for union," wrote Douglas Horton.[15] What happened in fact, however, is that most of the "mythology" that Congregational Christian and Evangelical and Reformed people believed about each other had not been swept away before 1957. *The "sweeping away" took place in the period of consummation of the union between 1957 and 1961 when the constitution was designed and adopted.*

This was borne out in the floor debate over the issue of "one homeland agency" in the 1959 synod sessions. So-called "CC" and "E&R" positions were not as clear-cut as many had believed. The *Basis of Union with Interpretations* had stipulated an all-inclusive homeland agency. However, in its proposed draft the Commission to Prepare a Constitution excluded concerns about higher education and institutional benevolent work (hospitals, homes for the aged, and so forth). Defending the exclusion were representatives of institutions of higher education and benevolent institutions, chiefly of Evangelical and Reformed background. Their concern was twofold. On the one hand, they had operated in a tradition that emphasized an *immediate* and direct relationship to the churches and consequently feared that a *mediated* and indirect relationship required by the one-homeland-agency concept would weaken their support bases and remove their freedom. On the other hand, some Evangelical and Reformed educational leaders saw a fundamental philosophical difference between their understanding of the church's responsibility in higher education and that of the Congregational Christian leadership, especially prevailing in the Board for Home Missions. Evangelical and Reformed tradition tended to emphasize a relationship of responsibility with a token amount of control between the church's structures and its institutions. In Congregational Christian practice such a relationship was seen as a possible threat to the independence and freedom of the institutions; as a result, voluntary support without organizational connection to the churches was encouraged.

On the other side of the issue were many who supported the one-agency concept on philosophical and theological grounds.[16] Among these were representatives of the Board for Home Missions (CC) and the Committee of Fifty, which included representatives of the Board of National Missions (E&R). These proponents claimed that the trend toward a single agency for the homeland mission of the church was flowing widely throughout Protestantism, and that the times demanded a unitary rather than a fragmented Christian witness.

It was clear to most delegates that more time would be needed for resolution of the issue. Representatives of the Board for Home Missions, supported by various other agency people, sought a delay so that further discussion with the commission could be carried out. In retrospect it is clear that the delay allowed the supporters of the concept to marshal sufficient sentiment to effect a change in the commission's thinking so that both higher education and benevolent work were finally incorporated in a constitutional provision for one homeland agency. Subsequent developments demonstrated, however, that the change did not lay the matter to rest.

Less obvious in all of the debate over the single-agency concept was an underlying polity issue having to do with agency accountability in relation to the General Synod. This had been an internal issue in the Congregational Christian fellowship where anti-union churches held to the position that the boards were responsible to the local churches and to the General Council as their representatives. Thus, while in the 1959 synod the concern about agency accountability seemed to come chiefly from the Evangelical and Reformed delegates, the issue was alive among the Congregational Christian people as well. For within church systems employing Congregational polity, the development and expansion of national-level program agencies in the first thirty-five years of the twentieth century had often posed the question of their accountability to the local churches. The resources and power of autonomous boards tended toward a domination of denominational affairs that left local churches and regional units on the fringe of decision-making. The reorganization of the National Council of Congregational Churches in 1913 provided certain informal constraints of accountability with respect to program boards. From that time until the late 1950s, however, the increased resources and *informal power* of these boards had raised concern about what some felt to be imperviousness to local church interests. Hence, in the debate over the issue of one all-inclusive homeland agency for the United Church, the threat of unaccountable *informal power* was perceived by delegates from both of the union partners. At the same time Harold E. Fey, editor of *The Christian Century* and observer at the synod, commented that

> the factor which caused postponement for a year of a decision by the General Synod on the constitution was the objection on the part of some Congregational Christian boards to being made fully responsible to the elected representatives of the churches, or to accepting the decisions of such representatives concerning their scope and work.[17]

This suggests quite clearly one of the strains to which Robert W. Spike referred a year later.[18] The traditional Evangelical and Reformed reliance upon constitutionally defined relationships encountered the Congregational Christian system of autonomous units cooperating. More than a year before the 1959 synod, the Committee of Fifty (the interim board of directors of the new UCC Board for Home Missions, with equal CC and E&R representation) had sent a

65

memorandum to the Commission to Prepare a Constitution that addressed the issue of accountability. The chief thrust of the memorandum was affirmation of the importance of clearly delineated responsibilities among the boards, the General Synod, and the Executive Council. In arguing for this the committee was making the point that any legal contractual way of specifying responsibility would impair the autonomy of the several units—the boards and the General Synod. The relationship proposed was one of mutual trust and common goals. How viable this could be over a period of time remained a concern for those who saw accountability in more legal terms.

It is important, however, to reiterate the point that the issue did not represent *simply* a division between the two uniting traditions. This was shown in the 1959 synod by an amendment that was offered to add to Paragraph 22 of the proposed constitution the words "such actions, decisions, or advice being *advisory, not mandatory.*" This was opposed by both groups of delegates. When debate over this issue continued in the 1960 Adjourned Meeting, those words were dropped, but only after strong concern was expressed about the General Synod's apparent impotence in the face of bureaucratic centralization in the boards.

There were other notable points of reconciliation of understandings and attitudes within the emerging fellowship of the new United Church as the Constitution and By-Laws were prepared and debated. Of strategic importance both theologically and structurally were new perceptions of the nature of the church. Although sharing a common Reformed tradition, the union partners had experienced in their individual histories some quite different accents in church organization. This was particularly true with reference to the reality of the church. At what point is the church most real as church? In the local setting, where people are gathered for worship? Or in the larger organization, in which local churches are simply components of the whole?

As Gerhard W. Grauer, chairman of the Commission to Prepare a Constitution, pointed out in his statement to the 1960 adjourned session of the Second General Synod, there were dangers in church union efforts of vitiating "the distinctive character of the Christian witness" through either an insistence upon one point of ecclesiology and theology or in a de-emphasis of the same.[19] The Basis of Union had established the principle that "the basic unit of organization of the United Church of Christ is the Congregation; that is, the local church" (Art. III A). By the time this principle was incorporated in the proposed Constitution and By-Laws (Art. IV, 7), there was a general consensus about its importance. Nevertheless, there were divergent points of view concerning the role of the local church within the organizational structure of the United Church. In short, if the *United Church* is composed of "congregations or local churches" (Art. II, 5), what relationship is to be maintained between the *parts* (each of which is fully the church) and the *whole* (which has no reality apart from its

66

components)? Two points of view prevailed and then were reconciled and affirmed.

On the Evangelical and Reformed side, which had traditionally placed emphasis upon the larger structural representation of the church (synods and General Synod), there was also a central article of faith: that the church is "gathered by the Son of God through Word and the Spirit." Hence the concern that the accent fall heavily upon the activity of Christ the Lord in and through the church in the local setting. This point gained recognition and affirmation in the Constitution and By-Laws in Article IV, 8:

A local church is composed of persons who, believing in God as heavenly Father, and accepting Jesus Christ as Lord and Saviour, and depending on the guidance of the Holy Spirit, are organized according to appropriate ecclesiastical and legal procedures for Christian worship, for the furtherance of Christian fellowship, and for the ongoing work of Christian witness.

The effect of this was to reassure those who were concerned to see the emphasis fall on God's activity through Christ as the distinguishing mark of the church and as the bond of unity between all local churches.

The point was made even more explicit in Article IV, 20:

The congregations or local churches of the United Church of Christ have, in fellowship, a God-given responsibility for that Church, its labors and its extension, even as the United Church of Christ has, in fellowship, a God-given responsibility for the well-being and needs and aspirations of its congregations or local churches. In mutual Christian concern and in dedication to Jesus Christ, the Head of the Church, the one and the many share in common Christian experience and responsibility.

These paragraphs in the constitution blended the accents upon the local church and the larger fellowship (expressed in denominational organization) without rigid definitions and legal language.

On the Congregational Christian side there was a similar reconciliation of divergent points of view. In view of Congregationalism's historic struggle to liberate the church from hierarchical domination, both ecclesiastical and political, it was not surprising that there was a prevailing concern to safeguard the *autonomy* of the local church. That concern was born in a zealous devotion to the lordship of Christ and a resistance to any form of authority over the local church that did not arise from within its membership. Thus, while Congregational Christian delegates could give wholehearted support to Paragraphs 8 and 20 quoted above, they were equally wholehearted in their support of Paragraph 21, which spelled out the significance of the autonomy of the local church:

Nothing in this Constitution and By-Laws shall be construed as in any way giving to the General Synod, or to any conference or association, now or at any future time, the power to abridge or impair the autonomy of any congregation or local church in the management of its own affairs. Nothing herein contained shall destroy or limit in any way the right of each congregation or local church to continue to operate in the way customary to it; to retain or adopt its own methods of organization, worship and education; to retain or secure its own charter; to adopt its own constitution and by-laws; to formulate its own covenants and confessions of faith; to admit members in its own way and to provide for their discipline or dismissal in any way not contrary to law; to call or dismiss its pastor or pastors by such procedure as it shall determine; to own and manage its own property and funds; to control its own benevolences; and to withdraw by its own decision its membership in the United Church of Christ at any time without forfeiture of ownership or control of any real or personal property owned or controlled by it.

While reassuring to some, to others the paragraph seemed to contradict the implied commitments of the earlier paragraphs of Article IV. Vigorous debate over the issue at the 1960 synod sessions resulted in agreements that made approval possible. At the same time many throughout the United Church found the paragraph controversial. As is often the case, the language required to develop effective safeguards for freedom seems to lack the possibility of positive construction. To those who found the paragraph disconcerting the problem was in that it seemed to elevate the principle of dissent above the principle of responsibility to the larger whole. The fact was, however, that commitment to the health of the larger communion of the church was dominant among those who supported the paragraph. Holding Paragraphs 8, 20, and 21 together is a prerequisite for understanding the achievement of reconciliation represented in the Constitution and By-Laws. Their seeming contradictory import reflected the overriding compulsions of the commitment to unity that led the delegates to affirm them.

Between the 1959 and the 1960 meetings of the Second General Synod, the Commission to Prepare a Constitution received over five hundred communications offering suggested changes. This input from individuals, churches, conferences, synods, and agencies did much to prepare the way for an ultimate reconciliation of divergent positions. No small part of that reconciliation was demonstrated in a communication signed by executives and leaders of all the involved agencies supporting the second draft of the constitution as it was to be submitted at the Adjourned Meeting.[20]

Two significant cautions were voiced also in the interval of the 1959 and 1960 sessions. J. Paul Williams expressed a concern that the new proposed constitution seemed to indicate overanxiety about the autonomy of the local church while paying little attention to guarantees for democratic procedures in the national-level structures.[21] Howard F. Schomer gently chided the Executive Council leadership for failure to trust General Synod delegates and the leading of the Holy Spirit in the life of the church.[22]

Although the focus of attention at the Second General Synod in 1959 was the proposed Constitution and By-Laws, the influentially moving event was the presentation and adoption of the Statement of Faith.[23] In his report to the adjourned session of the Second General Synod in 1960 about the preparation of the Constitution and By-Laws, Gerhard Grauer called attention to the fact that

> last year we sealed our union in a great act of faith, not by a creedal statement or a doctrinal pronouncement, nor even by legal enactment, but by a Statement of Faith. . . . Historians, we believe, will always point out that the Statement of Faith which really unites us was adopted before a constitution was adopted.[24]

There is little doubt that Grauer's perception was right: the union had been formalized by the votes of the Uniting General Synod in 1957, but the sealing or confirming of those formal actions of a deliberative body occurred in the unifying experience of a liturgical act—the recitation of the Statement of Faith the synod had voted to approve. By that act the synod found a solid base for its courage to deal with the difficult issues of constitution-making.

When Elmer J.F. Arndt, chairperson of the Commission to Prepare a Statement of Faith, presented the commission's report in its final form, the synod stood to proclaim:

> We believe in God, the Eternal Spirit, Father of our Lord Jesus Christ and
> our Father, and to his deeds we testify:

> He calls the worlds into being,
> creates man in his own image,
> and sets before him the ways of life and death.

> He seeks in holy love to save all people from aimlessness and sin.

> He judges men and nations by his righteous will
> declared through prophets and apostles.

> In Jesus Christ, the man of Nazareth, our crucified and risen Lord,
> he has come to us
> and shared our common lot,
> conquering sin and death
> and reconciling the world to himself.

> He bestows upon us his Holy Spirit,
> creating and renewing the church of Jesus Christ,
> binding in covenant faithful people of all ages, tongues, and races.

> He calls us into his church
> to accept the cost and joy of discipleship,
> to be his servants in the service of men,
> to proclaim the gospel to all the world and resist the powers of evil,
> to share in Christ's baptism and eat at his table,
> to join him in his passion and victory.

He promises to all who trust him
forgiveness of sins and fullness of grace,
courage in the struggle for justice and peace,
his presence in trial and rejoicing,
and eternal life in his kingdom which has no end.

Blessing and honor, glory and power be unto him. Amen.

Prepared by a commission of thirty members, drawn equally from the uniting fellowships, the Statement of Faith was offered to the synod as a testimony rather than a creed.* In language that exhibits the influence of the scriptures in which the accent falls on God's activity among his people, the Statement testifies to the divine shaping of the church for mission in the world. As such it expresses the faith of those who know themselves involved in a relationship with God's work for humanity. The delegates' response to the proposed Statement provided "the most dramatic moment" of the synod, when a unanimous vote brought a spontaneous singing of the Doxology. This enthusiastic response presaged widespread acceptance not only in the United Church but also in other denominations.

In many respects an equally significant action was enthusiastic endorsement of a "Call to Christian Action in Society," a document that set the tone for a major focus of concern in the new denomination.[25] With that "Call" and the Statement of Faith the new United Church found common ground that could be reflected in worship and in work, even while the debatable issues of denominational organization required more discussion. There was a common mind, expressed in the Preamble to the Constitution, that the purpose of the new United Church was "to express more fully the oneness in Christ of the churches composing it, to make more effective their common witness in Him, and to serve His kingdom in the world."

In summary, it is clear that the debates over the proposed Constitution and By-Laws reflect: (1) the ambiguous understandings of Congregationalism; (2) the recognized need to develop a viable denominational structure in the Congregational Christian fellowship; (3) the absence of a clearly articulated ecclesiological principle in the Evangelical and Reformed Church; and (4) the pressure of issues arising from larger and more complex organizational forms. The result insofar as the Constitution was concerned is demonstrated in a built-in flexibility that was a threat to some but a sign of promise to others in the new church.

When the Adjourned Meeting of the Second General Synod voted unanimously on July 7, 1960 to adopt the Constitution, the consummation of the union had passed a decisive point. Next steps included voting by the churches

*See Appendixes for a membership list of the commission.

and the synods, a process set for completion by 1961 but during which time some discouragement and anxiety again arose. The discouragement resulted from what seemed at first to be the slow response of churches in voting. Although the First Congregational Christian Church at Stockbridge, Massachusetts was the first to vote approval of the Constitution, by November 3, 1960 only 117 churches had voted, of which 95 were affirmative. By May 15, 1961, just seven weeks before the Third General Synod, the total number of Congregational Christian churches voting approval was 2,960 out of 5,458, with 23 of the 33 synods (E&R)* also approving. Up to that time 215 churches (CC) and one synod (E&R) had voted disapproval. It was clear that some effort would be required to secure a significant number of church votes by the June 1, 1961 deadline set by the General Synod. Approval of the Constitution signified membership in the United Church of Christ, hence a concern that a majority of the 5,458 Congregational Christian churches would take action before the 1961 General Synod declared the adoption of the Constitution and By-Laws.

Another source of anxiety was a growing uneasiness among some Evangelical and Reformed people about the structure proposed for the United Church. Many did not see the hope of a significantly new church organization being realized. Specific fears were: (1) that because of the proposed state-level conferences, the conferences of the Congregational Christian Churches would simply absorb the Evangelical and Reformed units; (2) that the limited authority of the General Synod was creating a power vacuum into which the highly organized boards and instrumentalities were already moving; and (3) that the locus of the church being the local church would result in a diffuse national identity that belied the reality of the denomination as the church.

The surfacing of these concerns was highlighted in a proposal by William L. Rest, president of the North Illinois Synod, that that synod decide not to vote on the proposed Constitution in 1961 and in the invitation to eleven other synods to likewise refrain from voting. The intention was thus to delay approval of the Constitution (since fewer than two thirds of the synods would have approved) and to keep the "structures resolutions" in force. This would have the effect of delaying consolidation of the boards and instrumentalities and would give the General Synod and the conferences more time to organize. Rest clearly did not want to damage the union. He was asking all Evangelical and Reformed ministers to face the question: "Is there anything we can do that will not wreck the merger and still stop this drifting into a congregational structure?"[26]

Throughout the debate over the Constitution and during the voting by the churches, anti-union forces in the Congregational Christian fellowship continued to express opposition to the formation of the United Church. Those efforts produced uncertainty and tension for many local churches as convinced

*In 1956 General Synod (E&R) combined the Iowa and Nebraska synods into a new Midwest Synod, thus reducing the number to thirty-three.

individuals on both sides of the issue sought to influence decisions. For some union opponents the proposed Constitution was confirmation of the fears they had expressed all along. The Committee for the Continuation of Congregational Christian Churches reproduced and circulated the letter of William L. Rest as evidence that the union was being engineered by ecclesiastical bureaucrats.

Despite the negative response in both of the uniting fellowships, the Third General Synod, convening in Philadelphia, July 3-7, 1961, was able to declare the Constitution and By-Laws adopted and in force. The co-secretaries, Nathanael M. Guptill and Sheldon E. Mackey, were able to report that 3,547 churches had voted approval, while 342 had voted disapproval, making the voting churches in favor 91.2 percent of the total, far above the 66.7 percent required.[27] In the Evangelical and Reformed constituency thirty-two of the thirty-three synods approved the Constitution, thus placing all local churches of that communion in the United Church. The one synod voting disapproval of the Constitution, the Magyar Synod, nevertheless explicitly stated that its vote pertained only to that document and not to the United Church.*

Adoption of the Constitution and By-Laws in 1961 signaled the consummation of the union affirmed four years earlier at the Uniting General Synod. The United Church of Christ emerged as a new form of denominational organization. Although bearing significant marks of continuity with the organizational traditions of the uniting bodies, the new structure was obviously a venture into uncharted territory.[28] It was built upon *reconciliation* rather than *compromise;* that is, reconciliation of concepts of order and freedom, authority and power, that had become rigidly encased in memories and habits of eras long past. That reconciliation symbolized a concept of Christian unity which needed testing; namely, organizational unity expressed in church union is possible only where commitment to one another as members of the Body of Christ has been demonstrated. In United Church of Christ experience that commitment was tested in three major steps: (1) the preparation and affirmation of the Basis of Union from 1942 to 1949; (2) the act of union in which adherence to the letter and spirit of the "structures resolutions" gave transitional continuity in 1957; and (3) the preparation and adoption of the Constitution and By-Laws as the final act of union consummation between 1957 and 1961.

Historical perspective affirms the appropriateness of such testing of commitment. Subsequent experience suggests the impossibility of drafting a constitu-

*The Magyar Synod had steadfastly supported the union but had also asked that it be exempted from realignment procedures which would disperse the Magyar churches into the regional conferences. It is also noteworthy that in all previous votes on the union the Dakota Synod had been the only negative voice. That synod, however, voted approval of the Constitution. This reversal was due to changes in pastoral leadership between 1947 and 1961.

tion, which would be more than a series of compromises, without the commitment that was exhibited between 1957 and 1961. Thus reconciliation made consummation of the union possible. Delegates to the Second and Third General Synods testified to a sense of "spiritual renewal" and "mutual invigoration" that marked their awareness of being *of* the United Church of Christ.

When the United Church entered the mainstream of American Christianity as a newly organized denomination in 1961, its significance was more in promise than in reality. While the process of the consummation of the union had been internally of critical significance for the church, the viability of the structure it had designed and adopted was not yet proved. The union had been consummated, but the church still had to be formed organizationally in that structure. The years of *formation*, 1961 to 1969, would demonstrate whether "in the United Church of Christ American Protestantism has the model of union it has so long needed."[29]

ORGANIZATIONAL FORMATION

Organizational formation in religious communities generally exhibits complex interplay of political, theological, religious, and social factors. In the experience of formation in the United Church of Christ the fourth factor, that of radical social upheaval, became decisive. Recognition of this is essential to any understanding of the formative years of 1961 to 1969. This in no way underrates the roles of the political, theological, and religious factors—all of which interact with the social.

In a traditional sense the ordering of the church's life by the ministry of Word and Sacrament goes on all the time. When organizational concerns are high in the community of faith, however, there tends to be less awareness of the influence of the church's religious and theological activity. This is particularly true when organizational formation is dominant in the church-union process. Political considerations seem to many people to be dominant since the pressure of old organizational models and habits often move the church in the direction of compromise and accommodation. A superficial glance at what transpired in the formation of the United Church of Christ might confirm that impression. However, the record of those decisive years suggests a time of dynamic development in which *both* organizational *and* spiritual formation took place in ways that gave the new church a distinguishing character.

Formation, whether organizational or spiritual, is brought about by both constant and variable disciplines. As the 1961 General Synod began to function under the newly adopted Constitution and By Laws, it was under the constant discipline of a structural design affirmed by the churches. Learning to use that design in ways that fulfilled the announced purpose of the new denomination and the expectations of its constituency required political sagacity and determination. Another constant was the faith professed. Obedience to the claims of faith in "God, revealed in Christ, and in the Holy Spirit" was an insistent appeal made by the co-presidents, Fred Hoskins and James E. Wagner, in their final messages. It was also the appeal made by Ben Mohr Herbster, who became president at the close of the synod sessions.

Variable disciplines in organizational and spiritual formation are provided by the demands placed upon the church as it seeks to fulfill its God-given mission in particular social and cultural contexts. Changing demands, fluctuating resources, and an often-faltering response to the Holy Spirit were of primary significance in the church's formation during the upheavals of the Sixties.

While the Third General Synod faced a weighty agenda of organizational chores, many of which would not be completed for several years, the delegates were given a glimpse of the way the church's mission was being shaped when Ben M. Herbster said in his acceptance speech:

The United Church of Christ will be able to justify all the "blood, sweat and tears" that have gone into the effort, during these past years, only if we shall be able to achieve a new devotion and loyalty to the demands of the Gospel of Jesus Christ. Those demands include, beyond a personal commitment to the way of Christ, also *an unending effort to guarantee to all men, women and children, here in America and to the ends of the earth, a chance to live in freedom, good will, justice and advantage.* . . . I pledge to all of you that we shall not be content as long as there are any disadvantaged people. We shall work, pray and strive that all men shall have a decent chance at life.[30]

Because of concern with a multitude of organizational matters, it is possible that the import of Herbster's words was not fully absorbed by those who heard them. The statement reflected the words of dedication with which the Second General Synod in 1959 closed its "Call to Christian Action in Society": "To these tasks we dedicate ourselves in the name of God who calls us to seek justice for all his children and to love our neighbor not only in word but in deed. In him is our confidence and our trust."[31] The significance of these statements along with the *Herald* editorial cited earlier in this chapter increases when they are considered in relation to the question of United Church of Christ identity.[32] The style of life and thrust of mission did not arise from a decision of the delegates. There was, in fact, quite minimal discussion about such matters. Denominational leaders were determining the direction of the new church body—*assuming* a consensus—and in so doing they were contributing to its spiritual formation.

That the delegates generally did not dissent from the directions indicated is evidence either of agreement or of indifference. Retiring Co-president James E. Wagner was sensitive to the latter problem, and in his last message from his position said:

I stress one other hope, . . . that by *every* corporate means available to us and by the rededication of our own personal habits, we shall seek for the

United Church [of Christ] an ever-deepening rootage of its witness and service in the Bible and in the great historic mainstream of the Christian doctrinal tradition. Protestantism has had constantly to face the Roman Catholic charge of an alleged "indifferentism" in Christian doctrine. Strangely enough, within the Protestant fellowship, every movement for Christian union has had to bear, in turn, from fellow-Protestants less concerned about or even vigorously opposed to the reuniting of the Churches, this charge of "indifferentism" respecting Biblical truth and Christian doctrine.[33]

Wagner's concern actually received little attention at the time. This is not to say that indifferentism prevailed, but preoccupation with other matters left the spiritual formation of the new organization to a few articulate leaders, who were in themselves symbols of spiritual strength and integrity. Abraham Akaka, synod chaplain and a clergy delegate from Hawaii, illustrated this in his enthusiastically received messages on the theme "Building a New Church," in which he called for a "discipline . . . [that] can deliver a blow against the forces of evil in the world."[34]

Learning to live under the newly adopted Constitution and By-Laws required, among other things, adjustment to new labels and new terminology. Some of these were unfamiliar to both traditions: Board for World Ministries, Board for Homeland Ministries, Stewardship Council, Council for Lay Life and Work, and Office of Communication. In all these names was exemplified an effort to recognize the changed circumstances of the society in which the church was about its mission. "World Ministries" seemed more appropriate than "American Board of Commissioners for Foreign Missions" (a name signifying a most distinguished history in missionary effort) or "Board for International Missions." Use of the word ministries rather than "missions" signified the new world situation for the church. Likewise, use of the new term ministries in designating the replacement for the Board for Home Missions and the Board for National Missions indicated not only a wider scope of program activity in the homeland but also a new concept of the mission of the church in the society: not simply church extension but the church ministering to human needs on all levels.

Perhaps no one of the new agencies provided by the Constitution and By-Laws exemplified the changes in national-level organization as much as did the Stewardship Council. Its forerunner was the Committee on Methods of Solicitation, Collection and Disbursement of Missionary, Benevolent, and Administrative Funds of the United Church of Christ. This committee, established by vote of the Uniting General Synod in 1957 under the provisions of Article IV, Sections K and L of the Basis of Union, presented a lengthy and detailed series of recommendations to the Second General Synod designed to implement the concept of a central treasury for the United Church. These recommendations had far-reaching implications with respect to budget, treasury procedures, stewardship, and promotion. From this committee also came the design of the Stewardship Council, an agency of coordination, education, and promotion, which symbolized the unity of the denomination in program support.

A distinctive break from a long-time tradition was the abandonment of separate organizations for laywomen and laymen. In the design of the Council for Lay Life and Work was the recognition of a changed society in which women were increasingly free from housekeeping models of church life. Equally important was a greater awareness of the ministry of the laity in the total life of the church—very much as a result of special studies done by the World Council of Churches and its predecessor movements.

Also reflective of a changed society was the provision for an Office of Communication as a denominational instrumentality. Designed not only to manage in a more sophisticated manner the church's public relations but also to lead the denomination in the use of the mass media for its ministries, this office from the beginning had a crucial role in the development of the United Church of Christ public image. As such it had exceptional impact upon the organizational formation of the church as well.

Organizational formation had to do not only with national-level agencies but also the realignment of regional groups—synods, conferences, and associations. Acting upon a provision of the Basis of Union, the Uniting General Synod in 1957 had authorized a study of all factors "involved in the realignment of Associations, Conferences, and Synods."[35] The intention of this action was to offer assistance in a process where the initiative lay with the regional groups themselves. Of particular importance was the subsequent action in 1961 of the Third General Synod, authorizing the continuation of the Committee of Nine to Study Realignment of Conference and Synodical Boundaries.[36] In this action the General Synod sought not only to provide assistance in the formation of new conference structures but also to give counsel about procedures, constitutional provisions, and "the importance of regionalism for program, fellowship and education."

In acting thus the General Synod exhibited an aspect of the organizational concept of the United Church that combined freedom and order. The continuing regional bodies were free to make their own decisions about their existence, internal affairs, and program. At the same time, expressive of the principle that autonomy did not isolate units within the United Church, the General Synod offered a means of order that gave regional units common purposes, designs, and patterns of relationships, which gradually established uniformity and mutuality. The effect was a creative use of principles of church order that were important to both former traditions: the freedom of autonomous units in the Congregational Christian tradition and the orderly procedures of the Evangelical and Reformed system. The wide acceptance of this among the conferences and synods is reflected in the report of the committee at the Fourth General Synod of 1963 that as of that date twenty-eight new United Church conferences had been formed. These combined the synods (E&R) and the conferences (CC) in most states. In a few cases where only Congregational Christian churches were represented, the conference (CC) acted officially to become a conference of the United Church of Christ. By 1965 forty-one conferences were organized as regional expressions of the United Church of Christ.

Attention must now be turned to two other matters that were of decisive significance in the formation of the United Church in the period between 1961 and 1969. The first of these has to do with the development of working relationships between the several autonomous organizational units that make up the United Church. The second has to do with the impact of a radically changed social situation upon the evolving organization of the denomination. They must be considered together. In both matters the United Church was severely tested. The consequences are shown in the organizational restructuring that took place in 1969-71.

Establishment of working relationships between the autonomous units of organization was essential to the reality of the United Church as a denomination. These relationships were described in the Constitution and By-Laws, but their utilization and fulfillment depended upon more than the written word. President Ben M. Herbster, whose term of office began at the close of the Third General Synod, recognized the crucial need for communication and correlation between the various units. He understood his office to have a major role in facilitating these relationships. Monthly meetings of the heads of the instrumentalities in his office were one effort to establish a sense of common purpose. By supplementing these with a heavy schedule of preaching and speaking engagements throughout the country, Dr. Herbster became something of a symbol of the reality of the United Church to many people in the merged communions who had very few other visible evidences of it.

Herbster's role in this formative period of the church's life deserves attention for still other reasons. He had served many years as a member of the General Council (E&R) and had been deeply involved in the discussions and negotiations leading to the union. Between 1957 and 1961 he served as co-chairman of the Executive Council along with Ashby E. Bladen. In many respects Herbster's role was mediatorial within the structures of the church and, in a symbolic way, in the church at large. He represented the kind of faith and active piety that appealed to many in the constituency, while at the same time displaying a Calvinist passion for the rule of God in the affairs of the world. This enabled him to give the church vigorous and prophetic leadership at a time when human needs presented the Christian community with a mandate that could not be avoided. The ground of Christian hope and responsibility for him was not humanitarianism however; it was in the reality of God's presence and work among God's people.[37]

This combination of prophetic concern and faith piety was exhibited especially at the Fourth General Synod in Denver when, reminding the delegates that "what we do and say here will have unmeasured consequences," he challenged the synod to deal aggressively and responsibly with the racial crisis confronting the nation.[38] Herbster was not alone, of course, in taking such a position. Other leaders in the church shared his concerns for social justice. At the same time he brought to that concern a style of Christian piety that was recognized and approved by many people in the churches.

Moreover, Herbster was sensitive to the importance of setting new directions for the new denomination. Social concerns in themselves were not new to either of the former communions. Both had national agencies for social action and had been vigorously involved in speaking to issues in the nation and in the world. The new directions of which Herbster spoke represented the hope and intention of involving the *whole* church in concerns about the conditions of humanity that touched the Christian conscience. Neither the Evangelical and Reformed Church nor the Congregational Christian Churches had ever been challenged so totally to deal with a social issue by steps that were designed to "transform our church life" and to "mobilize the manpower and the means of the Church" for its resolution.

Out of this concern came the emphasis upon Racial Justice Now, which eventually led into a permanent church agency for dealing with persistent and widespread forms of racial discrimination in the nation. Although not perceived at the time to be a potential problem for denominational organization, this creation of an ad hoc agency began almost immediately to pose questions about the structural relationships described in the Constitution and By-Laws. What was the relationship of ad hoc agencies to the one-homeland-agency concept that had been incorporated into the Constitution?

Another decision of the 1963 General Synod that had bearing upon the formation of the church's organizational structure established a pattern of biennial "Emphases." These were intended to focus the attention of the entire denomination upon important concerns. The first of these, the Urbanization Emphasis, adopted for the 1964-65 biennium, exposed the issue of agency responsibility in a way that had not been anticipated. Which agency is responsible when a concern of importance to the whole church cuts across areas of responsibility in several instrumentalities? Overlapping efforts and preoccupation with their own programs tended to inhibit the instrumentalities' and conferences' involvement in the task of mobilizing the whole energies of the church. When reporting to the Fifth General Synod in 1965, Donald L. Benedict, executive director of the Urbanization Emphasis Committee, stated: "If the United Church of Christ is serious about responding to the fact of urbanization, then, I believe, that a complete re-evaluation of the relation of our present Instrumentalities to needed functions must be undertaken."[39]

The problem of the relationship of autonomous instrumentalities to the General Synod had been heightened also in an unexpected way by the office of the

President of the Church. What was the president's role? Religious leadership? Institutional leadership? The public voice of the church? All were included in By-Law 182. However, the "style" of the president always redefines the role, especially where the organization is flexibly designed as was the United Church. When President Herbster assumed the role of prophetic leadership in setting the church in new directions, there was a subtle but significant shift in the church's self-perception; the involvement of the "whole Church" in a concern about the racial crisis and urbanization inevitably posed the question of a symbol of the "whole Church." The president was that symbol, but his power was limited to his gifts of counsel, advice, and persuasion. Who could mobilize the whole church? That was the problem raised by Benedict.

Concerns about the viability and usefulness of the organizational structure, so hopefully designed between 1957 and 1960, surfaced in another way at the Fifth General Synod. An overture from the Ohio Conference asked that the Executive Council seek the services of an advisory management consultant in evaluating problems of denominational organization. The thrust of this overture was strengthened in an unexpected way by an address on "The Church and the City" by Thomas G. Ayers, an active layman.[40] His proposal for a committee to make a structural review of the United Church organization was accepted by the synod. The Committee on Structure was constituted with Donald W. Webber as chairman and Ashby E. Bladen as executive secretary.

Although the Structure Committee did not complete its work until 1969, an interim report given to the Sixth General Synod of 1967 clearly indicated to the delegates that some structural changes could be expected. For its own guidance the committee had prepared a *Statement of Purpose and Mission of the United Church of Christ* emphasizing that "form and structure are essential . . . [but] will change . . . [and] must always be subservient to mission."[41] Touching the most sensitive area of organizational concern, the statement averred:

> The achievement of its purposes requires a structure of interrelationships which provides freedom through order, flexible enough to accommodate differences of understanding in a democratic process of decision making yet strong enough to assure mutual support and faithfulness. *The authority of the whole is the self-imposed willingness of each part to co-operate with the rest and to undergird and support the responsible leadership of those who represent the larger fellowship.*[42]

Two closely related issues were identified in the words "willingness of each part to co-operate" and "the responsible leadership of those who represent the larger fellowship." Inferentially, the first words refer to the instrumentalities and conferences and the latter to the Executive Council and officers of the General Synod. Agency accountability and the program responsibility of the General Synod had to be defined in ways that would not inhibit the mission of the church expressed through its representatives in the General Synod.

When the Tentative Report of the Committee on Structure was released in

79

November 1967 to various official bodies and instrumentalities, the first responses were negative and critical. A lengthy memorandum from twelve agency executives to the Executive Council asked that the agencies be given an opportunity to assist the Committee on Structure to revise its report before sending it to the General Synod delegates.[43] The Executive Council subsequently asked the committee to prepare a second draft of the report after consultation with the instrumentalities and conferences for submission to the council at its October 1968 meeting.

In the judgment of instrumentality heads, the Committee on Structure seemed to be recommending abandonment of an organizational pattern of "relatively autonomous units held together by a . . . common purpose and a common discipleship in a structure of responsible relationships." The question to be faced, they contended, is which ecclesiological principle is to prevail in the United Church. A major point in the Tentative Structure Report was that all activities and agencies of the United Church should be brought under the control of the "total Church." This introduced again an issue that had been debated in pre-union discussions and which continued to produce divided opinion. Was the committee implying that only the General Synod and the Executive Council represented the "total Church"? If so, then the "total Church" is never present in any or all of its parts—a contention of those who held to the concept of the local church as the *locus* of the church.

This internal debate within the United Church exemplified in a striking way some of the issues that were becoming prominent in religious organizations generally in the nation. Gibson Winter cited the fact that "the proliferation of agencies posed a serious problem of unity of command within the religious organizations, for agencies grew up before a corresponding ideology or ecclesiology was developed for their control."[44] He argued that "emerging problems of unity and coherence in organization create a need for a *theology of organization.*"[45] Was it the intention of the Committee on Structure to develop a new theology of organization for the United Church? Apparently critics of the committee's report felt this to be the case. At the same time, as indicated earlier concerning the debate over the constitution, there were many in the church who feared the absence of a new approach to denominational organization. Some who saw, as Winter argued, that "agency domination is a particular threat to Protestant denominations because many of them lack a principle of authority for religious organization beyond the 'gathered' congregation," were convinced that structural changes were needed to give the United Church a sense of acting as a whole church.[46]

It is not clear whether dissatisfaction with the organizational structure of the church at that time (1967-68) arose from theoretical grounds or from an experience of failure in the structure as it then prevailed. Instrumentality heads could rightfully point to their responsiveness to the General Synods of 1963, 1965, and 1967. At the same time the trend in American churches generally was toward organization by rational process, "subjected to a hierarchical principle of subordination, and integrated across extensive areas encompassing a multiplicity of activities."[47] That trend undoubtedly affected the United Church.

In its final report, dated February 1, 1969, the Committee on Structure argued: "There are manifestations throughout the Church of restlessness and impatience with organizational difficulties and the limitations imposed by some earlier compromises and arrangements. . . . It is essential that organization be subservient to mission."[48] In consequence of that conviction the committee contended that the difficult decisions the church must make had to be considered at the national level and not by any one unit of the church. The responsibility therefore belongs to the General Synod. But that body, since it meets only biennially, must entrust the implementation of its decisions to the Executive Council. In addition the committee claimed that "the President should have clear responsibility for positive program leadership or definite bases for supervision and co-ordination . . ." since now "his executive leadership depends too heavily upon effectiveness of personality and subjective powers of persuasion."[49] These two judgments of the committee concerning the roles of the General Synod and the president of the church constituted the background for a series of recommendations for structural change submitted to the church by the committee. Ten specific recommendations were incorporated in proposed amendments to the Constitution and By-Laws.

The response of the church as a whole to the proposals for structural change is treated in the next chapter. It is important, however, to be reminded that all the concern for improving the structure and organization of the denomination arose within the context of a decade of drastic social change. It is possible to speculate as to whether organizational restructuring would have come so early in the new denomination's history had there been a time of more stable social and cultural development. In the American system of voluntary social organization, response to external circumstance tends to be quick and often reactive. Conservative forces were indeed present in the society generally and also within the church. The evidence from the records of the United Church, however, suggests a predominant pattern of constructive response rather than reaction. That is, obviously, a judgment that can be evaluated fairly only from a longer-range perspective than is now possible. Furthermore, it cannot be claimed that the United Church succumbed to the fundamentalism of change, which showed itself in so many ways not only in religious but also in secular organizations. From another perspective, it must be admitted, the built-in conserving instincts of the church were at work and did resist demands for more radical change. This was exhibited somewhat dramatically in the Seventh General Synod of 1969.

Although the compass of this book does not include a review of the social changes and events of the Sixties that impinged upon the formation of the

United Church, it is important to indicate specific kinds of responses made within the church to those changes and events. Reference has been made to the racial crisis, which led to a major effort on the part of the whole church from 1963 onward. This led eventually to the establishment of the Commission for Racial Justice, the only instance of a structural response to a major social issue in the denomination. In this respect the Civil Rights Movement dealing with the racial crisis may be characterized as the *key* social issue that affected not only the United Church but all of American society. The impact of this was to be felt strongly from 1969 onward.

Other concerns were often related to the civil rights issue but received different attention. The Urbanization Emphasis, covering the period of 1964 through 1968, encompassed several social issues, including race problems, poverty, and health and welfare. A common practice in addressing other issues was to develop resolutions and pronouncements. Some of these called for specific action by the instrumentalities, while others were channeled through the office of the president of the church as expressions of the General Synod's mind about the issues. The Sixth General Synod in 1967, for example, reiterated a concern about the war in Vietnam that had been expressed in 1965. Other resolutions dealt with South Africa and the Peace Priority effort.

ECUMENICAL CONCERN

The focus of attention in this chapter has been on the organizational formation of the United Church in the context of rapid social change. No account of the period from 1961 to 1969 would be complete, however, without consideration of the denomination's concern about and involvement in ecumenical matters. Formed not only as a united church but also as a uniting church, this new church body had a claim to prove.

United Church involvement in ecumenical affairs as well as in church union planning was given organizational expression by an action of the Executive Council in June 1960, creating the Commission on Christian Unity and Ecumenical Study and Service. That body carried major responsibility for two proposals concerning further church union: from the International Convention of the Disciples of Christ and from the Consultation on Church Union.

An invitation to enter into union conversations had been communicated from the Disciples of Christ to the Uniting General Synod in 1957. In 1959 Gaines M. Cooke, executive secretary of that body, addressed the Second General Synod. As a consequence the new Commission on Christian Unity and Ecumenical Study and Service had as one of its first responsibilities the proposal for union conversations with the Disciples. Before these conversations were able to move to a definitive stage, however, the Consultation on Church Union (COCU) entered the scene and for nearly a decade altered Protestant plans for church union. The plan envisioned a multiparty union, which by 1969 included nine denominational groups.

82

In view of ever-widening opportunities for further explicit moves toward church union, the commission sought from the Fourth General Synod in 1963 a definitive statement about union. That statement, adopted by the General Synod, affirmed: "We believe that the Head of the church calls us to reunion, to renewal, and to the world. In the faith that God speaks a relevant and saving Word to the faithful, *the United Church of Christ is ready to lose its life, if need be,* that Christ's Church may become visibly one."[50] With this kind of commitment to union, the commission, under the leadership of David G. Colwell, assumed a position of leadership in the Consultation on Church Union.

Future historians may see something ironic in the concentrated attention given to church union during the Sixties, at the time almost all traditional institutional efforts in religion were losing ground. That irony seemed especially pronounced when the Consultation issued a plan of union in 1970 as public confidence in religious institutions was waning rapidly. The United Church, however, could point to its own experience in which union brought the renewal of vision and commitment required to address the turmoil and needs of the world. The new denomination stood as a witness to the validity of union.

The Sixties also saw important moves in the worldwide scene of ecumenical endeavor. Both constituent groups in the United Church had close ties to the World Council of Churches and provided important leadership. The ink was hardly dry on the newly adopted Constitution and By-Laws when delegates left for the Third Assembly of the World Council in New Delhi, India in mid-November of 1961. Of far-reaching consequence in the vast changes experienced by Western Christendom in this decade was Vatican Council II, convened in Rome in October 1962 and continuing intermittently for two years. Among official Protestant observers was Douglas Horton. From time to time other United Church people were accredited visitors.

Involvement in two worldwide confessional bodies had also been a pattern of ecumenical interest in the United Church parent fellowships. Through their General Council the Congregational Christian Churches were participants in the International Council of Congregational Churches, while the Evangelical and Reformed Church held membership in the Alliance of Reformed Churches Throughout the World Holding the Presbyterian System. The formation of united churches in Canada, South India, and the United States led to the merging of these two confessional bodies into the World Alliance of Reformed Churches in 1970.

Some diminishment of unity concerns and ecumenical commitment might have been anticipated in a newly united church body deeply immersed in its own organizational formation. While this may have occurred in some circles, the general posture of the United Church was one of staunch support of such enterprises. This was due in part to the continuity in the denomination's leadership where ecumenical involvement had been a long-time pattern. It was due also to experience. Despite the struggles and difficulties, the formation of the

United Church through the first decade of existence had been a demonstration to its own membership of the vitality that the union effort can provide. President Herbster gave voice to this in November of 1964 when he spoke on behalf of the World Council of Churches at a New York meeting:

There was a day when we thought we ought to join for economic reasons, for political reasons, for sociological reasons, and I would not minimize them. But . . . God calls us to unity. . . . Should not our love of Christ . . . make the ties that bind us together . . . strong enough to withstand the tensions that result from our imperfect apprehension of the things of God?[51]

Two years later, at Dr. Herbster's urging, the Executive Council addressed a special resolution to all instrumentalities and agencies asking them to work ecumenically in all matters. The two recognized instrumentalities, the Board for World Ministries and the Board for Homeland Ministries, responded with policy statements of commitment to collaborative work. It is evident from any reading of the activities of the various denominational agencies that an ecumenical stance prevailed. That this stance was also in the thinking of the delegates to the General Synods throughout the decade is shown, for example, in the Fourth General Synod's encouragement to the Commission on Worship to work cooperatively with the two major Presbyterian bodies. In the Seventh General Synod of 1969 a specific request was made that the preparation of a new United Church hymnal be an ecumenical venture. The result of this was the formation by the United Church Hymnal Committee of the Consultation on Ecumenical Hymnody involving ten denominations, including Roman Catholics and Lutherans.[52]

When the United Church of Christ celebrated its tenth anniversary in 1967, its basic formative period was drawing to a close. Organizational restructuring was in the offing but not yet clearly outlined. Major changes would occur in the next decade, some of them already foreshadowed by the tentative report of the Committee on Structure, but even more by the heightening tensions in the nation over the problems of civil rights and undeclared war. The impact of all these would be most dramatically expressed in the 1969 General Synod, but the full import of the moral and social revolution inherited by this young church body would be assessed slowly as a new decade dawned. In that time of testing of all social and religious institutions, the United Church would be questioning itself. What is its identity? What does it mean to be the United Church of Christ?

CHAPTER 4

IN SEARCH
OF IDENTITY

Particular events often serve as vantage points from which historical perspective is gained. For the United Church of Christ the 1969—or Seventh—General Synod was such an event; it was both the end of the beginning and a new beginning. There occurred in that synod a remarkable convergence of forces both within and without the United Church which marked the transition to a new period of development.

CONFRONTATION AND TENSION

Two dramatic moments symbolized that convergence: the appearance of James Forman and his presentation of the Black Manifesto on behalf of the Black Economic Development Conference, and the election of a new president for the church. They represented, on the one hand, the critical character of the social revolution under way in the nation throughout the Sixties and, on the other hand, an entirely new style of operating as a deliberative and legislative body of the church. In both instances there were unexpected elements, but at the same time the decade of the Sixties had given ample indication of the very forces that were thus symbolized.

Delegates gathering in Boston, therefore, for the Seventh General Synod had been forewarned to expect a different kind of synod. James Forman's supporters had received prime space in the news media by use of a sit-in in various national offices of major American denominations to underline the "reparations demands" of the Black Economic Development Conference. Both the Board for World Ministries and the Board for Homeland Ministries offices of the United Church had been occupied. Nevertheless, Forman's appearance on the speaker's platform at the synod with a group of supporters heightened the tension that had been nourished by reports and rumors throughout the opening hours of the session.

Whatever other significance attaches to the Forman episode, it is clear, in retrospect, that it helped move Black churches to center stage in all denominational considerations. Concern *about* the racial crisis of the nation had been high in the consciousness of the church since President Herbster's call to action in 1963. In succeeding years a small but growing number of Blacks had assumed leadership roles on a national level, especially through the official Committee for Racial Justice Now and later the voluntary and influential United Church Ministers for Racial and Social Justice.[1] At the Seventh Synod these Black leaders gained credence and power by their judicious use of the Black Manifesto occasion and won endorsement of significant proposals from the synod. Though small at first, a discernible shift of the dominantly white constituency's concern *about* the racial crisis to a concern *for* Black sisters and brothers can be traced in part to the work of the Black leadership at the synod.

Some of the same factors at work in relation to the rising Black consciousness of the church and the sense of crisis in the nation were evident in the election of the president of the church. Although there had been an election contest at the Third General Synod in 1961,[2] the Seventh Synod experienced for the first time a significant amount of pre-election "campaigning" by supporters of three candidates. Robert V. Moss, Jr., the president of Lancaster Theological Seminary, was the Nominating Committee's choice. When this was announced well in advance of the synod, the United Church Ministers for Racial and Social Justice sponsored the candidacy of Arthur D. Gray, a Black pastor from Chicago. A short time later the newly organized United Churchmen for Change announced the candidacy of Paul E. Gibbons, a young campus minister. The experience of vigorous campaigning by these groups at the synod, although unnerving to those delegates who considered it unseemly "politics," added to the atmosphere of tension and confrontation. Staid ecclesiastical traditions toppled before the winds of change. New modes of organizational procedure and parliamentary behavior replaced the temperate and reasonable habits of the traditional church assembly.

As much as anything else the election contest for the office of president reflected the radical changes in the church's self-understanding that were the source of the structure proposals developed since 1965 and implemented by this synod. Most apparent was the increased importance attached to the office of the president in the life of the church. In itself this was an indication of a whole new understanding of the place of the denomination's national-level organization. When viewed from the perspectives of the two major church traditions represented in the United Church, this change takes on a significance that deserves discussion later in this and succeeding chapters.

Of equal importance is the way the election contest for the presidency exhibited the impact of an increasingly visible pluralism in the church. Every synod had experienced sharp differences of understanding and judgment. In most cases such differences were resolved into a unity that often appeared as uniformity and conformity. Although that was an obvious organizational goal in a newly united church body, it was neither viable in the long run nor valid for a people professedly receptive to the guidance of the Holy Spirit. Moreover, it was bound to be irritating to the Blacks who found expectations of conformity to be a denial of their own cultural and personal self-awareness. As the demands of a pluralistic self-consciousness increased in the church, new dimensions of reconciliation and unity would have to be explored.

In many ways the 1969 General Synod miniaturized the nation's own traumatic experiences of the Sixties. Every one of the major elements of the national crisis can be identified in the United Church experience at Boston. Reference has already been made to the fact of increasing pluralism, the reality of which would confront the church and the nation for decades to come.[3] The problems of human existence resulting from the population explosion were compounded by a "culturally-outstripping" technology that made so much irrelevance of the elements of a so-called stable society. As one among other institutions of society, the church was affected by all this. As a community of faith, believing its life to be rooted in a transcendent reality, the church was faced anew with the task of knowing itself and its mission in relation to the society's agony.

Any assessment of the church's situation in such times must take into account its own loss of "place" in the society and the general loss of the certainties by which all human life finds its legitimacy.[4] American Protestantism generally, and the United Church in a particular way, were anchored in the structures of the society from colonial times. A major segment of the United Church, the Congregational, had a unique involvement in those structures of the colonial era and in much of the "establishment" throughout the first one hundred fifty years of the nation's life. The church's place in the society was firm and acknowledged by the general populace. But drastic change came. The technological demands and developments spawned by World War II created a society that does not stay "in place" but flows all over the land. Inevitably, the church, rooted in place as it served a stable residential population, began to know the meaning of rootlessness. In a related way the old certainties grounded in a style of social, moral, and religious life that was fostered by the church became irrelevant for many people. Added to that was the impact of the so-called "liberal" (and later, "radical") theology, which eroded confidence in the chief tenets of piety, the Bible and the transcendence of an all-powerful Deity.

It must be added here that the 1969 General Synod did not exhibit in its actions any profound sense of this loss of place and an eroded faith. If anything, the delegates engaged the issues with customary dedication. Not until after 1971 did the awareness of something lost begin to affect the deliberations of succeeding synods.

STRUCTURAL CHANGES
Confrontation was the dominant style of the Seventh General Synod. So commented the editorial reports in the *United Church Herald,* and added, "Sometimes, during the 18-hour days . . . , delegates lost sight of their lofty theme

'Obedience to Christ: Justice and Reconciliation.' "[5] Issues themselves were not always at stake. What provoked the most heated outbursts in confrontive debate were the *feelings* in Black and white relationships, and in youth-adult encounters. But, of course, important issues were up for debate, particularly in relation to the proposals for change in organizational structure. Altogether, an unusually large number of concerns received attention and, despite the exceptionally crucial structures issues, many of these were typical of the high level of awareness about social problems that had dominated other synods.[6]

Perhaps more important in the long run than confrontive style was the presence and increased activity of organized ad hoc groups or caucuses. These were to become increasingly characteristic of the political process of successive synods, again marking an important change.

> At a time when opinions vary and emotions flare, individuals can find satisfaction only when their appeals—given the strength of group sanction—reach officials and agencies in such a way that they cannot be easily dismissed. Group consciousness and participation are here to stay.[7]

Such organized groups were evidence of the pervasive pluralism referred to above. Individual judgment and concerns tended to be either submerged or had to be incorporated into the concerns of interest groups.

An example of organized group effort was that of the United Churchmen for Change, whose proposals for "wider representation in decision-making" and a Temporary Commission for Missionary Development of the Local Church reflected the nationwide trend toward greater youth involvement.[8] Although neither proposal was adopted as presented, both made an impact that was expressed in actions to specify quotas for youth representation and to provide funds through the Board for Homeland Ministries for ad hoc and "temporary forms of ministry."

Even more striking was the success of the United Church Ministers for Racial and Social Justice, who were able to secure General Synod approval of far-reaching patterns of dealing with the reality of the Black churches within the United Church fellowship. This group's strategy of working through the Executive Council proved to be an important element in their success. Advocacy by the Executive Council gave credibility to the proposals since delegates felt that the council's judgment was better informed. As a by-product of this involvement, the Executive Council was cast into a leadership role, which proved to be a pattern of things to come in succeeding synods.

The Seventh General Synod, memorable in many ways as indicated above, brought the organizational formation of the denomination to a point of completion not realized when the Constitution and By-Laws were adopted in 1961. This does not imply that equally important or even more radical changes were not likely in the future. The structure adopted in 1961 had built-in flexibility. It assured a permanent place for freedom and order in the organized national units of the church. At the same time it was experimental in its arrangement of autonomous administrative units with a supposed equality of power. The capability of such an arrangement was immediately tested by the critical events and circumstances of the Sixties. Gradual awareness that a "conglomerate of autonomies" would not suffice in such times led to the proposals that the Committee on Structure placed before the church and the General Synod.[9]

When viewed from the perspective of the 1961 Constitution debate, it is clear that the committee was proposing changes having drastic implications for the church.[10] From the point of view of any who were dissatisfied with the national structure, the timing of the report was particularly significant. The confrontations, the frustrations in the face of action-demanding issues, the recognition that the times required change—all came to the fore at the very synod hearing the report. Many delegates there became aware of the power vacuum in the church's national-level leadership to which William L. Rest had pointed eight years earlier.[11] In acting on the Executive Council recommendations growing out of that report, the 1969 General Synod effectively moved to fill that power vacuum. In so doing it sharply modified the initial patterns of autonomy and self-determination of the parts of the system called the United Church of Christ.

Acknowledging that United Church polity formally affirms autonomy and self-determination, the committee saw this polity informally "described and practiced." "What the Church is to be and the relation of the parts to the whole are less well defined than the freedom of the parts."[12] Expressing the hope that "the Church can formulate and achieve effective co-ordination while its several parts are truly free of central (authoritative) control," the committee made proposals for *coordination controlled by the objectives determined by the General Synod.* The key points in the recommendations were a clear affirmation of the General Synod as the *decision-making* body for national-level matters and the Executive Council as the *implementing* body for those decisions. They called for integrated and coordinated efforts authorized by the General Synod and managed by the Executive Council.

To achieve this operational system the committee spelled out what would be required. Both the General Synod and the Executive Council would need to undergo change. To accomplish credible churchwide decision-making it was proposed that "where policy is made at a national level there should be present as active participants the most informed, competent and knowledgeable people our local churches, Conferences and Instrumentalities can provide."[13] For implementation of General Synod decisions and for servicing the synod in making those decisions, it was proposed that the Executive Council be enlarged and reorganized. Of prime importance was the plan to broaden the representation on the Executive Council from the instrumentalities and conferences, thus "commanding the respect, adherence and cooperation of all parts of the Church" in handling major issues.

Delegates to the 1969 General Synod gave detailed attention to the amendments of the Constitution and By-Laws proposed by the Executive Council for implementation of the Structure Committee Report. Voting representation in the General Synod was enlarged to include the elected officers of the church, members of the Executive Council, and the moderators. To give continuity to the biennial General Synods the terms of delegates from the conferences were changed from two to four years, with the possibility of one additional term. The Executive Council was nearly doubled in size and included specifically six conference executives. For the first time in a national-level body specific quotas were determined concerning the representation of men and women; in this case, one third of the lay representatives were to be women.

Detailed bylaw amendments about the organization and responsibility of the Executive Council underlined the crucial leadership role being assigned to that body as the General Synod ad interim. A major objective in this structural change was the kind of coordination of all aspects of the church's national activities that could be accomplished through a sophisticated system of central administration. In this respect relocating the budget and finance operations from the General Synod to the Executive Council made this key responsibility less susceptible to the pressures of a large deliberative body.

Closely related to these provisions for the work of the Executive Council were those that assigned greater executive responsibility to the office of the president. As the chief executive officer of the General Synod, under the new responsibilities assigned to the Executive Council, the president could no longer rely so heavily upon the "effectiveness of his personality and subjective powers of persuasion." Specific authority was now assigned. This included the elaboration of a staff of assistants as needs required.

Many other amendments were required to implement the proposals of the Committee on Structure. While these deserve attention, it is more important for the purposes of this discussion to assess the significance of the sweeping changes made in 1969. Two perspectives suggest themselves in making this evaluation: first, from the point of view of general organizational principles; and second, from a consideration of the particular dynamics of organizational development in the United Church.

In the first case it is clear that the increasingly sophisticated organizational development of religious denominations in America was influencing the United Church. Changes in organizational structure were essentially pragmatic, reflecting the principle that "organization is the application of rational processes of coordination and communication to achieve clearly defined goals."[14] That principle had been employed with marked effectiveness in some of the autonomous units of the United Church, most notably perhaps in the two recognized program instrumentalities, the Board for World Ministries and the Board for Homeland Ministries. By applying it now to the national structure of the church, the General Synod was effectually establishing "a principle of authority beyond the 'gathered' congregation" that was intended to be expressive of the "whole" church, that is, of all the local churches *represented* through the conferences in the General Synod.

The establishment of a principle of authority beyond the local church *by a system of representation* while at the same time maintaining the freedom of autonomous units had an important consequence. Limited but creative use was made of the principle of representative government by giving greater control of the denominational or national-level organization to representatives of local churches *without* turning that authority around to be exercised on the local churches. In so doing it lifted up a principle of Reformed ecclesiology that frequently is obscured: the autonomy of the local church has reality when its freedom is responsibly exercised on behalf of the whole church. To put it another way, the local church has its being in an expression of the lordship of Christ, which is a responsible relationship to those organizational structures that express the being of the whole church. Given the limiting influence of human sinfulness, it is inevitable that the United Church does not escape the burden of misuse of this principle. Nevertheless, its significance requires recognition, for to the extent that it is effectually employed it represents critically important elements in the identity of the United Church.*

From this perspective on the new structural proposals, it is important to turn to a consideration of the particular dynamics of organizational development in the United Church since 1961. During that formative time the power centers of the church on the national level were the instrumentalities. They moved creatively and vigorously into programming designed, on the one hand, to build up the churches and, on the other hand, to extend the church's mission in new directions. At the same time other centers of influence were appearing in conference structures as those bodies sought to minister to regional situations,

---

*Historically in the churches of the Reformed tradition the crucial relationship between freedom and order has been distorted in a false antithesis—freedom versus order. In popular American religious thought, freedom was considered to be exemplified in Congregational polity, and order in presbyterial polity. This has led to damaging prejudiciality in the relationships of these Reformed bodies. The prejudices lie equally heavy on both sides and are a blot on the face of American Christianity.

The constitutional framework of the United Church of Christ is intended to maintain a responsible and creative tension between freedom and order. Freedom is not only safeguarded but made responsible by: (1) the basic ecclesiological principle that no human authority may usurp the authority of Christ in the life and work of the church expressed in the Word and the presence of the Spirit; and (2) an ordering of relationships between the units of organization in which binding constitutional requirements have not the force of legal constraint exercised by one unit on another but of assignment of responsibility (endorsed and voted by representatives of these units) to each unit. Thus, responsible freedom is dependent upon a voluntary assumption of responsibilities essential to the life of the church in all its component units.

which tended to reflect the diversity of the nation itself. Conferences enlarged their own staffs to meet these needs. This tended to place the conferences and instrumentalities in a position of involuntary competition. On the programming level the effects of competitive positions were ameliorated by cooperation and voluntary coordination. But on another level this competition worked generally to the disadvantage of the instrumentalities and to the advantage of the conferences. The conferences were in the strategic position of having the constitutional assignment of providing the structural relationship of local churches to the denominational organization. This included participation in the General Synod's budget process and in the channeling of funds to the denominational treasury.

Some indication of the ever-increasing role of the conferences is given in the distribution of funds contributed by local churches for Our Christian World Mission.* In 1962, the first year under the new unified treasurer's office, 67.2 percent of the total amount of $16,141,885 went to national-level offices and agencies, while 32.8 percent was retained by the conferences. By 1969 the conference percentage had increased to 43.1 percent, and by 1974 to 47.7 percent, a figure approaching one half of OCWM giving.[15]

Another way to estimate the changing roles of conferences, instrumentalities, and the Executive Council that resulted from structural changes is to note the budget of the Executive Council. In 1962 the council expended $576,654, or 5.3 percent of the total amount available to national-level structures. This amount reached $1,000,000 in 1971, or 11.2 percent. In 1974 the Executive Council had available $940,000, or 10.4 percent. Thus, the Executive Council's operating funds increased 73 percent from 1962 to 1974. The import of this is the changing role of the council—which is the General Synod ad interim—in relation to both instrumentalities and conferences.[16]

The influence factor of the roles of the instrumentalities, conferences, and the Executive Council fluctuates in consequence of other circumstances and developments as well. Not least important are the personal and professional qualities of staff people. More difficult to assess is the continually changing attitude in the society generally toward institutions and organizations. The erosion of organizational loyalties in the Sixties, which touched every religious denomination in varying degrees and has had drastic consequences for some, has been undoubtedly an inhibiting element in the formation of the United Church. National agencies often seem remote to local church people. This has been a most significant element in the rising influence of the conferences. At the same time the growing importance of the Executive Council—also remote as a national unit—seems at first to be an anomaly. However, any organization of national dimensions requires at least one unit in which local groups feel they have a voice. In the particular circumstances of United Church development the Executive Council is in fact more directly answerable to the constituency than are the instrumentalities. This was especially true after the 1969 restructuring.

*Hereafter identified as OCWM.

As a concluding comment on the restructuring, it should be noted that all changes pointed in the direction of wider and more balanced participation in the national-level organization. This became most significant in the General Synods of the Seventies in two ways. First, it gave impetus to the growing role of the biennial General Synod meetings as a public platform. The public platform is an essential element of the social structure in a viable pluralistic society. As social and value pluralism became more marked in the church, the sessions of the General Synod became the needed opportunity for expression and identity. This function of the General Synod gatherings constituted a new and, for many, a questionable development. The Seventies exhibit the strains caused thereby. Second, the accountability issue was given a partial resolution. Under the new bylaw amendments the Executive Council became fully responsible for implementation of General Synod decisions. With an expanded Executive Council, specifically representative of established and newly self-conscious groups, accountability was enhanced.

Newly designed organizational structures tend to exhibit their weaknesses before their strengths are proven. This became clear in the United Church as the conferences approved the amendments, and the new provisions went into effect by 1971. One important unanswered question was whether the Executive Council would become another "program agency," having essentially the same character as the instrumentalities and conferences. This question in many ways constituted a key political issue for the Seventies. The questions of authority and power remained critical and were subject to the new circumstances of the new decade. While some may interpret negatively the change from 1961 to 1969 in the role of the instrumentalities, it may be pertinent to note a response of Truman B. Douglass, then executive vice-president of the Board for Homeland Ministries, to a question put to him by the Committee on Structure:

> In my opinion the Board for Homeland Ministries will diminish its responsibilities for the purely maintenance functions of the existing denominational establishment. These will be increasingly the responsibilities of the Conferences. The Board will try to discover the significant frontiers of mission in our rapidly changing society and engage in the research, experimentation and development relative to the occupation of these frontiers.[17]

Organizational development, as assumed here, is a response to the times and not simply or primarily a result of political maneuvering. For that reason the questions of authority and power are the *appropriate* questions, especially in the church that acknowledges a transcendent authority while developing its organization for the times.

NEW STYLES OF ORGANIZATIONAL LIFE

Robert V. Moss,[18] elected to the presidency by the 1969 General Synod, saw that synod not a "Babel but Pentecost." He claimed: "Our sons and daughters have prophesied, our young men have seen visions, and our old men have dreamed dreams."[19] A key to understanding Moss's leadership style during the first half of the Seventies was provided when he put this positive faith construction on what many had felt to be disturbingly fractious and confrontive sessions. Confrontation and contention were not laid to rest, but a change to clearly constructive tactics among all parties gave a comparatively different character to succeeding General Synods.

Through the Sixties, when campus disruptions were common, Moss had been a scholar, teacher, and administrator, working with the generation whose habit of mind concerning institutions was highly critical and questioning. It was, therefore, quite characteristic for him to declare in his acceptance address to the synod:

> Insofar as I am able to commit myself to the future, I promise not only our young people but every member of this historic General Synod that I shall be in the forefront of *the fight of our youth* to determine their own destinies and to live fruitful lives in a world at peace. This may mean heartache, it may mean angry confrontations in the marketplace, it may mean the sacrifice of urgent church work . . .[20]

The Seventies did not turn out to be the era of the "youth" of the church, even though their concerns and involvement in national-level decisions were highly visible. Conferences sought to include "under-thirty" delegates, and the 1971 General Synod amended the constitution to provide that 20 percent of the delegates be of that age group. Commissions, committees, and established agencies did the same. By the 1971 General Synod the youth caucus demonstrated vigorous and well-considered participation. Their causes were strongly oriented to issues that tended to widen the traditional generation gap. At the same time their carefully managed efforts both on the floor and behind the scenes won the respect and support of large numbers of older delegates.

The nation's trauma over the Vietnam War was reflected in youth concern about the church's position on issues of justice to war resisters, amnesty, justice to minorities, and military domination of the government. The Kent State University tragedy gave substance to their claim that freedom and justice in the land were losing out. The release of the Pentagon Papers confirmed the sense of a people who were victims of their own government. In these and related instances the under-thirty generation felt a betrayal that destroyed a traditional confidence in democratic institutions. Therefore, whenever a public forum, such as that which a General Synod seemed to provide, was available, this generation brought its concerns out in the open. While youth concerns were thus often in the forefront, other developments in the General Synod's style of operation provided additional attention-drawing power. Often used by pressure groups for their own purposes, sometimes used in the name of humanity, and used in the name of Christ, the General Synod by 1971 was viewed by many in ways that contrasted sharply with those expressed in its design of a decade earlier.

94

As the Eighth General Synod gathered in the summer of 1971, there were many indications that a new style of synod deliberation and action was taking over. If the Uniting General Synod of 1957 exhibited the church being "shaped by God's deed in Christ," the Eighth Synod demonstrated that the "world was setting the agenda for the Church." Very early in the sessions Jacob B. Wagner, chairman of the Executive Council, referred to the fact that "this is a highly politicized Synod" and called upon the delegates to remember even then that the church is "the beloved community of Christ."[21] Politicizing, of course, was sharply on the rise throughout the land. Its appearance in ecclesiastical deliberative assemblies was a new experience for many delegates, and it seemed to bear out the increasing pluralism of beliefs, values, and life-styles in the church that was causing fundamental questioning. Many could agree with Avery Dulles, S.J., Roman Catholic scholar, who commented that "Christians commonly experience the Church more as a companionship of fellow-travellers on the same journey than as a union of lovers dwelling in the same home."[22]

In planning the 1971 sessions of the synod, the Executive Council instituted procedures that were intended to use the politicized situation to advantage while giving greater opportunity for delegate participation and voice. Four issues were assigned priority time in the agenda: the health of the local church, the faith crisis, racial justice, and peace and United States power.[23] Delegates, in groups of twenty, discussed these concerns as Exploration Groups and brought pronouncements and action proposals to the floor of the synod. Although the procedure was new to the delegates, it had the effect of providing a balance of concern between church matters and social issues. Moreover, it set a pattern for wider delegate involvement in future synods.

This step had other implications. From the very beginning the United Church General Synods had employed the review-committee system in which the reports of the instrumentalities, commissions, and officers of the church were assigned to delegate-composed Review and Report Committees.[24] These committees then brought recommended actions to the floor of the synod, often becoming advocates of the special concerns of the groups and agencies whose reports they had reviewed. In this way the General Synod expressed "ownership" of the work of the agencies. Abandonment of this system may have tended to enlarge the distance between the denominational agencies and the local churches represented by the delegates. Although in most cases thereafter these agencies were given a hearing in the synod sessions, the absence of the advocacy of a committee of delegates tended to inhibit the agency relationship with the synod.

However, the new procedure of delegate involvement was of strategic importance. It forced cause-oriented groups to bring their concerns to intensive discussion and debate by smaller units of delegates. It made use of the adversary relationship in group discussion to great advantage. This brought more carefully considered and supported proposals for action to the floor of the synod for open debate. Issue Exploration Groups thus brought necessary focus to the assembly's debate and enabled the synod to identify and define goals and objectives for the denomination in the next biennium.

A significant change in the standing rules of the synod, adopted in 1971, underlined the reality of pluralism in the church. "The General Synod, recognizing the existence of authentic, responsible pluralism in matters of Christian conviction, judgment, and action and in order that it may consider substantial minority positions," amended its rules to provide an orderly and assured way for such positions to receive consideration.[25] In succeeding synods this rule was used to advantage for keeping delegates aware of divergent positions that otherwise may have been overlooked.

Concentration on four major issues and the use of a new procedure for deliberation resulted in somewhat less attention to the work and concerns of the ongoing agencies, with two major exceptions. Both of these had implications of significance for the future of the church.

In the first instance, considerable discussion arose when the Commission on Christian Unity and Ecumenical Study and Service offered a resolution concerning A Plan of Union proposed by the Consultation on Church Union.[26] While citing a concern about the polity proposed in the Plan, the resolution urged careful consideration with particular reference to the concept of the extended parish system. Delegates sensed the implications of the proposed Plan and asked for more assistance in considering it.

The second instance related to an action of the 1969 General Synod, endorsing a proposal from United Church Ministers for Racial and Social Justice that efforts be undertaken to establish a Black university. The matter had been referred to the Board for Homeland Ministries, but UCMRSJ* representatives had asked the Executive Council to review what was being done. The Executive Council's report to the synod prompted sharp criticism of the board's handling of the matter from Black church leaders. The synod's response was to refer the entire matter to the Executive Council for action and report at the next General Synod.[27]

Two major developments affecting the local churches grew out of the Issue Exploration Groups at the 1971 synod: increased responsibility for the Task Force on Leadership Development and a program for dealing with the Faith Crisis in the coming biennium. Both of these had long-range effects, the first leading eventually to the establishment of the Office for Church Life and Leadership and the second to the Faith Exploration program handled initially by the Council for Lay Life and Work.

Throughout the synod sessions the critical concerns of Black church leaders

*United Church Ministers for Racial and Social Justice.

were highlighted and considered. Of special importance was the desperate financial plight of the Black colleges related to the American Missionary Association.[28] The synod's response to this was a resolution asking the Executive Council to implement a major financial campaign for these schools.[29] This prepared the way for what came to be known as the 17/76 Achievement Fund, established in June 1972 by the Executive Council.

The public platform character of the General Synod became even more pronounced in 1971 than in 1969. In addition to issues that received attention in the Issue Exploration Groups touching upon racial justice and peace and United States power, other concerns given platform attention were: Angela Davis, Daniel and Philip Berrigan, American Indians, Mexican Americans, status of women in society, abortion, and South Africa. The support given to these causes—many of which would reappear in successive synods—prompted expressions of concern from articulate laypersons. John H. Esch voiced a feeling commonly expressed in local churches but not often at the General Synod. Affirming the diversity of concerns within the church, he claimed that General Synod actions and pronouncements tended to leave many persons of opposing positions alienated from the church they supported. Stating that "I feel very strongly that the Church must speak out in a loud voice of concern for the problems of our day," Esch called for an emphasis upon understanding, commitment, and individual responsibility in seeking solutions to problems. "The Church does not tell him how to think, but it demands that he does think on these things. The Church does not tell him what to do, but . . . he must do something. The Church does not act for him at the top, but it demands that he act."[30]

Esch's position represented a widespread conviction in the churches. However, cause-oriented platform presentations did not often elicit such opposition voices, thus leaving many people somewhat alienated. Also an exception of special interest because of the continuing intensive debate over the issue was the response of Robert M. Bartlett, a medical doctor, who challenged the "Freedom of Choice concerning Abortion" proposal that received synod support.[31] Causes that had received considerable public attention through the media generally received support from the majority of General Synod delegates.

Changes in the role, influence, and makeup of both the General Synod and the Executive Council—begun in 1969 and completed in 1971 with ratification of the amendments to the Constitution and By-Laws—brought a significantly different character to the organizational operation of the United Church on the denominational level. Most noticeable was the function of the Executive Council. When the 1969 General Synod referred matters to the Executive Council for implementation, that body was not prepared to handle the responsibilities directly. With the reconstitution of the council by 1971, through enlargement and restructuring, the focus of expectations and objectives fostered in the General Synod was upon that body. As the General Synod ad interim, the council represented to the entire denomination a center of authority and power not previously known and, for that matter, not a part of the tradition of either of the former bodies.

Among the standing committees of the reorganized Executive Council that helped to set new directions in the denomination was the Committee on Structural Planning. Maintaining a continual review of the organizational operation of the national-level agencies and units, this committee led the Executive Council to propose a series of structural changes from 1971 onward. The net effect of these again was to enhance the influence of the Executive Council. Increased influence could have meant Executive Council domination of all denominational affairs. The newly constituted council, however, saw coordination rather than domination as its role. At its first meeting following the 1971 General Synod, President Moss spoke of the opportunity afforded by the church's structural changes and commented: "It is possible that 1971 will be regarded as the year in which this denomination completed its union and became a new kind of communion on the American scene."[32] J. Martin Bailey editorialized about the promise of the new situation in light of the internal struggles of the previous decade:

Ironically, the issues which have been most threatening to our denominational life also have provided the cement which has bound our fellowship together. . . . To a degree few would have predicted, this internal strife itself brought the 40 independent conferences and 10 national agencies closer together.[33]

Major developments in organizational structure in the years following the 1971 General Synod provide examples of the new significance of the Executive Council in its denominational leadership role. The first was a response to the synod's action strengthening the local church, which called for a task force to "study and evaluate leadership development" in the United Church, with special reference to the respective roles of the Council for Church and Ministry and the Council for Lay Life and Work.[34] From this assignment came a proposal to the 1973 General Synod to establish the Office for Church Life and Leadership, accountable to the Executive Council in its developmental phase (which was to extend to 1977) and subsuming in its overall design the functions of the Council for Church and Ministry, the Council for Lay Life and Work, the Committee on Theological Education, the Commission on Worship, and the Theological Commission.

Establishment of this new agency of the denomination had the effect of implementing in part a concept proposed several years earlier by the Committee on Structure. At that time (1967) the committee had tentatively proposed the establishment of a third major program board to concern itself with "church ministries" as distinguished from "homeland" and "world" ministries. Although rejected then, the concept reappeared as a result of the growing concern for more intensive and extensive servicing of the local churches and the conferences. Institutional vulnerability, so glaringly demonstrated in church statistics throughout American religious bodies, became a cause for alarm as the Seventies unfolded. One clear need seemed to impress itself upon delegates and officials alike: better lay and professional leadership. The new agency, then, was designed to "combine in one nationwide office the policy-making, operational, and administrative function for leadership development in the United Church of Christ."[35]

A second major development marking the new style in United Church organization and operation was the establishment of the Office for Church in Society by the 1975 General Synod.[36] Social concerns had been formally lodged in the Council for Christian Social Action until 1972. As an autonomous unit of the national organization, this council and its able staff had been aggressive in its efforts to address wide-ranging social issues. At the same time, however, the General Synod and other agencies were likewise involved in such concerns. The increasing problems resulting from this arrangement and growing awareness of need for a new style led to reorganization. The Executive Council in 1972 asked the council to undertake a four-phase developmental process for the design of future steps. From this came the establishment of the interim Center for Social Action of the United Church of Christ, which functioned from 1973 to 1976. By constitutional amendment this was replaced by the Office for Church in Society to "assume the leadership function for social action concerns in the United Church of Christ, to provide resources to national, Conference and local churches and to strengthen the co-ordination of social action activities within the denomination."[37] In this arrangement the focal point for social concern and action was located in a responsible relationship to the Executive Council and thus in coordination with the office of the president.

A third development accentuating the role of the Executive Council and especially the office of the president was the establishment of the Council for Ecumenism to replace the Commission on Christian Unity and Ecumenical Study and Service.[38] The composition of the new council was in marked contrast to that of the commission, which had been elected by the General Synod. Members of the council were appointed by the Executive Council, chosen from among the delegates previously selected to represent the United Church of Christ in the several ecumenical organizations of which the United Church is a member. Its function was chiefly advisory to the president in all ecumenical matters.

These organizational changes in the first half of the Seventies serve as indicators of the character of United Church denominational structure as it approached the end of the second decade of its existence. What once seemed to

99

some as a "conglomerate of autonomies" became by circumstance and design a hierarchical structure of national organization. The circumstance had been provided by the pressure of rapid and drastic social change upon institutions. Viable organizational response to rapid change required a structural cohesiveness beyond that which is provided by voluntary cooperation. The design was adapted from "management science techniques," which require "needs assessment, priority setting, systems planning and program budgeting."[39] In this respect the United Church followed the trend among all major religious organizations in the midtwentieth century.

NEW CONCERNS

At the beginning of the foregoing review of organizational developments in the Seventies, reference was made to the fact that the decade did not turn out to be the era of the youth as many might have expected. As a matter of fact, the Seventies will be shown as the era of women's rights and concerns. While the cultural phenomenon of feminism requires more careful and intensive analysis than can be given here, it is especially important to see its impact on the churches as an example of cultural conditioning. Parallels between the so-called Women's Revolution and the Black Revolution are frequently cited. Their combined influence on the Christian movement in the Western world at least is likely to be more dramatic and far reaching than any other in the present century.

The cause of women surfaced in the United Church at the 1971 General Synod through formation of a women's caucus. When the synod adopted an official pronouncement on "The Status of Women in Church and Society," the United Church nationwide was alerted to the presence of a new major concern that would eventually affect every local church.[40] Even more important was the establishment of a Task Force on Women in Church and Society, another ad hoc arrangement that led eventually to the provision within the continuing structure of the General Synod of an organizational instrument for a particular cause. Implementation of the goals announced in the 1971 General Synod was accomplished in 1973 by a detailed authorization to the Executive Council for steps to "eliminate sex and race discrimination in every area of its life."[41] Related to the women's cause but having wider consequences for every aspect of the church's organizational life was a paragraph in the General Synod's action: "The Bylaws will be changed so that the elected membership of boards, councils and commissions shall be equitably representative and consciously balanced between youth, women, men, Third World people, clergy, etc."[42]

Other actions resulting from the work of the Task Force on Women in Church and Society were aimed at equal opportunity for women in the church: ordination, theological education, and agency and judicatory staff positions. Finally, the synod ordered the use of inclusive language in all printed materials issued by official units of the United Church. The work of the Task Force on

Women came to an end at the 1975 General Synod, when wide-ranging instructions were given to the various agencies of the church to eliminate inequities, and the Executive Council was authorized to provide an affirmative action officer, attached to the president's staff, for monitoring and consultative responsibilities. The same authorization included an advisory commission to work with the new office.

Concerns arising from the increasing pluralism of the society continued to manifest themselves throughout the first half of the Seventies. At the 1971 General Synod voice without vote was granted to specified representatives of six special interest groups. At the 1973 General Synod the number of recognized groups was twelve; in 1975 nine were recognized. Of special interest were those representing new racial and ethnic groupings: the Council for American Indian Ministry, the Council for Japanese American Congregational Churches UCC, the Hispanic Caucus of the United Church of Christ, and Pacific Islanders and Asian-American Ministries.

The Council for American Indian Ministry, sponsored by the Board for Homeland Ministries, received official recognition as a special ministry of the United Church by General Synod action in 1971. Subsequent authorization was given for two representatives of this council to sit in an advisory capacity with the Executive Council. In the same action the council was designated as the agency for allocation of United Church resources to American Indian work.[43] In a presentation to President Moss at the same sessions, Mitchell Whiterabbit, speaking for the council, said: "During your tenure . . . the American Indians have surfaced and become visible in the life of our Church. . . . You have brought us recognition. We hope that . . . we will become partners with full participation in the life and structure of the United Church of Christ."[44]

This tribute from the Council for American Indian Ministry symbolized the effectiveness of a new leadership style emerging from the enlarged role of the Executive Council. It was evidence of collaboration, coordination, and collegial sensitivity among the national offices, agencies, conferences, and local churches. As a result the confrontive and contentious tactics that characterized the 1969 and 1971 General Synods became unnecessary. As a denomination the United Church appeared to be much better equipped to be responsive to the concerns of a highly diverse constituency.

In several ways the spirit among delegates at both the 1973 and 1975 General Synods was evidence of the "cement that holds our fellowship together."[45] Openness, shared concern, and a sense of the common bonds of unity in Christ made it possible to address difficult and divisive issues without rancor and bitterness. This did not mean absence of friction or a diminution of passionate commitment to causes. But the wounds of the Sixties, when insensitivity was battered by the inescapable and justifiable claims of the disadvantaged and oppressed, were being healed by a new sense of being human. The synod could and did affirm that as the gift of the Spirit of God. At the close of the 1975 General Synod, a message from President Moss to the churches conveyed the sense of a new discovery:

> For five full days we were confronted from our seats . . . by a huge red and blue banner with the words: "Jesus Christ frees and unites," and the symbol of the United Church of Christ. The text and that symbol were burned into our hearts and minds. I believe we were united in Christ as no General Synod has ever been before. Our differences were open and candid, without rancor. We were free of the separate personalities of our parent Congregational Christian and Evangelical and Reformed traditions, and were unhampered by our racial, ethnic and sexual differences. After 18 years of turbulent, exciting life, *the United Church of Christ has crossed the threshold of maturity.*[46]

The importance of this affirmation is heightened when it is placed in the context of the general religious situation in American life in the first half of the Seventies. That situation exhibited unique and severe problems of religious identity and commitment that affected the majority of American religious bodies. The problem of identity had many ramifications for the United Church, however.

THE QUESTION OF IDENTITY

It is possible to interpret the entire period of 1965 to 1975 in the experience of the United Church of Christ as a search for identity. That is the nature of formation, whether in individual or group experience. A growing congruence of self-perception and style of operation in any organization is an important component of its vigor and strength when it is symbolized in shared affirmations. President Moss pointed to this in his opening address to the 1975 General Synod: "There is a consciousness emerging within this fellowship which we call the United Church of Christ that the style of life which seems to be growing among us is rooted essentially in the freedom and the unity which Jesus Christ alone can give."[47]

Those who participated in the 1973 and particularly the 1975 General Synod could affirm that statement because it expressed something experienced. Observers over the years could verify a growing sense of identity that touched base with the hope of a "new fellowship" in which "the principle of the autonomy of the local church understood in terms of its historical and theological development . . . and the principle of the mutual accountability . . . would not only co-exist but [in a sense] strengthen . . . one another."[48] Delegates to the General Synods, both regular and associate, along with other persons in official positions in the denominational structures, could identify themselves within a commonly perceived style of organized church life. To the extent that this perception existed, it was possible to speak of United Church identity.

102

Nevertheless, the question of identity was not resolved for large segments of the United Church. On the local level, in small and large communities, in urban and rural centers, churches drew their identity from quite different sources, most of them unaffected by a new style of life such as that experienced in national gatherings. In many cases local churches were still known in their communities by their former affiliation with either the Congregational Christian or Evangelical and Reformed traditions. But in style of church life even those traditional distinctions tended to be blurred by the pervading characteristics of main line Protestant churches. For the average local church member the name United Church had little content. Some indeed felt it to be sharply lacking in the particularity of other church names that designated either polity or confessional distinctions.

If United Church of Christ identity is rooted in the freedom and unity that Jesus Christ gives, making possible a faithful use of the tension between local church autonomy and mutual accountability, then the critical problems facing the denomination lie in the life of the local church. This was perceived in the decision of the General Synod to establish the Office for Church Life and Leadership, a national-level agency designed to work closely with conferences in the servicing of local churches. It was likewise the concern behind the 1967-68 biennial emphasis, "The Local Church in God's Mission," and the Faith Exploration program initiated by the former Council for Lay Life and Work. These were efforts not simply to bring local churches and denominational structures closer together but to undertake a shared enterprise in those matters that are of critical importance to the existence of the community of faith, which the local church manifests.

Even as such efforts were being made to address the particular aspects of the identity question in the United Church of Christ experience, other aspects of the general religious situation in American churches provided urgent practical concerns for both the denominational organization and the local churches. Two of these, intimately intertwined, must be considered in depth to gain additional perspective on the identity question. They were (1) steadily declining membership in most major American church bodies and (2) diminishing financial support. These realities, which impinged sharply upon United Church activity in the late Sixties and the early Seventies, heightened the question of denominational identity directly and indirectly. They posed the issues of *survival* and *relevance*, which, Gibson Winter argued, are "inseparable aspects of religious identity."[49]

Issues of both survival and relevance were sharpened by the statistical trends in American churches since 1960.[50] The membership of the ten largest church bodies peaked in 1967 at 77,666,223. United Church of Christ membership peaked two years earlier at 2,067,179. The downward trend continued from the mid-Sixties to 1975, when the total United Church figure was 1,818,762—a 12 percent loss in ten years. A parallel decrease in financial support in all denominations added focus to the questions of survival and relevance. From 1964 to

1972 basic support dollars for the national agencies of the United Church decreased 11.8 percent. Some of that decrease had resulted from a shift of funds to conferences. When the inflation factor was applied, however, the decrease was 39 percent.

Equally striking was public awareness of a changed attitude toward the place of religious faith and the role of religious institutions in the society. The news media regularly headlined the difficulties faced by the churches. The Gallup Poll underlined the dramatic reversal of public religious interest by reporting that 67 percent of the population in 1968 saw a decrease in religious influence as compared with 14 percent in 1957.[51]

The realities of declining membership and waning support were felt on many levels in the United Church by 1972. In May of that year the Executive Council was forced to reduce allocations to the various agencies sharply. For some people the situation was explainable by the denomination's deep involvement in social concern. Sheldon E. Mackey, executive secretary of the Stewardship Council, replied by citing a study which disproved that interpretation and placed the responsibility on the feeling that "the church is not important in modern life."[52] J. Martin Bailey, in a *United Church Herald* editorial, took a somewhat different stance in reflecting on the situation:

It seems clear that we were wrong in assuming that many thoughtful persons would be attracted to our ecumenically-oriented, socially-progressive denomination. Youth and unaffiliated admirers of our efforts to be his servants in the service of men and women have not flocked to the United Church. . . . We have much to offer such persons. But we have lacked one thing. *We have failed to invite friends and neighbors to share with us "the cost and joy of discipleship."* Such Pentecostal enthusiasm for fellowship seems to have gone out of style.[53]

Bailey was touching upon a theme that became widely supported in the two succeeding General Synods: the need to pay close attention to the disciplines of witnessing and thus inviting others to share in the cost and joy of discipleship. In a background statement on the vitality of the local church, prepared collaboratively by the five major national agencies for the 1975 General Synod, an effort was made to affirm the public reputation of the United Church as an open and inclusive communion with deep commitment to the rectifying of societal problems, claiming that

in [that] commitment the United Church of Christ has paid the telling but not unforeseen price. Some predict that we are pricing ourselves out of existence. They are too hasty. . . . They infer that this price is not commensurate with the "true" meaning of the Gospel. Those who espouse this doctrine want cheap grace. They . . . forget that the Lord has called his Church to engage in redemptive suffering.[54]

In a similar background statement on evangelism it was acknowledged that evangelism had not been a dominant strain in the United Church's predecessor denominations. Rather there was a persistent concern for the Holy Commonwealth. But

the United Church of Christ is in fact a united and a uniting Church with many strands and voices comprising its fabric. *Major attention needs to be given to United Church identity in the context of mission.* At present, the many-faceted character of the denomination's identity makes difficult recruitment of members and the sustaining of institutional strength.[55]

Survival and relevance, the components of religious identity, were the manifest concerns behind these statements and their subsequent utilization in program planning. Compounding the problem was the circumstance affecting other major Protestant bodies in varying degrees, but more severely the United Church: the gradually dwindling number of members with roots in the predecessor denominations. The particularity of the Puritan and continental Calvinist strains embodied in those traditions, although not completely lost, was of diminishing influence. The same was true of the other strains—Lutheran, Christian, and Methodist—except in certain geographical enclaves. Thomas C. Campbell and Yoshio Fukuyama, in their study *The Fragmented Layman*, allude to the difficulty that heterogeneity of religious backgrounds makes for accurate judgments about the United Church.[56] Identity on the national and the local level would not come easily to a church body whose historical rootage had been cut off by social and cultural mobility.

A final contributing factor to the identity problem in the early Seventies was the pervasive sense of a loss of faith in the society. Manifested in the general American religious scene by so-called radical theology and the death-of-God accents, the loss of faith experience in the United Church of Christ bore few distinctive marks. Nevertheless, the steady mixing of faith affirmations with messages of human improvement and psychological well-being did little to counter the declining sense of the transcendent dimensions of the faith. Knowledge and understanding of this dimension of the faith tended to be theologically deprived as the cult of experience dominated. Theological criteria for evaluating the meaning of the gospel in given life situations often gave way to "feeling" criteria. The authority of the faith for life was in one's experience of the faith, with little or no attention given to the authority of the tradition of the community of faith, the Bible, or faith statements by which groups were identified.

For many people in major American denominations "the experience of religious faith" had no transcendent referent at all; the experience was in the realm of interpersonal relationships. To find religious identity in "loving and caring" relationships did not necessarily require a particular religious community or a particular faith in a transcendent deity. Thus, the church as a community of faith lost its meaning for many people. Other communities and other relationships supplanted the church in the lives of people who, in a society of pluralistic value, had many options.

MATURITY AND ACHIEVEMENT

As the United Church approached the end of the second decade of its existence, then, it faced many of the same uncertainties as other church bodies. The question of identity was also shared, even though there were particular aspects traceable to its unique history. Denominational identities are rooted in history: confessional and theological, ethnic and social, ecclesiastical and political. In this ecumenical age, when crossing denominational lines is commonplace, traditional identities have muted significance. Hence, denominational identities were in crisis in the Seventies. Names that expressed historical developments had diminishing significance for local church members. Names that denoted a confessional family were probably more meaningful, but seldom in a substantive sense, for the translation of such confessions into contemporary relevance was difficult and not often undertaken. Churches that bore names indicating a particular ecclesiastical structure or liturgical practice tended to have a somewhat greater significance with respect to the internal life of the church, but little relevance in the general society.

Nearly all major church bodies in America gain some identity through hymnals, service books, and liturgies. Although many of these share some common materials, each draws upon its own tradition for those elements that are distinctive. In this respect the United Church of Christ presents something of a paradox. Its constituent bodies represent quite diverse understandings of the liturgical life of the church. On the Evangelical and Reformed side there was a significant liturgical tradition, although there were no mandatory formularies for worship. On the Congregational Christian side there was a historically rooted antipathy to fixed liturgies and a long tradition of freedom to shape the practices of worship to local need and inclination. When the United Church was formed, the principle of local church freedom with respect to forms of worship was included in the Constitution and By-Laws.

Concern about worship and its practice in the local church led, however, to the establishment of a Commission on Worship, charged to "pursue a scholarly study of worship and to give leadership to ministers and churches in the conduct of worship." The mandate specifically included the responsibility to draw upon "the treasure of the historic and universal Church," while not disregarding "the best in the traditions" of the uniting constituencies. The commission was to "prepare or propose for the General Synod's approval and commendation, books of worship, hymnals and other orders" for the church.

The eighteen-member commission, initially appointed by the Executive Council and later elected by the General Synod, began its work in 1961. In

106

1964 *The Lord's Day Service* was published and distributed by approval of the Executive Council as a trial effort intended to stimulate interest and response. This was followed by *Services of Word and Sacrament I and II* in 1966 and in 1968 by *Services of the Church*—the latter a series of booklets containing all major services and rites. The *Services of Word and Sacrament I and II* were incorporated in *The Hymnal of the United Church of Christ* in 1974. The hymnal represented the culmination of twelve years of work in producing materials for worship.

Although these materials were widely distributed and used in local churches, thus contributing in a small way to United Church identity, it is impossible to assess their real impact. Diversity of practice will continue to characterize United Church worship, even as it does in those bodies that have traditionally employed uniform materials and shared a common heritage.

As the unfolding story of its development in the preceding pages shows, the particular aspects of United Church identity have to do with the effort to devise and implement a viable form of denominational organization for a people whose dominant heritage called for a church committed to God's mission in the world. That mission, drawing heavily upon the Calvinian accents upon God's sovereign rule in the world, was bent naturally toward a concern for the transformation of society and less toward the evangelistic effort to "win souls for Christ." This suggests that United Church identity may never be susceptible of a simple and singular description as that which is implied in terms such as Presbyterian, Lutheran, or Episcopal. It reflects neither a confessional nor a cultic pattern of church life. Rather, United Church identity, as it became manifest between 1957 and 1975, demonstrated the continuing characteristic of organizational flexibility under the mandate of God's mission in the world. While this was a handy means of identification in relation to other church bodies, it became increasingly the essential element in United Church self-understanding. This was the thrust of President Moss's address at the opening of the Tenth General Synod in 1975.

Eighteen years of development and testing had resulted in substantial achievements. The newly framed partnership style among national offices, instrumentalities, and conferences had done much to close the traditional gap between national and local units of church life. As detailed earlier, the two centers of major influence coming to prominence in the Seventies were the Executive Council and the conferences. Conference collaboration brought the denominational concerns closer to the local churches. Of equal importance was the growing capability of the conferences in their servicing of the local churches. Denominational cohesiveness and strength were the result.

No interpretation of the significance of United Church development during those years would be accurate without acknowledgment of the key role played by Black churches and Black leadership. Their influence in the shaping of the

United Church was disproportionate in relation to their numbers[57]; it rested upon the providential convergence of high-quality Black leadership and the emergence of a new sense of pluralism within the community of faith. This contribution of the Black churches within the United Church fellowship was not lessened by the continuing need to address the many problems remaining within and without the churches. That responsibility belongs to the church for decades to come. It was the Black effort that moved the United Church into the new age and opened doors to wide-ranging opportunities to deal with racial and social injustice within as well as without the community of faith.

In many respects the influence of the Blacks in the church paved the way for another movement of far-reaching significance that gained almost immediate support—women in church and society. No church body in the nation responded as completely and quickly to the Women's Movement. Its effect upon the denomination was immediate, showing in greater representation on all levels, drawing upon new leadership among women, changing attitudes, and invigorating the fellowship with a new sense of wholeness. Future historians will have a better perspective on the influence of this movement, but as of this writing the Women's Movement would seem to be changing the church more dramatically than anything since the sixteenth century.

A closing statement on the development of the United Church of Christ could very well end at that point. However, the word united in the name of the church suggests some final consideration of the original announced intention of this church body to be a "united and uniting" denomination.

Reference was made earlier to President Moss's comment on the 1975 General Synod in which he expressed the judgment that the synod was "free of the separate personalities of [the] parent Congregational Christian and Evangelical and Reformed traditions, and . . . unhampered by . . . racial, ethnic and sexual differences." The evidence was in the spirit of the synod, but that in itself was a reflection of a reality that had showed itself again and again through the years, especially in relation to the potentially divisive moments when "racial, ethnic and sexual differences" were at the heart of the debates. The will to be a united church, for which the empirical evidence was strong throughout the union negotiating period, was demonstrated repeatedly after the union was consummated. To be united was not only a dream and hope; it was the article of faith, not always explicitly acknowledged, at the very heart of the church's sense of being the church. In the crucial moments it was the discovery of being one in Christ that brought reconciliation and healing and made the United Church a reality.

The intention to be also a uniting church was conditioned by other circumstances that inhibited active efforts in that direction. Reference was made in the previous chapter to the effect of the formation of the Consultation on Church Union on conversations with the Disciples of Christ and to the 1963 General

Synod's reaffirmation to commitment to union. Events in 1971 and 1972 led to a redefinition of that commitment. The submission of the first draft of *A Plan of Union* by COCU caused the Executive Council to release in May 1972 a detailed critique of the *Plan*.[58]

Calling for a reassessment of the concept behind the Consultation on Church Union, the Executive Council argued that the times required a new approach and asked that the emphasis in COCU be upon the renewal and mission of the church.[59] Preoccupation with organizational structure as indicated in the *Plan of Union* seemed to the Executive Council to be nonproductive. United Church experience provided the background for this proposal. Although years of effort had been given to organizational design in the United Church, the principle had been consistently held that organization is subservient to mission. Whatever influence the United Church would have in the consultation would derive from its own proven experience.

A decision of considerable significance in 1972 provided an interesting commentary on the Executive Council's memorandum to COCU. That decision moved the United Church of Christ into a joint effort with the United Presbyterian Church to publish a new church paper combining the *United Church Herald* and *Presbyterian Life*. Although many factors, chiefly of an economic character, entered into this decision, the proposed publication was primarily an effort to combine larger resources in meeting the needs of the churches for a church paper addressing the laity. "Treating the essentials of the Christian faith from the perspective of lay persons in a new journal of 'evangelical' intention seemed most appropriately a joint effort with a church body standing in the general Reformed tradition."[60] The new journal was to be published in two editions carrying news items appropriate to each denomination but utilizing much common material.

Cooperation between these two church bodies had been common practice for many years on many levels, but the new journal, named *A.D.*, seemed a harbinger of things to come, not necessarily of union but of those things that express the unity of God's people in Christ.

SUMMARY

This historical account of the development of the United Church of Christ has omitted a wealth of important and fascinating material relating to the work of the conferences, the instrumentalities, and the ad hoc agencies created from time to time. The focus has been on the development of the organization. To that extent the account is limited. At the same time it is a necessary portrayal of the converging events, movements, ideas, and commitments that make up the institutional church. It is legitimate at this point to ask: "Why this particular convergence?" To some extent the question has been answered by identifying movements and conditions prevailing in the second quarter of the twentieth century, when the United Church was born.

However, no period in history stands in isolation. Those forces at work in American Christianity in the twentieth century had roots in earlier periods. When these are examined, further light is thrown on the birth and formation of the new denomination. It is important to a fuller understanding of the United Church that these roots be identified and traced back into the history of Western Christendom. That is a task for the following chapters.

CHAPTER 5

WHY THE UNITED CHURCH OF CHRIST?

Historical narratives have limited interpretive value. They do not answer all the questions that can be raised about the meaning of the direction of events and decisions. Thus, the foregoing account of how the United Church of Christ was conceived and shaped leaves the question of "Why?" largely unanswered. If anything, the question of why the United Church exists at all may have been sharpened by the review of its development.

Roger Shinn wrote:

The United Church of Christ is, by most reckonings, an improbable collection of exceedingly diverse people. The sociological wisdom often used to explain groupings of people does not tell why so strange a combination of denominational families and ethnic groups came together to form this church.[1]

The improbability of the United Church has on occasion been observed by outside commentators, but it continues to be of interest as well to those within its membership who have involved themselves deeply in its work and life. In so many respects it is not different from other main line American Protestant churches with which it shares a common heritage. At the same time its diversity, its history, and its problems suggest that as a particular configuration of denominational life on the American scene there are shaping elements of a distinguishing character. To argue distinction in this sense is not to claim a uniqueness of quality. It is, rather, to point out that in *any* denominational configuration of church organization in a voluntary society it is necessary to identify points of distinction simply for better understanding.

It follows, then, that an important task remaining in this book is to go behind the events, decisions, and general organizational development that make up the story of the United Church and to interpret the shaping elements in American Christianity that come to focus in this denomination. These were identified in the Introduction as the concern for Christian unity, extensive organizational development, and religious and cultural pluralism. The impact of each of these upon the newly developing church was remarked in the narrative account. At the same time new questions were raised continually. Why did the Congregational Christian Churches have so much difficulty clarifying the ambiguities of their denominational life? Why were they so polity-conscious and yet seemingly confessionally indifferent? Why was the Evangelical and Reformed Church apparently so flexible in matters of polity? Why did it appear to be confessionally indifferent when it had such a rich confessional tradition? For example, agreements on how to state the content of the faith professed were reached with comparatively little effort. Was the theological development of the merging communions so much of one piece that there were no differences to be debated?

These questions and many others are posed by the "facts of the case" as reviewed in the preceding pages. They are not easily answered, and no claim is being made here that they will be answered fully in this chapter. Nevertheless, the story of the shaping of the United Church of Christ would be incomplete and perhaps misleading if no effort were made to interpret those shaping elements within the context of the particularities of the Congregational Christian and the Evangelical and Reformed histories. Those histories, however, will not prove helpful without seeing them also from the perspective of significant motifs in American Christianity generally. Once this is done it will be possible to consider those histories more directly and point to some answers for the questions listed above. Such an examination of these elements requires reference to sociological, theological, and historical material. Beginning with largely descriptive insights from sociological studies, the following account moves into a more interpretive style of theological and historical analysis.

SOCIOLOGICAL PERSPECTIVES

Sociological analyses of American Christianity in the past four decades have contributed helpfully and abundantly to new perceptions of church life and organization. Two facets of these analyses are of significance to an understanding of why the United Church came into being: (1) identification of sociocultural influences with respect to Christian unity; and (2) identification of religious factors in the United Church, exhibited in the parent bodies, which are shared in varying degrees with other church groups but which at the same time point to elements of the heritage that bind the United Church together.

A recurring theme in sociological studies of American church life is the divisive character of social differences. The classic assessment of this tendency was made by H. Richard Niebuhr in 1929.[2] Debate about the relative weight of the role of social differences as compared with the role of theological differences in denominational distinctions goes on simply because they are also relative to other influences at any particular moment in history. This is illustrated by the fact that Niebuhr's book was published at a time of a rising sense of the "scandal of a divided Christendom." It pointed a finger of judgment at the churches for their failure to deal with the reality of social differences and the consequent divisive and discriminatory impact.

112

Thirty years later Robert Lee, working within a changed social milieu and observing the surge of interest in church unity in American Protestantism, began to inquire as to the reasons for that phenomenon. He argued:

The essential soundness of Niebuhr's book in theory and application has been widely upheld. . . . If we accept Niebuhr's pioneer work as basically sound, and if we apply the analysis of social sources to the current scene, then it seems plausible that current patterns of church unity reflect a unity that has developed in American culture during the intervening years. . . . Our thesis is that the increase in church unity springs in considerable measure from the pressures of a growing cultural unity within American society.[3]

In support of this thesis Lee details areas of significant social change: race, class, sectionalism, and nationalism. In each there were changes toward elimination of conflict and narrow self-awareness and loyalty, and toward a greater sense of social unity. He saw signs of increasing cultural unity in common values, styles of life, mass communication, growing mutual dependence, and the all-pervasive organizational revolution.

From the vantage point of the mid-Seventies it is possible to say that the growing cultural unity Lee described was in fact more fragile than his evidence seemed to indicate. The Sixties brought to the American people an overwhelming sense of social and cultural disunity. Racial conflict and sectional self-consciousness seemed to tear the garment of social unity to threads. National unity was threatened by the Vietnam experience in ways that created high levels of anxiety and self-concern.

Yet, Lee's thesis as it stood in relation to the decades between 1930 and 1960 needs to be taken seriously. The experience of the recovery from the Great Depression of the Thirties, of the unifying national effort in World War II, and of the burgeoning affluence and self-confidence of the Fifties did point in the direction of a growing cultural unity. Furthermore, the evidence is ample that ecumenical interest, as expressed in cooperative efforts and even organic union, was nurtured by the same conditions that pointed toward cultural unity. Not the least important of these was the increased tendency of denominational organizations to find their models in the more extensive and complex forms of social organizations.

That the Congregational Christian Churches and the Evangelical and Reformed Church were affected by these developments cannot be denied. In those church bodies the influence of the organizational revolution was felt continually in the period under consideration. In two different settings Douglas Horton cited advantages to be expected from a larger and better organized denomination. In his pamphlet *Of Equability and Perseverance in Well Doing*, published in 1950, Horton had argued that the older form of Congregational organization, developed in the days of an agrarian economy, was inadequate for "out-guessing and out-maneuvering" the anti-Christian forces of the time. He asked for church organization with flexibility and with authority to act where action was needed. Later, writing in *The Christian Century*, he declared:

The most obvious advantage of the union is the least important and has been the least frequently mentioned: the union will constitute an out-and-out benefit to the business life of the two communions. All the features of denominational life which depend upon what is commercially the size of the market or the breadth of the financial base will be profited.[4]

The union of the Evangelical Synod and the Reformed Church in the United States in 1934 resulted in a national organization capable of enlisting the resources of a relatively small denomination in tasks of a size that compared well with much larger church bodies. The organizational development of this denomination will be treated more fully in chapter 7, but it is important to note here that traditional polity considerations tended to be minimized as the two bodies grew together in common concerns and responsibilities. The result was an organizational structure, adopted five years after the union was formed, that reflected current models of voluntary organizations rather than a traditional church polity model.

A pragmatic attitude toward polity in both of these church bodies was paralleled by another aspect of cultural unity; that is, the diminution of the role of ethnicity in denominational differentiation. Ethnic differentiation had been important in the beginning years in the formation of the Reformed Church and the Evangelical Synod as communities of German immigrants. But accommodation and acculturation reduced the ethnic sense as generations came and went. Assimilation within the mainstream of American culture and church life was especially noticeable after World War I. Although some traditions continued to be cherished and the German heritage was held in honor, the Evangelical and Reformed Church in many places throughout the nation increasingly showed itself to be very much a typical American Protestant denomination. This was true, of course, of other ethnically oriented church bodies as well.

To cite cultural influences toward church union and toward Christian unity in the broader sense is not to argue that such influences were of a primary character. The concern for Christian unity has its primary sources in the faith itself. At the same time cultural influences of the kind discussed above do apparently add momentum—and opportunity—to the organizational expression of unity. In a society where church structures are designed in the context of a voluntary system, cultural changes seem to have a rather immediate impact upon church organization. This was especially true in the years 1930-60.

A second facet of sociological analyses is of importance in understanding the United Church of Christ. This has to do with the identification of factors of religious orientation that the United Church of Christ shares with other American Protestant church bodies but which need to be singled out as constituting elements of *affinity* for union. That is to say, that although these factors cannot

114

be claimed as primary agents in church union, they have to do with a *religious orientation without which the union would have been highly unlikely.* During the late 1960s Thomas C. Campbell and Yoshio Fukuyama undertook a study of the patterns of lay attitudes and church participation in the United Church.[5] The study addressed two questions with respect to American culture:

The first is, under the conditions of differentiation, is there any significant diversity of forms of church participation *other than* the diversity that reflects closely the forms of cultural diversity? The second is, can one discern any conscious or unconscious consequences of the diversity of forms of church participation that are not "explained" by the cultural diversity underlying it?[6]

These questions were then addressed in relation to three hypotheses, the first two of which have had fairly wide use in sociological studies and have yielded findings that could be employed to check the validity of the data gathered:

[1] Differences in an individual's social situation result in different modes of religious orientation and social outlook.

[2] Participation in religious organizations is a phenomenon which can be meaningfully described along at least four dimensions: organizational, religious knowledge, belief and devotional orientations.

[3] Different church participation orientations have different consequences for behavior and attitudes on social issues.[7]

The third hypothesis was the most important for determining whether the church participant's religious orientation had any significance for involvement in the issues of the society. Using four standard types of church participation, the study defined religious orientation in terms of organizational involvement, religious knowledge, devotional orientation, and belief orientation. Analysis of responses from more than eight thousand laypeople in both urban and rural churches yielded data in support of the hypotheses. Of chief importance for understanding the United Church is one singular finding that deviates from most popular assumptions; that is, *that church participation measured by the Index of Devotional Orientation correlates with attitudes that challenge cultural values.*[8] By devotional orientation is meant church participation expressed in a concern for the church's fostering of the devotional life, a definition of a Christian as one who is involved in daily prayer and Bible-reading, who supports church prayer meetings, and who is "searching for ways to sense an *instrumental* role in God's action."

The significance of this for the United Church is underlined when it is placed alongside statements in both the Preamble of the Basis of Union and the Preamble of the Constitution and By-Laws. In the former the "instrumental role" of the church (the body of believing Christians) is accentuated:

Believing that denominations exist not for themselves but as parts of that Church, within which each denomination is to live and labor and, if need be, die; and confronting the divisions and hostilities of our world, and hearing

115

with a deepened sense of responsibility the prayer of our Lord "that they all may be one"; [we] *do now declare ourselves to be one body.*

The same themes are caught up in the Preamble of the Constitution and By-Laws in such lines as: "in order to express more fully the oneness in Christ of the churches composing it, to make more effective their common witness in Him, and to *serve His kingdom in the world.*"

Added to this announced intention are the actions of the Third and Fourth General Synods, which set the United Church on a course of challenging cultural values, of concern for social justice, of devotion to God's kingdom. The sense of being the *instrument* of God's mission and work in the world was dominant.

Two conclusions suggest themselves when the Campbell-Fukuyama findings are considered in relation to the announced and practiced intentions of the United Church to be instrumental in God's work in the world. First, the religious orientation of United Church people constitutes an important element of affinity without which the union of the Congregational Christian and Evangelical and Reformed Churches would not have been possible. *This shared attitude toward their role as Christians and as church people made other differences tolerable.* Perhaps even more important is the fact that this shared understanding of responsible Christian life contributed strongly to the "will to unite," which was cited in earlier chapters as a crucial element in overcoming the obstacles to union in the 1940s.

Second, the roots of this particular religious orientation of United Church people, although identifiable in the parent bodies, are to be found in other segments of American Protestantism as well. It is to this conclusion that attention must now be given. This is supported by research findings about United Church members who were "converts," so-called, from the Presbyterians, Baptists, Methodists, and Lutherans.[9] A large portion of the United Church constituency came from these other church families.[10]

This suggests that further understanding of the United Church requires moving beyond the sociological insights to a consideration of the *sources* of the dominant religious orientation of American Protestantism. These sources lie deeply within the diverse American religious traditions. To uncover and interpret them it is necessary to use a combination of theological and historical analyses. In so doing it will be important to bear in mind the concern to know the specific ways in which the merging communions that formed the United Church were shaped by and helped to shape that orientation to religious practice which challenges cultural values.

A HISTORICAL-THEOLOGICAL PERSPECTIVE: THE ENGLISH REFORMED TRADITION

A theological analysis of the religious orientation of American Protestants yields perspectives that make the United Church less improbable than is sometimes

116

assumed. The common heritage is all-pervasive. It should not be surprising that a predominantly Anglo-Saxon church body would be able to strike a common course with a German-background group if attention is given to their involvement with the dominant theological motifs in American Christianity. The element of *affinity* to which sociological research points has theological roots widely attested to by scholars.

This does run counter to some commonly held assumptions about the United Church. James H. Nichols, for example, in commenting upon the concern of the Congregationalists to be a uniting fellowship says: "In looking about for a partner toward the end of the 1930's, they came upon the Evangelical and Reformed Church. *It was less a matter of affinity* or of long association than that these were the two denominations most disposed to merger in principle who were not otherwise engaged."[11] It can be argued on the contrary, however, that while these two denominations were in fact "most disposed to merger in principle," as H. Paul Douglass[12] pointed out, the *affinity element* is essential for understanding the United Church. To understand that element it is necessary to examine the dominant characteristics of American Protestantism by moving back from the sociological data about it to its historical development.

It is worth noting that this was the procedure H. Richard Niebuhr followed forty years ago in his effort to interpret the meaning of American Christianity. In the preface of his book *The Kingdom of God in America,* Niebuhr expressed dissatisfaction with the limitations of the study he had made in *The Social Sources of Denominationalism,* a book he had written eight years earlier:

Though the sociological approach helped to explain why the religious stream flowed in these particular channels it did not account for the force of the stream itself; while it seemed relevant enough to the institutionalized churches it did not explain the Christian movement which produced these churches; while it accounted for the diversity in American religion it did not explain the unity which our faith possesses despite its variety; while it could deal with the religion which was dependent on culture *it left unexplained the faith which is independent, which is aggressive rather than passive, and which molds culture instead of being molded by it.*[13]

The religious orientation in which church participation "results in the transformation of social attitudes" and which stands in tension with culture is not uniquely American. However, it is in America that the impact of this orientation is most evident. Neither the story of the nation itself nor of its religious life can be told apart from attention to the way in which this particular understanding of the Christian life was expressed. In a general way all Protestant movement in this country was affected by it. *In particular ways it is responsible for the traditions that flowed together in the United Church.*

To clarify this it is important to indicate and interpret three major theological themes: the sovereign rule of God, the lordship of Christ, and the transformation of all life. The emergence and dominance of these themes in the Protestant

117

movement introduced what scholars have called the Puritan Epoch.* In a unique way the roots of American Protestantism lie firmly imbedded in the English Reformation, that is, in the Puritan movement of the late sixteenth and early seventeenth centuries. It was there that the Reformed tradition, nurtured from its soil in both Switzerland and Germany, generated a dynamic thrust that has greatly affected all Western culture since that time. Sydney Ahlstrom characterized it as

> essentially a Christian revival in which the biblical understanding of man and history was forcefully proclaimed. This meant a renewal of concern for *this* life, *this* world, and all their impinging problems, moral and social. Other religions may be other worldly; but the Jew, the Christian, and even the Moslem are all impressed by the prophetic demands of the Bible and its peculiar concern for the irreversible course of history, in which men participate in this world as morally responsible persons.[14]

What flowered in England was a faith that refused to bow to tyranny and despotism, that would not yield the ordering of life to human contrivance, because God is sovereign. God's sovereign rule of the world of human beings is neither arbitrary nor capricious but a faithful work of divine mercy as revealed in Jesus Christ.

The Calvinist sense of God's sovereignty gave to the Puritan Reformed movement in England the irresistible power of a "possessed people." Confessing with John Calvin, "We are not our own. . . . On the contrary we are God's, to him, therefore, let us live and die. We are God's; therefore, let his wisdom and will preside in all our actions,"[15] they had a profound and radical sense of responsibility and destiny. Such a movement filled the immense spiritual vacuum left by the trivialization of the gospel in the medieval church. In place of the vacuous authority of the established ecclesiastical system, which took away the will to be responsible, the Reformed faith found the authority of the Word of the sovereign God a source of freedom and responsibility.

With this sense of being responsible to the sovereign rule of God, the Puritans could not tolerate what they felt to be the corruption and the misuse of authority in the Church of England. When their efforts at reform were frustrated or compromised, they saw no alternative but to look for another opportunity in which to fulfill their responsibility. That opportunity was being offered in the wilderness and boundless expanses of the New World across the seas. To that new land they came not so much to escape an intolerable situation as to fulfill

*While Niebuhr discusses these themes explicitly in *The Kingdom of God in America,* the reader who wishes to gain the full flavor of the argument should also use: Perry Miller, *Errand into the Wilderness* (Cambridge: Harvard University Press, 1964); Alan Heimert, *Religion and the American Mind* (Cambridge: Harvard University Press, 1966); Sidney Mead, *The Lively Experiment* (New York: Harper and Row, 1963).

118

what they believed to be the mission to which God had called them. They had a vocation. They came on an "errand into the wilderness," as Samuel Danforth called it in his election-day sermon in 1670[16]; to be "as a city set upon a hill," to use the words of Governor Winthrop of Massachusetts Bay Colony.

The spread of the Puritan Reformed movement to a new land led to a development of faith in the rule of God which was not without the ambiguities that attend all human enterprise. While these must be recognized, they are not the focus of attention in the effort to understand a major consequence of that faith in regard to the church, that is, the autonomy or independence of the church in relation to the culture. The autonomy of the church as a consequence of faith in the sovereign rule of God eventually contributed to such formal concepts as separation of church and state, religious liberty, and freedom of worship. Its significance for the major concern of this chapter, however, lies in another direction.

Although the meaning of the sovereign rule of God underwent considerable change from colonial days to the present, its influence upon the American Protestant understanding of the church's autonomy in relation to culture continues to be normative. That is to say, the church's independence from any form of external control and the sense of being responsible to God are firmly fixed in the attitudes of church people. Admittedly, it is not likely that the ground of this in the sovereign rule of God is widely recognized today. Nevertheless, the unconscious influence of this principle, so important in the Reformed tradition, is evident in attitudes among church people today and certainly in the United Church.

This is the import of the Campbell-Fukuyama findings concerning those who scored high on the Index of Devotional Orientation.[17] This style of church participation, reflecting a sense of being responsible to God, correlates with a positive and concerned stance toward social problems. From that finding Campbell and Fukuyama argue that the devotional orientation implies a necessary sense of a transcendent reality.[18] The sense of a transcendent reality was deeply imbedded in the American religious consciousness by the emphasis of the Reformed faith tradition on the sovereign rule of God *in all aspects of life.*

God's sovereign rule in all of life was expressed in a special covenantal relationship in Puritan Reformed thinking. This covenant with those whom God called was both assurance and obligation. This sense is most vividly expressed in Gov. John Winthrop's words to the people on board the ship *Arbella* as they were about to land in Massachusetts Bay in 1630:

Thus stands the cause between God and us, we are entered into Covenant with him for this work, we have taken out a Commission, the Lord hath given us leave to draw our own Articles we have professed to enterprise these Actions upon these and these ends, we have hereupon besought him of favor and blessing; Now if the Lord shall please to hear us, and bring us in peace to the place we desire, then hath he ratified this Covenant and sealed our Commission, (and) will expect a strict performance of the Articles contained in it, but if we shall neglect the observation of these Articles which are the ends we have propounded, and dissembling with our God, shall fall to embrace this present world and prosecute our carnal intentions, seeking great things for ourselves and our posterity, the Lord will surely break out in wrath against us be revenged of such a perjured people and make us know the price of the breach of such a Covenant.[19]

Covenant theology had roots in the thinking of John Calvin, the French-Swiss Reformer. Calvin interpreted the covenant in biblical terms as God's promise to his people which he obligates himself to fulfill, as given in Genesis 17 and Jeremiah 31, and actually *fulfilled* in the incarnation, death, and resurrection of Jesus Christ. The sacraments are the seals of that fulfilled covenant. L.J. Trinterud has called attention to the different accent in covenant theology among the Rhineland and English reformers, some of whom tended to consider the covenant a conditional promise on God's part. God has kept his part of the covenant by what he has done in Christ, but the covenant was not regarded as complete or effectual unless there was a responding promise of obedience from the believer. In that way the covenant became for some a "mutual pact or treaty." Trinterud comments: "The burden of fulfillment rests upon man, for he must first obey in order to bring God's reciprocal obligation into force. Theologically, of course, the difference between these views is of the greatest moment."[20]

In Rhineland Reformed thinking and among many Puritans, however, the emphasis *was not upon the believer's obligation alone*; it rested upon what the divine initiative provides so that the obligation can be fulfilled. It is the gracious gift of the sovereign God that makes a human response possible. That gift is Jesus Christ, himself, who by his Word and his Spirit is present in the hearts of those who believe. By baptism the believer enters the covenant relationship; by participation in communion at the Lord's table the believer is sustained by the presence of Christ.

This leads to consideration of the second major theological theme in the Reformed tradition that has shaped the common religious heritage of American Protestants and the United Church, namely, the lordship of Christ. The rule of God and the rule of Christ were synonymous for the Puritans; the first implied obligation, while the second implied possibility; one was law, the other was grace. The rule of the sovereign God was not to be flaunted; God's law was the essential restraint of all human lust for power and autonomy, thereby assuring freedom. Restraint, however, did not produce goodness and justice. Only the presence and reign of Christ in the human heart could make this possible.

Where Christ is Lord the human heart knows no coercion of the law but only the constraint of Christ's love. "The love of Christ controls us," said the apostle Paul in his second letter to the Corinthian Church. This was the meaning of the lordship of Christ for those who believed in the sovereignty of God.

Two important implications of Christ's lordship for the people of the Reformed persuasion were his headship in the church and his empowerment of the individual believer in a life of freedom. In these convictions too there were ambiguities that became prominent in later stages of Protestant development in America. Nevertheless, they have continued to be characteristic of the Christian movement in this land.

While the sovereignty of God meant the independence of the church from any form of external control, the lordship of Christ meant that the shape and function of the believing community were to conform to Christ its head. All Protestant church bodies did not agree about the implications of that for church organization, but the chief effect in all was restraint of the power of the clergy. If Christ is head, no person may arrogate to himself or herself in the church the authority that belongs to Christ. The practical corollary of restraint of the power of the clergy, however, is the enhancement of the power of the laity. The organizational patterns of American Protestant churches exhibit the full range of attempts to express the authority of Christ in relation to the authority of believers, both clergy and lay. In this respect the institutional form of the church always represents for Christians a fundamental dilemma in their relationship to Christ.

For the individual believer the lordship of Christ meant an inward presence that brought harmony and peace to the heart. The consequence was a release of energy for willing the good and doing it. Apart from the freedom Christ gives from self-serving and self-justifying necessities, there is no possibility of loving one's neighbor. As H. Richard Niebuhr put it, liberty as a presupposition or self-evident right of human beings was not accepted by the Protestants of this tradition; rather, freedom was the goal that could be envisioned for those who knew the lordship of Christ.[21]

To know, that is, to experience the releasing freedom of the lordship of Christ was not, however, simply a matter of human choice. The initiative for the pressing of Christ's presence and liberating love upon the human heart was that of the sovereign God. It was grace, God's grace alone, that opened the door of the kingdom of freedom, justice, and righteousness. As is well known to students of American Christianity, in the nineteenth century this emphasis upon the divine initiative was gradually transferred to an emphasis upon human initiative under the impact of the Second Great Awakening. Nevertheless, the initial stress upon God's sovereign grace forms the substratum of the faith expressed in those whose church participation is characterized chiefly by the Devotional

Orientation underscored in the Campbell-Fukuyama study. In this orientation the life of the Christian in Bible study and prayer reflects a dependence upon and loyalty to the divine sovereignty; it reflects an ultimate trust in a goodness and freedom beyond human capability but which can be known in a life surrendered to Christ's rule. Thus, the *effect* of Christ's lordship in the life of the Christian is expressed in obedient response to the divine purposes.

In much of American Christianity, especially in the last one hundred fifty years, the experience of Christ tended to be increasingly a private and individual matter. When this is the case, the "instrumental" role of the Christian in relation to God's purposes is atrophied. This can be attributed to the loss of the sense of God's sovereignty and an increase of the role of human initiative. That the devotional life can move in the direction of a purely private experience of Christ is well attested. It is a risk that the church has always known; in that risk the church easily becomes a convenient organization to suit individual desire. This can be countered only by accentuation of the rule of God, which leads to a sense of corporate responsibility and involvement.

The third major theological theme of the Reformed tradition as it is seen in the American Protestant movement naturally follows upon the discussion of the lordship of Christ, namely, the transformation of life according to the divine purpose. In fact, none of these themes can be considered in isolation. The vision of the transformation of all life, that is, not only of the individual but of society as well, can be traced all through the Judaeo-Christian tradition. Its meaning for Christians is explicit in the person of Christ in whom the New Creation can be known by those who enter his rule. But the New Creation is never a private estate for the self-satisfied. Its reality is in the world reconciled to God by sovereign grace, *and in the sense of being enlisted in the service of reconciliation.*[22]

Following in the tradition of Calvinist teaching, the Reformed movement as it developed and extended its understanding of the divine sovereignty saw the transformation of the society as the church's responsibility and goal. That transformation was not to be accomplished by law (except where the law is required for the restraint of evil) but by the reign of Christ in human hearts. This, in turn, was dependent upon the extension of Christ's love through obedience, care, and concern for all human beings and the society itself.

The extension of Christ's rule so as to bring freedom to all inevitably meant more than missions of mercy. The altruistic motive was not enough. For the person under the control of Christ's love there was always the responsibility of standing against those cultural attitudes and values that violate and destroy the human spirit and often the human body. But again, this was more than a responsibility of the individual Christian; it was the reason for the church's being, which by its very nature expresses the reality of the rule of Christ. It was therefore the responsibility of the church; that was its vocation.

The hinge upon which all this turns is the sovereignty of God. Trust in that sovereign power is possible because of the rule of Christ in the human heart. Evidence of that sovereign power is the transformation of life through freedom from the inward bonds of sin and the outward barriers of society's injustices and unjust patterns of order.

A HISTORICAL-THEOLOGICAL PERSPECTIVE: THE GERMAN REFORMED TRADITION

Such a survey of the major themes of the Reformed faith as they were shaped on the American scene from earliest colonial days does not tell the entire story about the United Church. It accounts for only one component of the element of *affinity* with which this chapter is concerned. Concentration upon that component—the shaping of the Reformed faith under the Puritan movement—was necessary because of the way in which it literally prepared the fertile soil of the American religious situation for other Christian groups. The other aspect of the element of *affinity* becomes visible in the religious ethos and theological motifs characterizing the Evangelical and Reformed Church, which found the "fertile soil of the American religious situation" proper for its own implantation.

Partly because of a later arrival upon the American scene but also because of its history of development in different ethnic, political, and social circumstances, the Evangelical and Reformed relationship to the general American religious situation requires separate attention. Although the story of the Evangelical and Reformed group is the subject of a later chapter, it is necessary at this point to indicate two interrelated circumstances that have important bearing on the subject of affinity for union.

First, the German immigrations from which this church body was drawn were spread over a period of more than two hundred years. Some differentiation of the stages of immigration is clearly required for a constructive interpretation of the religious temper and theological orientation of these German people. Those who came in large numbers into William Penn's colony, the Virginias, Maryland, New York, and the Carolinas during the colonial period (especially in the early 1700s), were subject to influences that were very different from the ones experienced by those who arrived a century later and participated in the westward expansion of the nation. Another level of differentiation is indicated in the waves of immigration in the late nineteenth century.

A second but related circumstance was the influence of the religious, political, and social turmoil on the Continent of Europe. Although seemingly a permanent feature of the German people's life, this turmoil reached peaks of intensity that produced important theological trends. Political and religious strife, often indistinguishable in the war-ravaged Germanic lands, did not crush the dynamic intellectual and cultural movements to which so much of the Western world is indebted. From these came vital thrusts of German theological scholarship, which began to affect American theology in the nineteenth century especially and increasingly thereafter.*

As a union of the Evangelical Synod of North America and the Reformed Church in the United States, the Evangelical and Reformed Church represented a fusion of the two major church movements originating in the sixteenth-century Reformation in Germany and Switzerland, namely, Reformed and Lutheran. The Reformed faith of the forebears of German and Swiss people of the Reformed Church in the United States developed a distinctive character in the Rhineland region of Germany and in the German cantons of Switzerland under the influence of Ulrich Zwingli and, later, of John Calvin. The Zwinglian and Calvinian streams of Reformation tended to flow together in the Rhineland after 1560 largely through the efforts of Peter Martyr, John á Lasco, and Theodore Beza, all co-workers of Calvin.[23] Their work was supported by Heinrich Bullinger, of Zurich, who was Zwingli's successor. Most influential of all in many respects were Martin Bucer at Strasbourg and Philipp Melanchthon, a Lutheran.

The dominant characteristic of the Rhineland Reformed movement was its irenic and mediatorial spirit, which focused upon the unity of the faith. Calvin's doctrine of the Spiritual Presence of Christ in the eucharist was a focal point of mediation between the memorialist position of Zwingli and the Real Presence position of Luther. Beyond this, however, was a little-noted fact of the work of all the Reformers, that is, the immense effort they gave to the reconciliation of differences for the sake of the unity of the church. It is ironic that the Protestant world has tended to build its monuments on the failure of those efforts rather than upon the convictions that prompted them. The irony is the greater when it is remembered that "the divisive forces in politics were often too strong for the unitive forces of religion."[24] Nevertheless, this concern for the unity of the church remained a major feature of the Reformed tradition in the Rhineland from whence came the Reformed people, who, along with their Lutheran neighbors, settled in large numbers in Pennsylvania.

Two other features of the Reformed tradition in Germany require a more extended discussion—church order and the practice of Christian piety. These were especially significant for the colonial experience of the German Reformed people in America, conditioning them for existence in a land where the initiative for the life of the church fell directly upon the laity.

Church order, of course, in sixteenth-century Germany had its foundation in civil order. The ruler of the province was as responsible (in principle if not in

*Philip Schaff was the initial key figure in this influence, although he represented only a portion of the growing thrust of German theology. Schaff was known as the ecumenist of the Reformed tradition. His work with the German Reformed Church in the period of 1844 to 1870 left an indelible imprint on its theological work. Schaff's contributions are discussed later in this chapter and again in chapter 7.

124

fact) for the spiritual and ecclesiastical affairs of the people as for civil and political matters. However, in those provinces, where the Reformed faith was dominant, Calvin's teachings about church government introduced a countervailing principle that gave to the German Reformed Church movement a distinctive type of church order. Although it can be seen only in its embryonic stages in the area of the Rhineland known as the Palatinate, this developing church order became a pattern or model of sorts for the people who emigrated to America. Its principal supporter was Elector Frederick III of Heidelberg. In every congregation a consistory comprised of equal numbers of clergy and laity was formed for the purpose of order and discipline in the church.

The concept of church discipline exercised by persons elected by the congregation contrasts sharply with the prevailing custom of the Lutheran and the Zwinglian Reformed churches. It was a direct development of the Calvinist Reformed concept of the lordship of Christ in the church, which would not tolerate either arbitrary clergy or lay control. The consistory, including both, was to act in conformity with the Word of God to maintain order. Many years later this Calvinist principle of church order, based on the lordship of Christ, gave the German Reformed immigrants in Pennsylvania a form of organized church life comparable to that of their Puritan neighbors.

Any discussion of the practice of Christian piety in the tradition of Western Christendom must run the risk of misunderstanding because of the distorted connotations of the term. The difficulty is especially acute with respect to the strain of piety in the German Reformed tradition in the Rhineland during the nineteenth century. That strain of piety was of an activist type, which spurred and supported educational and missionary work. To differentiate between this and what is generally known as Pietism it is necessary to go behind the images of the Lutheran Pietism of the seventeenth century represented in Philipp Spener and August Francke, which were chiefly a reaction to rationalism.* The sources of Reformed piety of the Rhineland lie in the creative blend of the fundamental energies of Reformation thought and teaching in the sixteenth century. They found expression in the *Heidelberg Catechism*, produced in 1563, the classic symbol of the German Reformed faith.

Activist piety drew its strength from the Reformation conviction of God's justifying and sanctifying work in Christ by which the human mind and heart are transformed. The *Heidelberg Catechism* casts this conviction in personal terms, which makes it a powerful devotional classic, a means of nurtured faith and commitment. William Toth, writing of its spirit, claimed:

*Eighteenth-century Pietism affected both the Reformed and the Lutheran churches. I am defining "piety" as that self-disciplined set of attitudes and habits of mind formed by a sense of belonging to God and expressing itself in life-long discipleship under Christ; and "pietism" as a manner of life that seeks in attitude and habit to conform to images of holiness and to require such conformity of others who wish to be called Christian.

The . . . Catechism . . . stimulates the conviction that Christianity, vastly more than a system of doctrine, must be a Godward orientation of the soul of man that culminates in the *transformation of human activities according to the designs of God*. Its genius lay in the irenic spirit that cultivated the love of essentials—*beyond the churches the church* and beyond the scriptures the historic stream of faith and experience. "It was Lutheran inwardness, Melanchthonian clearness, Zwinglian simplicity, and Calvinistic fire, harmoniously blended."[25]

Melanchthon's role in the evolving spirit of the Reformed Church in the Rhineland deserves attention because of his commitment to a mediatorial responsibility between the Lutheran and the Reformed positions. As a young, brilliant, and trusted colleague of Luther, he maintained contacts with Calvin and other Reformed leaders in an effort to demonstrate the unity of the church. As confidant and counselor of Elector Frederick III, his irenic yet clear exposition of Luther's teaching made him an invaluable ally in peace efforts. It was Melanchthon who contributed to the catholic spirit of the Heidelberg Catechism through his influence on its authors, Zacharias Ursinus and Caspar Olevianus.

Reformed piety depended upon catechetical teaching. Bard Thompson has called attention to three propositions of Reformation theology behind this use of catechisms:

(1) The Word of God presents itself as an inexhaustible resource to the believer; it cannot all be heard in one sermon, nor fathomed at one reading. (2) The believer who takes the Word seriously must become captive to it, forever remaining its pupil and disciple. (3) The true relationship between the believer and scripture is not one of private opinion, but a lifelong discipleship which gives depth and seriousness to religion and energizes the priesthood of all believers.[26]

Catechetical instruction centered in the homes as the heart of family worship, even while the Catechism was used in the church's worship, usually just before the sermon. The results were crucial for a faith that was informed, grounded in the scriptures, yet corporate, not private. From childhood on the community of faith learned that "before the Word of God, *the believer's responsibility was not one of private judgment, but one of serious discipleship.*"[27]

These foundations of the strain of Christian piety persisted among the German Reformed people and gave them a sense of self-identity as they settled in the New World. While the further development of that story must be reserved for a later chapter, its significance for the major theme of this chapter must be underlined. This strain of Reformed teaching and practice was carried to England, where it fed the Puritan movement. When it reached American shores in the German Reformed migration of the early decades of the 1700s, it found a developing Protestant ethos in which it was at home, although it had little direct contact with New England Puritanism.

A HISTORICAL-THEOLOGICAL PERSPECTIVE:
THE GERMAN EVANGELICAL TRADITION

Tracing the elements of *affinity* in American Protestantism that are essential to understanding the United Church requires, finally, a careful look at the Evangelical Synod component of the Evangelical and Reformed Church. Although arriving much later on the American scene, approximately two hundred years after the English Puritans and one hundred years after the German Reformed people, the German Evangelicals brought to the new denomination a distinctive strain of church life. Two developments in the German church situation of the late eighteenth and early nineteenth centuries—Pietism and unionism—throw light upon this. Carl E. Schneider, church historian, calls attention to the perspective that must be maintained, however, in viewing these developments:

The German immigration to the Western frontier during the first three decades of the nineteenth century was occasioned by the peculiar converging of political, economic, and religious influences. *In no wise was the immigration of these years related to the German arrivals of the seventeenth and eighteenth centuries.*[28]

Pietism, the first concern here in the period under consideration, had evolved from a confessional and scripture-centered practice of Christian piety in sixteenth-century Rhineland to a nonconfessional and experiential style of piety in the period from about 1670 through the eighteenth and early nineteenth centuries. Although in both forms the personal sense of God's redeeming grace was strong, in later Pietism the experiential accent was dominant.* Countering the rising tide of rationalism, later Pietism turned to an intensification of the devotional life by ascetic and emotion-stirring disciplines instead of the discipline simply of confessionally oriented scripture study, which was characteristic of Reformed piety in the sixteenth century.

Religious formalism and rationalistic theology constituted a powerful threat to both the Lutheran and the Reformed churches, sometimes resulting in a reduction of the animosity that had existed between them since the late sixteenth-century doctrinal disputes. A revivalistic spirit, particularly in western Germany, accompanied the efforts of pastors from both church groups to counter the inroads of rationalist thought. Such combined efforts produced extra-church societies, which published tracts and generated missionary endeavors.[29]

Discontent with the German church situation, combined with severe political and economic conditions, led vast numbers of Lutheran and Reformed pietists to look to opportunity in America. However, a second development in the German church situation—unionism—is closely related and must be taken into account.

*The parallel with American experiential pietism in the Great Awakening of the mideighteenth century is obvious, of course. Spiritual revivalism was not confined to America but could be found in various forms throughout western Europe as well.

Union of the Lutheran and the Reformed churches in Germany, so earnestly desired and sought by the Reformers, had never been achieved. Although the pietist movement brought peace and cooperation in many areas, in others an unfortunate and spiritually debilitating hostility persevered. Apparently, union remained beyond the reach of concerned Christians. It did not, however, escape the attention of the political and civil groups for whom German nationalism had become an inspiring ideal. This nationalist spirit, combined with union concerns kept alive by such leaders as Friedrich Schleiermacher, led to the effort of Friedrich Wilhelm III, the king of Prussia, to unite the churches. The result was the birth in 1817 of the Church of the Prussian Union, called "Evangelical" to point to its basis in the fundamentals of the gospel without Lutheran or Reformed distinctions. Unfortunately, there were then three "churches" in Germany since many individual Lutheran and Reformed churches refused to be united. Extreme Lutheranism resulted in widespread separatism.[30]

After 1830 the civil government's response became increasingly harsh toward dissenters from the union. Even as the United Evangelical Church movement spread into other regions of Germany, religious controversy between the different groups and parties increased. America, with its vast unsettled "West," seemed to beckon and offer hope to the warring parties. Among the immigrants who came were people for whom the United Evangelical Church concept offered the kind of freedom and opportunity earnestly sought by the Pietists, especially from the area of Württemberg in western Germany. The cause of church union was imbedded in the pietistic consciousness of these people for whom the gospel was liberty. By maintaining communication with the Church of the Prussian Union in the homeland and by drawing much of its pastoral leadership from the Basel and Barmen mission societies, which were pietistic, the developing Evangelical church movement (known as the *Kirchenverein*) in America was openly pro-union.

Discussion of the sources of the spirit of the German Evangelical Synod must refer to what has been described as its "nontheological temper." Motivated by its pietistic spirit to meet the religious needs of the German people in America, especially in the West, the *Kirchenverein* resolutely maintained independence from divisive confessional or doctrinal debates. Schneider claimed that "in the process of this adjustment to American conditions an irenic theological consciousness evolved, which, in spite of certain dogmatic features of the latter part of the period, remained the dominant characteristic of the Evangelical Church in America."[31]

At the same time, according to Schneider, the *Kirchenverein* was cognizant of the role of confessional statements and doctrinal positions in countering the faith-dissolving diversity of purported Christian teachings on the frontier. In 1847 the *Kirchenverein* (church union or united church) adopted a confessional paragraph that placed it "among the Churches in which the historical continuity

128

with the Reformation was to be maintained." That paragraph accepted the symbolic books of the Lutheran and Reformed churches "in so far as they agree; but where they disagree, we adhere strictly to the passages of Holy Scriptures bearing on the subject, and avail ourselves of the liberty of conscience prevailing in the Evangelical Church."[32]

This temper of the *Kirchenverein* had important implications for the later church union concerns of its successor Evangelical Synod. As is discussed somewhat more fully in a later chapter, the spirit of that synod was exemplified in what Walter Brueggemann, in writing of Eden Theological Seminary, has called "an evangelical pietism by which I mean a radical commitment to Christian faith in the reformation categories of 'grace alone' and 'faith alone' but in a mood which is concerned with a trusting commitment to the will and power of Christ without need to be theologically precise or doctrinally defensive."[33] Absence of concern for theological precision was increasingly evident in nineteenth-century American Protestantism. It reflected not only the temper of such groups as the German Evangelical people but also of the more indigenous denominations spawned by the energies of the Second Great Awakening.

Attention thus far in this section has been focused upon the major common themes of American Protestantism and their parallels in the roots of the constituent parts of the United Church. A brief recapitulation may help focus upon themes that have continuing significance but which, in their ongoing American development, appear in quite different form. The shared tradition of the Reformed faith, from both England and Germany, underlines the themes of God's sovereignty, Christ's lordship, and the possibility and obligation of the transformed life. Derivative themes and accents included the nature of the church as a called people, free from external control but covenanted in a responsible relationship with Christ by which the transformation of life could be extended to all society. Running through both the English and German traditions in the United Church background is an accent on the practice of Christian piety, which in later generations often shaded off into the cloying pietism that in its individualistic form has been a bane to Protestantism. A final theme was that of union. What happened to these themes and derivative accents can best be traced in the following chapters on the individual histories of the union partners.

A HISTORICAL-THEOLOGICAL PERSPECTIVE:
THE MOVEMENT TOWARD CHRISTIAN UNITY

Before reviewing the individual histories of the Congregational Christian Churches and Evangelical and Reformed Church, another task remains with reference to the dominant features of the religious orientation of American Protestantism. It is appropriate to reflect upon those features in relation to the modern movement toward Christian unity in the midst of which the United

Church was born.* What significance do they have insofar as it is possible to trace their common lineage? Is there evidence that these fundamental features have a role in the church union expressions of Christian unity? Are not pragmatic organizational considerations more critical in this time? `

Negative responses to the first question can be easily anticipated. For example, Charles Johnson, commenting on the experience of the Consultation on Church Union, had this to say in 1973:

The historic issues which spawned the separate denominations just aren't involved in the lives of those who have succeeded to the original inheritance. It might have been assumed that the Consultation on Church Union's resolution of traditional differences would expose the common foundation upon which a uniting church could be built. Yet this did not turn out to be the result. *My own hunch is that what was exposed was not the essentials of a common faith but how little was left to the children of the faith that motivated the fathers.*[34]

Minimal concern for the faith shared has seemed to characterize much of the effort to give institutional expression to Christian unity. This seemed to be true in the formation of the United Church, where little time was needed to find a common faith basis. Nevertheless, the conclusion may be premature that concern for structure signifies minimal concern for the faith to be expressed. Albert Outler, a noted Methodist ecumenist and theologian, has commented: "*Structure* was the uncharted rock on which COCU stove in its bottom. *Structure* is the will-o'-the-wisp that has lured almost every church in Christendom into expensive reorganizations."[35] *Ambivalence* about the place of structure reflects, of course, the dilemma of the Christian movement as it faces the institutional necessities of society. *Ambiguities* in the efforts to resolve the problems of structure in relation to the unity of the church represent human sinfulness and pride as well as the human desire in faith to be responsive to the gospel imperative.

Throughout Christian history this *ambivalence* and these *ambiguities* are prominent characteristics of the church's life. Protestantism itself, as indicated earlier in this chapter, has from its beginnings illustrated the point. It is possible to conclude, with a cynicism that may be more an expression of unbelief than of simple human weariness, that Christian unity is not worth the effort put into it.

Close examination, however, of the experience of the United Church of Christ (and of other union achievements too) reveals not simply the ambiguity of union efforts but *the reality of the unifying power of the gospel at work*. The significance of this becomes clearer when it is viewed within the context of the modern ecumenical movement as it is dated from the midnineteenth century to the present. For this movement has been—despite the charges of failure re-

*See Introduction, pp. 13-18.

peated by critics—a witness in the modern world of the unifying power of the faith.

It is time well spent to indicate some aspects of that movement, exhibited clearly in the United Church, that are often overlooked. Willem A. Visser 't Hooft, for many years the general secretary of the World Council of Churches, puts the point to be remembered thus:

The ecumenical movement was never concerned with unity alone. Since the days of the pioneers ecumenical workers have known that to unite the churches-as-they-are is not worth the trouble. *Unity is only desirable as an expression of a deep transformation of the churches, in other words as the outcome of their common renewal.* A united church is not necessarily a renewed church. *But real renewal must lead to unity.* For genuine renewal means *rediscovery of the fundamental mandate of the Church, and that mandate includes to live as the reconciled people of God.*[36]

Renewal based upon the gospel mandate to live as "the reconciled people of God" has been the persistent and dominant theme of the concern for Christian unity as expressed in the ecumenical movement. The "rediscovery" of this mandate is responsible for the dynamic impulse toward unity that has affected not only Protestants but Roman Catholics as well in the modern era. Vatican II could not have occurred apart from the impulse. Christian unity formed under that mandate has been experienced "as a mutual rediscovery of brothers who have never lost their kinship."[37]

In many respects the experience of Evangelical and Reformed and Congregational Christian people coming together in the United Church of Christ was just such a mutual rediscovery of a kinship that had not been especially visible to themselves or to others. Most important in the rediscovery were those elements of affinity that through the years had become the common treasure of American Protestantism but which had their roots in the struggles and life of the German, Swiss, and English forebears in the Reformed tradition. The thrust of the concern for unity illustrates the pervasive, even though probably unconscious, influence of the faith in God's sovereignty, in the lordship of Christ, and in God's power to transform human life. In its seventeenth- and eighteenth-century expression, that faith demonstrated its English Puritan heritage. It is in the nineteenth century that it was fused with and modified by other influences, including that of the German heritage.

Reference has already been made to the church union tradition of the Evangelical Synod as it came out of a fusion of Reformed and Lutheran churches in Germany. Requiring further attention, however, was an ecumenical development in England, which had far-reaching effect in both America and Europe. It constitutes a kind of "forerunner" experience among the churches that later became so deeply involved in the twentieth-century ecumenical movement.

Due largely to the theological genius and indefatigable efforts of Philip Schaff, a considerable ecumenical influence was extended by the movement begun in England in the midnineteenth century by Presbyterians and Congregationalists. This was the formation of the Evangelical Alliance in 1846. Characterized as "the explicitly ecumenical agency of the benevolent empire of voluntary societies,"[38] the Alliance did not represent a union of organized churches but of concerned Christians from churches of different polities. It had evolved as a result of the experience of hundreds of voluntary societies and drew its membership from various churches. Moved by evangelical fervor and piety, these societies devoted themselves to many forms of missionary work and tract publication. The stated intention of the Alliance was expressed in a resolution:

The Church of the Living God . . . is one church, never having lost, and being incapable of losing, its essential unity. Not, therefore, to create that unity, but to confess it, is the design. . . .

That this conference . . . feel constrained to deplore its existing divisions, and to express *their deep sense of sinfulness in the alienation of affection by which they have been attended,* and of the manifold evils which have resulted therefrom.[39]

The significance of the Alliance probably lies chiefly in the way the members had "rediscovered their kinship" and were responding to the mandate to "live as the reconciled people of God." In this way the *reality of the church as the Body of Christ* transcended ecclesiastical and organizational structures. When American participation in the Alliance was interrupted by the temporizing of the churches over the slavery issue, it appeared that this ecumenical effort had foundered on the rocks of the critical social issue of the Western hemisphere. It was Philip Schaff, formerly a professor at Mercersburg Seminary (forerunner of Lancaster Seminary) and then at Union Seminary in New York, who became the key figure in the Alliance on the American side. Schaff's personal vision of ecumenism extended beyond that of the Alliance to an expression of unity that involved church structures.[40]

Schaff's ecumenical involvement brought him into contact also with the Church Union of Prussia and, in that connection, with the *Kirchenverein* in America. Of greatest importance, however, was his role as a theologian of the Mercersburg Theology in the German Reformed Church during the twenty years he served as a teacher and scholar at the seminary in Mercersburg. Along with John Williamson Nevin he became a major force in the broadening of the ecumenical spirit, giving to it a catholic vision that has remained to this day. Although his teaching (and that of Nevin as well) stirred controversy within the German Reformed Church, it permanently affected that communion's vision of responsibility in Christian unity.

This can be seen especially in George Warren Richards, who became one of

132

the early leaders in the effort to develop the United Church of Christ.* His special contribution lay in the recognition that the cause of Christian unity could not be advanced without the forming of a new organism rather than simply a new organization. A new organism could be developed only from that which is in essential continuity with the Christian tradition (catholic substance), while at the same time eliminating the ephemeral forms of given historical circumstance (here was the Protestant principle at work). He saw the kingdom of God as the "vital principle" at work in modern Christianity.[41]

The focus of the foregoing discussion of ecumenical perceptions and Christian unity efforts from the midnineteenth century until the third decade of the twentieth has been upon the unifying power of the gospel. That power was at work as a countervailing force to the growing denominationalism in the United States. It represented an ever-increasing awareness that denominations in themselves tended to frustrate responsiveness to the mandate of unity. Involved in this awareness were the denominational leaders themselves, whose participation in unity talks, while advancing their own denominational causes, often reflected the ambiguities cited earlier.

Everett C. Parker, director of the United Church Office of Communication, wrote in 1968 about the situation prevailing in the 1930s and 1940s:

There was much talk of cooperation. . . . Actually, the denominations went their individual ways in a polite but fierce competition for the choice suburban "high potential" sites. In other fields of church life, programs were expanded and budgets increased from year to year. Denominations staked out their own principalities and *began to look upon themselves as powers.* There was much jockeying for enhancement of denominational prestige. *The church became highly visible through the development of bureaucratic structures.*[42]

The situation to which Parker refers illustrates another aspect of the "scandal of denominationalism." As real as it was, however, the fact remains that precisely in such times *church union as an expression of Christian unity* reached a peak of no small proportions.

Twentieth-century ecumenism has its own distinctive marks: conciliarism and church unions. These deserve attention as the more immediate frame of reference for the shaping of the United Church of Christ, but their relationship to

*Richards, intensely active in the several union movements of the early decades of this century, wrote an article entitled "Ways of Church Union" (April 1928 *Christian Union Quarterly*) about organic union in terms that reflect the Mercersburg (particularly Schaff's) influence. For him organic union meant the forming of a new organism by a vital process or act of God, which then is able to form a "corporation" according to its own genius. In this one sees the conceptual basis of the Evangelical and Reformed union in 1934 and the E&R insistence as per the Basis of Union that no structure be built until after the United Church of Christ had come into being.

the preceding period of ecumenical endeavor discussed above must be kept in view. For the twentieth-century accents do in fact represent but a further development of the concern for Christian unity. The changes that took place show the impact of the growth of a technologically advanced society in which the betterment of human living continues to be matched by an increase of misery and tensions for ever larger proportions of the human family.

The formation of the World Council of Churches in 1948 marked the climax of the conciliar expression of unity. Beginning with the World Missionary Conference in Edinburgh in 1910, conciliar efforts were built on the thrust of the voluntary movements so prominent forty to fifty years later. In the subsequent founding of the International Missionary Council, in the Faith and Order Conferences of 1927 at Lausanne and 1937 at Edinburgh, and the Life and Work Conferences at Stockholm in 1925 and at Oxford in 1937, the worldwide Christian community discovered its unity in common concerns and tasks.

In the span of thirty-eight years between the conference at Edinburgh in 1910 and the First Assembly of the World Council of Churches in 1948 at Amsterdam, two world wars devastated western Europe. The Christian community worldwide was confronted with humanity's desperate need for healing. Voiced in the theme of the World Council Assembly at Amsterdam, "Man's Disorder and God's Design," and echoed in the council's continuing work was the conviction that the unity of the church in Jesus Christ is for the "healing of the nations." Growing recognition of the instrumental role of Christian unity accompanied the rising awareness of the critical nature of the fragmentation of the world following World War II. The mandate for unity was seen as grounded in the compassion of Christ.

There was a shift, then, from the evangelizing concerns of the voluntary societies, which had been the major thrust of ecumenism up to World War I, to a concern for the physical as well as the spiritual needs of human society. Western Christendom's response to this shift brought into critical focus once again the issue of a viable church structure for mission. Denominations that had been developing their organizations to cope with pressing needs of a different kind in a fragmented world became increasingly aware of their limitations. The issues were practical as well as theological. Pragmatic reason pointed to the wasteful and confusing overlap—and often downright competition—of denominational bureaucratic structures. Cooperation was possible but often came only under economic pressure.

More important was the sharpened theological awareness that the healing of society's wounds requires the church's own demonstration of the reality of that healing in its own shape and action. In a voluntary society the denominational form of the church provides the community of faith with an instrument for corporate action as well as for the experience of identity. But while denominational forms do enable the faith community to *exhibit* the larger reality of the

134

church for its members, they also *inhibit* the healing reality of Christ's body for the world. This dilemma became a matter of conscience to a degree not known before among American denominations. It was a potent force in the surge of church unions between 1919 and 1960.

Circumstantial factors in the movement toward unity as indicated above do not, of course, account for the initiative, disciplined effort, and concern demonstrated by the churches. For all the ambiguities discernible in their ecumenical effort, there is also evident an overwhelming balance of a sense of a "people possessed and called" to a task and a vision that continually transforms life where it is touched. The search for a viable structure for the church as shown in the church union accomplishments can be understood only by recognizing the influence—mostly unconscious—of the dominant Protestant ethos identified earlier in this chapter.

The church can tolerate the insecurity of structural tentativeness only when it knows itself under the *lordship of Christ*. Christ's rule in the church, known through Word and Sacrament and experienced by the work of the Spirit, requires the risking of everything, including organizational security, for the sake of the world for which Christ died. Having experienced and continuing to experience his *transforming power*, the church views the suffering, fragmented, and alienated societies of the world as the object of Christ's compassion, seeing no human being beyond redemption. For the world, as well as the church, is under the *sovereign rule of God*.

Church union, then, is an expression of the sense of its members that they are not their own; they are in the service of God, who reigns in their lives through Christ. They are, therefore, not content with a world that does not yet know the transforming power of Christ. God keeps the churches in ferment under the mandate of unity.

The United Church of Christ was born within this time of ferment generated by the mandate of Christian unity and the consequent denominational self-examination. In the midst of that ferment the Congregational Christian Churches and the Evangelical and Reformed Church *rediscovered their kinship*. Up to the midtwentieth century neither time nor circumstance had permitted that discovery. Drawn together in a time of great human need for the healing that only the gospel can offer, a shared religious orientation, and a common theological tradition, these two communions were able to transcend the differences their individual histories had produced and to experience a renewal the vitality of which is evident to this day.

This chapter has traced and described the forces, ideas, and movements that are an integral part of the story of the United Church of Christ. The validity of this kind of answer to the question "Why the United Church of Christ?" must be tested against the evidence offered in the account of its formation given in the first four chapters. Even then some questions remain about the long period of development of the two uniting communions. It is appropriate, then, to sketch out, with a selective use of a vast body of material, the historical development of denominations known until 1957 as the Congregational Christian Churches and the Evangelical and Reformed Church. To do that is to uncover the unique features of the kinship which these groups have rediscovered as the United Church of Christ.

CHAPTER 6

FROM MOVEMENT TO DENOMINATION: THE CONGREGATIONAL CHRISTIAN STORY

Congregational origins are the subject of an immense body of research. As a movement nurtured in the English Puritan Reformation, it shared with other groups claiming that heritage some concepts of the nature of the church and its organization that in one form or another have affected much of American Protestantism. At the same time scholars have found in Congregational development some of the most distinctive ideas of Puritanism.

Debate rather than agreement, however, has characterized much of that research over the past fifty years. Even at this date a clear picture of Congregational origins is not easily gained. There is general agreement that historians writing in the late nineteenth and early twentieth centuries were inclined to read into the early New England life some of the prevailing nineteenth-century democratic accents on individual rights and religious liberty. However, H. Shelton Smith points out that "one of the surprising turns in contemporary historical research concerns the origin of Congregationalism," in which that tendency is challenged.[1] Some new and helpful perspectives are now available for understanding this particular expression of Reformed church life. They are of especial significance for understanding why it was possible for Congregationalists to join with the Evangelical and Reformed Church in forming the United Church of Christ.

Denominational models of church life inhibit the effort to understand Congregational origins. Such models have only nineteenth- and twentieth-century frames of reference; they are inapplicable to the early seventeenth-century milieu of religious organization in which the Congregational models of church life began to evolve. The Puritan movement, which eventually gave birth to such models, had little concern in the beginning for the framing of a new type of church organization. As Edmund S. Morgan has pointed out, divisions among the Puritans over the "form" of the church became acute only after they achieved control of the English Parliament in 1641.[2] At that time quite diverse points of view began to develop.

Then some Puritans preferred to leave each individual church independent of outside control, while others thought that the ministers of the churches should be organized into presbyteries, consociations, and synods in order to enforce orthodoxy among themselves. Those who held the latter view became known as Presbyterians; those who held the former were called Independents or Congregationalists.[3]

Behind these gradually diverging points of view, however, were some shared convictions about the nature of the church, which had been hammered out of the struggle to cleanse the Church of England throughout the latter half of the sixteenth century. Much of the impulse for this came from the influence of John Calvin in Geneva, Ulrich Zwingli in Zurich, and Martin Bucer and Peter Martyr in the Rhineland. It was to these Reformers that many English Protestants fled in 1553 when Queen Mary restored Catholic practice. After Mary's death these exiles brought to the motherland strong convictions about the internal independence of the church that they had learned in the Rhineland. They knew the church as a people gathered out of the world by the preaching of the gospel who, in the unity of the Spirit, strengthened one another, enabling all to frame their lives by the Word of God. God's sovereign rule through the Word would not tolerate either ecclesiastical or political interference.

These shared convictions were used in a variety of ways. Many Puritans remained faithful to the Anglican tradition, seeking to purify the church from within. Others organized new congregations after the model of church government in Calvin's Geneva; these were the Presbyterians. Those most influenced by the Rhineland Reformers were the Independents or nonconformists. They held that the "visible church is a *particular congregation*, never a diocesan or national body," having full power to order its life because Christ is Head of the church.[4] For these Independents the church was gathered by mutual covenanting, based upon the covenant of grace that God had made known through the Word and sealed in the sacraments.

These foundational ideas about the church were shared by the Separatists. They differed from the Independents in their relationship to the Church of England. As the name implies, separatism meant complete separation from the Church of England, denying that a corrupt church could be the true church. Independents, while asserting the right and obligation to govern their life in the church under Christ, did not deny that the true church could also be found within the Church of England.

As the Puritan movement flowed to New England shores, its undifferentiated forms of church organization were tested in completely new circumstances. Out of that testing came the basic strains of Congregational church life.

ORIGINS OF THE NEW ENGLAND WAY

The cartographer's tracing of Congregational origins pinpoints sites on both sides of the Atlantic. Each site is significant for particular developments in the Puritan movement as it faced the need to shape a church in conformity with its vision. England, Holland, and New England witnessed and shared in the struggle of totally dedicated Puritans to be obedient to their convictions. Not given to reticence about their views, they have left a wealth of detailed, but sometimes confusing, printed materials by which later generations can enter into their journeys.

Although Elizabeth, who succeeded Mary on the throne in 1558, was Protestant, her regime continually frustrated the hopes of nonconforming Puritans. The result was another exodus to the Continent in the early 1600s, largely, but not exclusively, of those who were known as Separatists. Sometimes known as Brownists (after Robert Browne, of Norwich) or Barrowists (after Henry Barrow, the most rigid Separatist of them all), their location in Holland was significant. There they were free to organize, discuss, debate, and reorganize. This resulted in a mellowing of positions about the church, which eventually brought nonseparatist and separatist strains of thinking closer together as the movement began toward America.

John Robinson, however, is the focus of attention in Holland. This dedicated Puritan pastor brought most of his congregation from Scrooby, England to Amsterdam in 1608 and then to Leyden in 1609, where they remained for eleven years. There they sought to be a disciplined body of believers gathered by the Word, formed by the Spirit, and leading a holy life. From the strong Reformed influences of the Rhineland, they learned "the principles of mutual edification and fraternal correction" so essential to the community of faith.[5]

Separatist though he was, Robinson was not intolerant of nonseparating Puritans. In Holland he had intimate ties with Henry Jacob and William Ames, two outstanding thinkers of the nonseparatist tradition who had fled to Holland because of the threats of the English ecclesiastical authorities. Current scholarship agrees that this association led finally to some modification of Robinson's separatist views.[6] In particular, Jacob's influence on Robinson can be seen in the latter's change of attitude toward the Church of England, a change noted by others. More important is the evidence in the *Seven Articles* of the Leyden Church, signed by Robinson and William Brewster, a ruling elder of the church. Articles four, five, and six exhibit an attitude toward the Church of England and the authority of the bishops that belie a rigid separatist position.[7] This document, prepared apparently about three years before the journey to Plymouth, not only shows the influence of Jacob and Ames as powerful thinkers but also the fluid character of Puritan understandings of the church at that time, both among Separatists and non-Separatists.

Americans generally, not only Congregationalists, find the stirring account of the pilgrimage of the Leyden congregation to the New England shores a treasured document.[8] Told by William Bradford, governor of Plymouth Colony, the story of that epic voyage is eloquent testimony of the indomitable spirit of those

Puritans who knew themselves as "not their own but God's." "They knew they were pilgrims," wrote Bradford as they left Holland. Their place in Congregational origins was anchored at Plymouth Rock, but the extent of their role in the forming of the American Congregational tradition can be traced only by turning first to the other and larger migration of Puritans, who settled in Massachusetts Bay Colony nearly a decade later.

Nonseparating Puritans were more numerous in England and later also in New England than were the Separatists. Their journey to the New World had a pronouncedly different motive from that of the Separatists. They came, as Samuel Danforth said, "on an errand into the wilderness"; their aim was example and reform not separation. The Church of England was their spiritual mother, as Gov. John Winthrop emphasized. Winthrop's *A Modell of Christian Charity* gave clear indication of the colony's purpose and role.[9]

A comparison of Winthrop's document and Bradford's account of *The Mayflower Compact* provides illuminating perceptions of both the different concerns prevailing in these two colonizing efforts and their different self-understandings as Puritans. Winthrop illustrates the profound sense of going to the New World "under orders." There was a task to be done, a commission to fulfill. In consequence, the document is strongly homiletical, using a hortatory style that culminates in a warning: "for wee must Consider that wee shall be as a Citty upon a Hill, . . . soe that if we shall deale falsely with our god in this worke wee have undertaken and soe cause him to withdrawe his present help from us, wee shall be made a story and a by-word through the world."[10] Winthrop sought to mold these Puritans into a body of vision-oriented colonists.

Bradford's account of the Leyden pilgrim's approach to the colonizing task is largely descriptive, but it includes *The Mayflower Compact*. That compact had been made necessary by the fact that among the *Mayflower* passengers were many "strangers"—not of the Leyden Church—who had joined the ship in England. "Occasioned partly by the discontented and mutinous speeches" that some of the "strangers" made, the *Compact*, according to Bradford, was "the first foundation of their govermente in this place."[11]

The *Compact* was, as H. Shelton Smith points out, nothing more than a church covenant adapted for civic use.[12] Its distinction is in the establishment of a "civill body politick" based on social contract and not upon the authority of civil magistrates appointed by the Crown. This in itself differentiated the Plymouth Colony from the Massachusetts Bay Colony, where civil authority continued to be derived from the Crown and was linked to ecclesiastical authority. From the beginning the Plymouth Puritans were a covenant-based church. The covenant was the "authority" that founded order in the life of the church.

When the nonseparating Puritans settled in Massachusetts Bay, they were not as clear in their thinking about the issue of the authority by which the church could define itself. If the church is, as John Field claimed in 1572, a "company or congregatione of the faythfull called and gathered out of the worlde by the preachinge of the Gospell, . . . " who were the faithful?[13] The Separatists had answered that by a consistent use of the covenant. The Bay Puritans had not been as consistent simply because through years of struggle in the mother country they could not fully reconcile their Puritan understanding of the church with their loyalty to the Church of England. Edmund S. Morgan claimed that by their refusal to separate from the Church of England, the nonseparating Puritans deprived themselves of the opportunity to put their ideas fully into practice. . . . There is evidence that a few ministers gathered together special groups from within a church or from several churches. The members bound themselves to one another by covenant but also remained as members of their regular parish churches.[14]

Their arrival in New England gave nonseparating Puritans their first experience in forming the church. Their principles were clear enough, but what would be their practice in a land where the mother church did not exist and where long-time parish memberships did not prevail? Could they form the church under the principles enunciated by Henry Jacob, one of their number, who is sometimes called the father of Congregational church theory? His summary included:

(1) The visible church is a particular congregation, never a diocesan or national body; (2) the church is formally gathered through mutual covenanting; (3) the church is composed of holy or regenerate believers; (4) the supreme head of the church is Jesus Christ, from whom the church has immediate and full power to order its entire life, without determination or control by any overhead body.[15]

These were principles affirmed by all Puritans, including the Separatists, but only the latter group had practiced the principles consistently by going first to Holland, then to Plymouth. Now, in Massachusetts Bay, the non-Separatists were in the position of doing what many of them, when in England, had criticized the Separatists for doing.

What happened at Massachusetts Bay continues to be surrounded with questions and speculation. Two quite opposite points of view are held: one insisting that the nonseparating Puritans there established a distinctive form of church order[16]; the other contending that by reason of a visit from the Plymouth Colony, the Bay people were converted to a separatist position.[17]

That the Plymouth Separatists did not influence the founding of the first church in the Bay—Salem—would seem to fly in the face of facts. In 1629, when Salem was founded, leading members of the Plymouth Colony were present. Edmund S. Morgan argues convincingly that the Bay Puritans probably sought and willingly received counsel from these visitors about voluntary church organization, in which the Plymouth colonists were experienced.[18] The constituting of the church by entering into a covenant with God and with one another and the ordaining of a pastor and a teacher were marks of separatist influence. There was, however, no claim of separation from the Church of England. In fact, John Cotton, who came to the Bay four years later, took great care to deny that there had been any undue separatist influence from Plymouth in his tract *The Way of the Congregational Churches Cleared* (1648).[19]

What, then, were the features of church life worked out by the Bay Puritans that so affected New England for generations? In seeking to answer that question it is important to bear in mind that the Congregational Way in New England evolved over a period of years, so that some distinguishing features did not appear until fifteen years later. During that time there were changes in both the Bay and the Plymouth settlements and consequently some distinctions appear blurred.

It is clear that Bay Puritans were not Separatists in the sense of separation from the Church of England, while Plymouth Puritans were clearly Separatists in that sense. But both groups were "separatists" in the sense of being "called out" of the world, separated from worldly behavior. The distinctive feature of Bay Puritanism, which became, in John Cotton's words, the "Congregational Way," was the accent on the covenant of grace. It is God's grace working in the human heart that generates faith. That faith, then, obligates the Christian "to joyn willingly together in Christian communion and orderly covenant, and by free confession of the faith . . . , to unite themselves unto . . . visible congregations."[20] When Cotton accentuated faith as God's work, he was implying criticism of the Separatists, who, although in agreement about grace as essential, tended to emphasize the fruits of grace by their requirement of a church covenant aimed at good behavior. For Cotton that meant the Separatists were establishing the church on a covenant of works rather than on the covenant of grace.

The Congregational Way as developed by Bay Puritans laid stress, then, not on the church covenant as the foundation of the church but upon the covenant of grace, which made a saving faith possible.[21] The church covenant was simply an implementing device for the assembling into a body (congregation) of those who knew grace or, in other words, had "saving faith." Again, then, the question was: Who has this saving faith? As Congregational church life developed in the first decade of the Bay Colony's existence, the "testing" of persons seeking admission to the church for the purpose of identifying "saving faith" became a complex and restrictive procedure. Its subtle intention was to see that the church was made up only of "Visible Saints." The experience of saving faith became the major concern of the Christian, and the definition of that experience was the concern of the churches, especially of the ministers.

Formalizing the order of church life called "congregational" took place at Cambridge. A "synod," that is, an assembly of "elders and messengers" of the churches, gathered to consider their direction and the problems that defied mutual counsel on a voluntary basis. Called originally by the General Court of the Bay Colony in 1646, the synod's work was not completed until the third session, in 1648, when it produced what is known as the *Cambridge Platform*. Distinguished by its delineation of the Congregational understanding of church government, the *Platform* represented the fruit of the efforts of Bay Puritans to be responsible to their vision of God's will for the church.[22]

THE CONGREGATIONAL WAY TESTED

The *Cambridge Platform* has been called New England Congregationalism's "monument." That designation has an unintended appropriateness when it is remembered that monuments often honor achievements past and gone. Up until the time the Cambridge Synod formulated the *Platform*, the vitality of the Congregational Way developed by the Bay Puritans had been evident in the numbers of people gathered into churches. More than fifty churches could be counted as the product of the zeal and dedication these colonists brought to their calling as Christians. But the problems that prompted the calling of the synod in the first place were not soon to be solved. The Congregational Way entered a time of testing, which brought far-reaching changes both to the form of the churches and to their faith.

Any survey of the writings of the latter half of the seventeenth-century New England experience readily shows the nature of that testing. Caused by a combination of social and religious circumstances—second-generation lack of spiritual fervor, growing religious pluralism, declining Puritan influence in England—this testing is shown in two defensive developments: the Half-Way Covenant and the Reforming Synod of 1679.

The first was a compromising solution to the problem presented by church members who, although in the covenant, were not in full communion because they had not given evidence of "saving faith," but who still wanted their children baptized. These "half-way" church members could hardly be denied the desire for their children's baptism without driving them out of the church. In 1662 elders and messengers from the churches gathered in Boston to act in concert to authorize such baptisms. This action, the so-called Half-Way Covenant, was a break in the exclusivistic pattern of the early Congregational Way. Inevitably, it had a liberalizing effect and began to sap the vitality that the churches had known.

The second defensive development—the Reforming Synod of 1679—was called out of a concern to improve discipline and order in the churches. Although accompanied by a day of fasting and prayer in the churches, the synod's efforts were nonproductive. Nothing came of the reiteration of the demand for faithfulness to the *Cambridge Platform*; that monument seemed to have turned into stone.[23]

This breaking away from tradition generated storms of controversy. One liberalizer who was more influential than the others, Solomon Stoddard, was at the heart of the dispute. At the Northampton church, where he served nearly sixty years, Stoddard demonstrated a concern for evangelism that bore fruit in several periods of spiritual awakening among the people. But Stoddard became increasingly dissatisfied with the restrictions of the Bay traditions and especially with the Half-Way Covenant. He refused to debar from the eucharist those who had not been able to make a confession of a saving faith (an ever-increasing number) but who had owned the covenant. He saw the eucharist as a converting ordinance whose nurturing effect should be withheld from no one who had made even a beginning profession of faith.

Two powerful cultural and religious developments of the turn of the century, extending nearly to the Revolution, that drastically changed the Congregational Way even as they did all of New England social and political life, were the growing strength of the Enlightenment in England and the rise of revivalism, known in America as the Great Awakening. On the Continent of Europe, but especially in England, the Enlightenment heightened human critical sensitivities and so produced increasing human self-confidence. Christian churches, which had so long dominated not only the spiritual but the intellectual life of western Europe, responded sometimes with resistance but also with accommodation. Out of resistance came efforts at spiritual revival. Out of accommodation came intellectual trends in theology that brought much internal struggle for the churches. The influence of these movements flowing to America from Europe is seen in the changes that took place in the eighteenth century, before the Revolution.

Not only did the churches of Massachusetts suffer spiritual decline, but all the way down the Connecticut River Valley to New Haven the loss of spiritual vitality had made inroads that were of great concern. While the struggle against liberalizing trends in Massachusetts never seemed to reverse the spiritual decline in the churches in that period, a different experience developed in Connecticut. The critical turning point was the convening of a synod at Saybrook, by order of the General Assembly of the colony, and the adoption in 1708 of what was known as the *Saybrook Platform*.

THE WAY REDESIGNED

The influence of the *Saybrook Platform* has been variously assessed, but it is clear that the document was produced by (and itself produced) forces that were to have a long-range effect in the shaping of Congregationalism. Sydney E.

144

Ahlstrom, writing on the 250th anniversary of the synod, makes this evaluation:
Few New Englanders could have foreseen that the turn-of-the-century decades which lay ahead were to witness a permanent bifurcation of that old Puritan region which in 1648 had sealed its spiritual unity in the Cambridge Platform. . . . It is, I think, sufficiently clear that a critical "time of decision" had arrived in New England; . . . there began to emerge two ecclesiastical and intellectual provinces which in time would become still more clearly defined and sharply opposed.[24]

Most significant for consideration of the emergence of the Congregational Way into the Congregational Churches as a distinguishable church body in America were the polity principles laid down by the synod and adopted by the Connecticut General Court in New Haven. For the voluntary and fellowship responsibilities between the churches as set forth in the Congregational Way of the *Cambridge Platform*, Saybrook substituted procedures emphasizing the obligation of "consociation" of neighboring churches. The purpose of consociation was mutual assistance in all church matters and an orderly procedure for adjudication of dispute. This telling—and controversial—provision called for "the sentence of non-communion" against pastors and churches who refused to submit to consociation.[25]

Commentators, then and since, have pointed to the so-called "Presbyterianizing tendencies" in the *Saybrook Platform*. Obviously, the effort was directed toward the protection of the churches more than toward their control. Nevertheless, the threat of control was there, resulting in a cautious interpretation of the more ambiguous portions of the *Platform* so as to preserve the independence of each church. In any case, the *Saybrook Platform* accomplished much of what was intended: orderly procedure and, above all, mutual support.

Testimony to the appropriateness of both the intention and the accomplishment lies in the predominant influence *Saybrook* had in the shaping of Congregationalism over the following one hundred fifty years. Apart from *Saybrook* or a similar arrangement, it is doubtful that the Congregational Way could have maintained and extended itself as the nation expanded westward. Three kinds of benefits accrued to the Congregational churches as a result of the influence of the *Platform*.

First, consociation and its related provisions enabled Congregational churches to withstand the divisive forces brought into the church and the culture by the two Great Awakenings, the Revolution, and the slavery issue. Second, consociation equipped these churches to deal constructively with the rising religious pluralism that eventually took away the privileged majority position the early Puritans had enjoyed in Massachusetts and Connecticut. Third, by their experience in consociation these churches were able to respond to the missionary challenge of the westward expansion of the nation. An example of the latter is the *Plan of Union* of 1801 with the Presbyterians, which was designed for cooperative work on the frontier.*

Of equal interest but of less significance for the shaping of Congregationalism for the future were certain events that occurred in Massachusetts during the same period as the Saybrook developments. Liberal trends had alarmed the more conservative Boston clergy for some time. Matters came to a head when some of the more aggressive laypeople, who were not afraid to challenge the older clergy, broke with tradition and took the lead in founding the Brattle Street Church. These "innovators" called a Presbyterian minister to serve the church and introduced the use of the Lord's Prayer in the regular worship. In what seemed to add insult to injury, this group issued a *Manifesto* that caused Increase Mather and his son, Cotton, to react in true conservative style.

Out of the ensuing pamphlet war and debate came a set of *Proposals*, produced by a convention of ministers of the Boston area in 1705. Essentially these *Proposals* sought to achieve the same kind of restoration of order and cohesiveness among the churches that was to be found in the *Saybrook Platform* of Connecticut. But the *Proposals* met with immediate resistance, much of it led by John Wise, whose book *The Churches' Quarrel Espoused* had a powerful role in reshaping Massachusetts Congregationalism in a liberal direction. The significance of Wise's book lies in his use of Enlightenment thought, with its accent on natural law, to support the New England Way. Here was the movement of accommodation that introduced vigorous strains of European (especially English) rationalism into American church life.

However, Williston Walker, noted Congregational historian, claimed that the failure of the conservative forces (the Mathers and their supporters) to achieve what the Saybrook Synod had accomplished was not due simply or even primarily to John Wise's influence; rather, it was a result of the aloofness of the civil authorities in Massachusetts. They did not support the cause of the majority of concerned clergy in the same way that the Connecticut General Court acted for the churches.[26] Perhaps the real import of John Wise as spokesman for the rising liberal movement was his shift of authority in the church from its Puritan base in the authority of Christ expressed through the scriptures and the experience of a saving faith, to a base in the will of the people—in short, in church democracy. The event that brought radical change to church life in Massachusetts was the founding of the Brattle Street Church in 1699; the rationale

*The *Plan of Union* will be discussed later in this chapter. It is important to point out in this connection, however, that early New England Puritan colonists did not differentiate so absolutely between Presbyterian and Congregational ways. Presbyterian Puritans in New England generally were members of the established churches, which were Congregational. Presbyterian self-consciousness among the Puritans gradually increased, especially after the heavy Scots-Irish immigration into the Middle Colonies in the early 1700s. The first Presbyterian churches were founded on Long Island around 1640 by some New England Puritans.

was provided by John Wise in 1713 and more fully in 1717 when he published *A Vindication of the Government of New-England Churches.*

Thus, the redesign of the Congregational Way in Connecticut and Massachusetts during the late seventeenth to the eighteenth century exhibited two quite different sets of energies. In Connecticut these energies reflected a beginning resurgence of spiritual fervor that drew heavily upon its long-time tradition of Puritan faith, while at the same time adjusting to the challenges of a changing religious and cultural situation. In Massachusetts these energies reflected the introduction of the intellectual perspectives of the Enlightenment, reinterpreting the New England Way in categories that were to become a permanent feature not only of American intellectual life but of its social and political experience as well. The Massachusetts experience symbolized in a small way the interaction between the Protestant faith and the Enlightenment that has characterized the nation's cultural development up through the nineteenth century.[27] It would be incorrect, however, to conclude that this remained isolated from the Connecticut experience. The Great Awakening of the mideighteenth century proved to be the event and the force that brought these two sets of energies together in New England.

CONGREGATIONALISM IN TRANSITION

American religious history draws more of its central themes from the Great Awakening of the 1730s and 40s than from any other event or movement. While it is possible to exaggerate its impact, there is greater likelihood of underestimating it because of the stereotypes so often employed to describe it as a religious phenomenon. It was a complex convergence of religious, social, intellectual, and political forces that defies simple analysis. Such a statement is intended as a caution in viewing the Awakening in terms that are simplistic.

In New England the central figure was Jonathan Edwards. His thought and work gave the Awakening a stamp that was not matched by any other person, even though in the Middle Colonies especially there were powerful leaders whose revival work had begun nearly a decade earlier. Of Edwards' influence on Congregationalism, Sydney E. Ahlstrom has written:

A new and irrepressible expectancy entered the life of the churches. A national sense of intensified religious and moral resolution was born. . . . Evangelicalism in a new key was abroad in the land, and its workings had a steady internal effect which was nowhere more apparent than in the Congregational churches.[28]

The significance of Edwards for the Congregational churches is to be seen not only in his spiritual insightfulness and intellectual brilliance but also in what he represented. He was a product of Yale—not of Harvard which even then was the venerable bastion of the Puritan tradition. He was a grandson of Solomon Stoddard, whose liberalizing tendencies had been abhorred by Boston conser-

147

vatives. Edwards represented the redesigned Congregational Way of Connecticut.[29]

His ministry in Northampton, where his grandfather had once served, is cited as the start of the Great Awakening in New England. But times of spiritual revival had been known there even under Stoddard. More important for understanding Edwards' part in the Awakening are his writings, the most important being the *Treatise on the Religious Affections* and *Some Thoughts Concerning the Present Revival of Religion in New England*. His legacy to American Protestantism was a modified Calvinism that incorporated experiential religion (that is, the factor of the experience of God's work in the human soul) into the mainstream of the Reformed faith. In that emphasis Edwards provided a rationale for a dominant characteristic of the Puritan faith, the experience of saving grace. What happens within the human spirit as a result of faith in God's justifying work in Christ is the key to understanding justification. Sanctification, then, as the direct work of God's grace through the Spirit, assumed a major place not only in the Reformed tradition of the Congregational churches but also in much of American Protestantism. The distortions that Edwards' legacy has suffered resulted from the failure to heed his insistence upon God as the active participant in the transformation of the human spirit: God as the initiator, God as the designer, God as the one toward whom all things move. Recent scholarship attests to the stature of Edwards' work and his role in shaping American religious life.

No powerful spiritual or intellectual movement ever leaves unmixed blessings. The Awakening in New England, in the Middle Colonies, and in the South left many different marks.* Because it was a movement of great vitality, evidences of it can be traced for many decades. Among the Congregational churches—concentrated as they were in New England where the religious, social, and political traditions already had long histories—the negative aspects of the Awakening seem prominent. Theological divisions already in existence before the Awakening were sharpened by it. Edwardean thinking was known as the New Divinity; then there were the liberals on one side and the Old Calvinists on the other. Such theological divisions had both positive and negative effects. On the whole, the intellectual vigor of the Awakening remained with the Edwardean group.

Of greater significance generally for the Congregational churches in New England was the resurgence of separatism. Always a latent force in churches of the Congregational Way, the separatist impulse in Connecticut was strengthened when many churches resisted the so-called presbyterianizing

*Readers are referred, in addition to books cited, to: Alan Heimert and Perry Miller, *The Great Awakening* (Indianapolis: Bobbs-Merrill Co., 1967); Edwin Gaustad, *The Great Awakening in New England* (New York: Harper & Row, 1957).

Saybrook Platform. Heightened emotions and renewed insistence upon evidence of saving faith brought on by the Awakening resulted in a movement toward "believer's baptism." Nearly one hundred "separated" churches in New England became "Baptist." Beyond that was a persistent separatistic tendency in many churches.

The positive effects of the Awakening's energies were exhibited in the vitality of the churches as they began to extend their horizons in missionary and evangelistic zeal. Lefferts Loetscher points out that: "The Awakening elevated the common man. By giving him a self-authenticating religious experience it made him independent of professional ministers and church synods. *Lay activity and lay authority in the church increased.*"[30] This accentuation of the laity's place in the church marked a definitive break with the long Western Christian tradition of the central role of the clergy. The Reformation had not removed the clergy from the center since the all-important task of interpreting the Word as the chief authority of life was reserved to them. But when the Awakening moved the believers' experience of regenerating grace to center stage in the life of the churches, they no longer depended upon the authority of the Word and its preacher. Protestant churches to this day struggle with the consequent ambiguities about the role of the clergy. At the same time their experience of the new place of the laity subsequent to the Awakening has been marked by vigorous involvement in the churches in ways that gave a new face to American Protestantism.

A concluding word about the effect of the Awakening on the church life of New England, particularly the Congregational churches, most naturally falls on Jonathan Edwards' vision of "the social redemption of humanity." That vision was based on his understanding of God's sovereignty. He saw the divine purpose of redemption not in individual terms only but in corporate and social terms as well. The Reformed faith had for him, as for so many before him, an ultimate focus upon the transformation of life and the society. That legacy remains a motivating force in the nation's idealism as well as in the churches' commitment to active social efforts.

Congregationalism in transition between 1720 and 1800 was affected by influences other than the Great Awakening. Social and political trends from Europe made their mark. Of equal importance was intercolony awareness of common concerns, an awareness that increased with the Great Awakening but which was enhanced by growing communication and trade. As the colonies moved toward independence from the mother country and into the task of forming a new nation, the energies of the churches tended in directions of support. The surge of philanthropic and educational enterprises spurred by the Awakening continued. Even as it did, however, the spiritual life of the churches waned. Changed social, economic, and political circumstances were partially responsible. At the same time the intellectual revolution produced by the Enlightenment gradually eroded the more orthodox faith of the churches that had been revived by the Awakening. When independence came and the Revolution was over, the churches were suffering a spiritual malaise of considerable magnitude.

CONGREGATIONALISM IN THE ERA OF DENOMINATIONS

Congregationalism in the nineteenth century reveals its distinctive character on the American scene when viewed against the backdrop of the proliferating denominational organizations of that period.* Four especially formative developments must be taken into consideration: disestablishment, the use of voluntary organizations, the Second Great Awakening, and the westward expansion related to the *Plan of Union* in 1801 with the Presbyterians.

Disestablishment came slowly for New England Congregational churches. For nearly two hundred years they had been in the privileged position of being the "official churches" of the colonies. Not until 1818 did Connecticut cut the churches loose from the state. Lyman Beecher, one of the most vigorous clerics of the time and, at first, a strenuous opponent of disestablishment, later declared it to be "the best thing that ever happened in the State of Connecticut" because "it cut the churches loose from dependence on state support" and "threw them wholly on their own resources and God."[31] Massachusetts was the last of the New England states to enact disestablishment, in 1831.

Relationships among Congregational churches in New England were not significantly changed by disestablishment. Thrown "on their own resources before God," the churches managed very well. Changes came chiefly as a result of two other closely related developments: the use of voluntary organizations to carry on missionary and philanthropic activity and the westward expansion of the nation. The opening of upper and western New York State following the peace with England attracted many New England Congregationalists. As early as 1798 a missionary society was formed in Connecticut. Voluntary support was the key to the capability of the churches to meet the needs of newly organized congregations on the western frontier.

In 1801 a *Plan of Union* was adopted by the Connecticut Congregational Association and the Presbyterian General Assembly for the express purpose of collaboration in missionary work in the new Northwest Territory. By a sharing of

*Organization of churches into regional (and later, national) bodies came slowly but was hastened by disestablishment after the nation's constitution was adopted. In the Anglican (Episcopal) churches the first American bishop was consecrated in 1784, and by 1789 the Protestant Episcopal Church in the USA was organized. Methodist Church organization dates from the famous Christmas Conference in December of 1784. Although Puritan Presbyterians had organized Presbyteries much earlier, it was not until 1789 that a full Presbyterian government was established. Churches of Continental lineage did not organize as larger bodies until the 1820s and 30s.

missionaries and ministers there was hope that the pressing needs of the new churches could be met. The *Plan of Union* symbolized Congregationalism's recognition of the new era of religious pluralism in which new forms of regional and national church organization would be necessary to meet the religious needs of a growing population. The emerging new form was the denomination. Many years were to pass, however, before Congregational churches would move specifically in that direction. Churches dependent upon a connectional system, such as the Presbyterian and Methodist, were rapidly becoming purposive organizations with a national character. Because local independency was cherished by Congregationalists they were at a disadvantage in relating to a connectional system. The consequence was the eventual breakdown of the *Plan of Union*, which resulted in many Congregational churches in New York becoming Presbyterian.

The moving force behind denominational expansion was the Second Great Awakening. In New England the Second Awakening began as early as 1792 at Yale but did not touch the churches extensively until 1798 to 1801. In contrast to the western frontier phase of this Awakening, the New England experience was marked by quiet zeal and fervor, without the emotional phenomenon encouraged by the revivalists of the First Awakening. New England's Awakening at the turn of the century resulted in a remarkable outpouring of lay energies in voluntary societies for missionary work, education, publication, and moral reform. It fired the zeal of the Connecticut Missionary Society. The new spiritual fervor of the churches resulted in the establishment of the American Board of Commissioners for Foreign Missions in 1812 and of the American Home Missionary Society in 1826. Although interdenominational at first, these societies were later supported almost solely by Congregational churches.

Thus, evangelistic and missionary zeal rooted in the Second Awakening, coupled with the expanded use of voluntary societies, accounted for New England's Congregational contribution to the forming of the near West in the first half of the nineteenth century. Churches were organized as far west as the Mississippi River and beyond by midcentury. Sydney E. Ahlstrom, in remarking about the extension of the Puritan heritage westward, wrote:

The emergence of such "little New Englands" had a striking effect not only on the religious nature of the western communities, but also on their political, economic, and cultural life; for this reason, it constitutes a highly significant factor in any estimate of Puritan influence on American life.[32]

Apart from the *Plan of Union* of 1801 there is little in the first four decades of the nineteenth-century Congregational expansion to indicate a concern about Congregationalism as such. The Congregational pattern of local church life was ideally suited to the needs of newly developing communities as New Englanders moved into New York, Ohio, Michigan, and farther westward. Moved by the fervor for the gospel generated in the Awakening in their home communities, Congregationalists "gathered" into churches for worship and education. Ministers (clergy) were needed, but it was lay initiative that counted. Cooperation with other New Englanders, especially those of Presbyterian leanings, was natural.

Congregational self-awareness was heightened in these new communities by strife and division within the Presbyterian Church. Cooperation under the *Plan of Union* became more difficult. Because their Presbyterian partners were often embroiled in their own controversies, Congregationalists became more aware of *their* own church tradition. On a comparative basis the Congregational form of organization offered a freedom that was attractive to those who found the voluntary system of organization a way of accomplishment. Growing self-consciousness about polity, then, was the result.

From self-consciousness about traditions, to considerations of polity, and thence to a gradual adoption of a denominational character and form of organization was the movement resulting from expansion westward.[33] Although the first state conference of Congregational churches was organized in Maine in 1826, that level of organization received its greatest impetus from the rapid expansion in the midwestern states many decades later.[34] In many respects, however, growing national consciousness as a "denomination" preceded state-level organizations of churches. Only associations of ministers were generally accepted on a statewide basis.

National consciousness and a national-level organization of churches were not the same thing for Congregationalists. The traditional emphasis upon and concern for the local church continually inhibited the concept of a larger organization of churches. Gaius Glenn Atkins and Frederick L. Fagley have argued that national consciousness was inhibited by:

(1) The tradition that the duty of the local church was for the religious leadership in the local community;

(2) The fear that a national organization would interfere with the freedom of the local church;

(3) The continuing influence of the writings of Rev. John Wise in Massachusetts and other New England states;

(4) The unconstitutional action of the Massachusetts General Association in establishing the American Board; and

(5) The unfortunate results that followed establishment by the Connecticut Association of the Plan of Union.[35]

National organization, if it was ever to be, had a powerful history to overcome. Only in the later part of the nineteenth century, when the energies of the western churches began to be felt, would that occur. On the expanding frontier, history tended to be left behind.

CONGREGATIONAL CHURCHES AS A DENOMINATION: TO BE OR NOT TO BE

Within the complex of religious, cultural, and economic forces that moved Congregational churches toward the denominational form of organization were some impulses produced in reaction to adverse events and circumstances. Two of these may be cited: the Unitarian break in Massachusetts and the *Plan of Union* debacle.

Liberalizing trends in Massachusetts have already been noted for their influence upon New England Congregationalism, effectively distinguishing between the churches affected by the Enlightenment, on the one hand, and the Great Awakening, on the other. Boston was the center of liberal influence, although not all the churches there belonged in that category. Unitarian perspectives emerged within the rather widespread theological milieu of Arminianism in the late eighteenth century.[36] Fed by the Enlightenment and shaped in reaction to the Great Awakening and Edwardean Calvinism, the Arminian theology of the liberals developed in a direction that affirmed the growing self-image of the American as a new kind of person—not caught in the bondage of a depraved nature but free and capable of the good. Human ability, so limited in the traditional Calvinist view, was not without the possibility of sin but could be nurtured in the good by the grace of God.*

Such views were the core substance of Boston sermons for more than fifty years. Received with approval, especially among the more affluent, they created an atmosphere that was increasingly content with the privileged place of the churches in Boston society. This made them fiercely zealous of Congregational independency and autonomy. The event that precipitated the sharp break with the more orthodox congregations was the need for two appointments to be made at Harvard College. The undercurrent of orthodox resentment toward liberal thinking came out into the open when appointments were called for publicly in the orthodox tradition. Immediate and vigorous response from the liberals opened the debate that came to be known as the Unitarian controversy. Ranged on the orthodox side were such figures as Jedidiah Morse, Leonard

*The Arminianism of the New England liberals must be defined within the context of the social and cultural development of Boston and its environs. This is the argument advanced by Conrad Wright (*The Beginnings of Unitarianism in America* [Boston: Starr King Press, 1955]), who wrote: "Arminianism was not a disembodied set of ideas; adopted for various capricious reasons by scattered individuals. It was part of the culture of a group. . . . The New England liberals were called Arminians, not because they were influenced directly by Jacobus Arminius (1560-1609), the Dutch Remonstrant, but because their reaction against Calvinism was similar to his" (pp. 5-6). American Arminianism was a distinctive product, then, of the Puritan ethos and its amalgamation of the Enlightenment thrust with the new self-perceptions of the American as a person. Wright's book is also invaluable for understanding the whole range of Unitarian concepts of the period.

Woods, and Moses Stuart. On the other side, charged with being Unitarians, were William Ellery Channing, Henry Ware, Samuel Thatcher, and others.

The break between churches of the Unitarian perspective and those of the orthodox tradition became visible in 1820, when Channing called for "a means of intercourse" among those who shared his views. Atkins and Fagley comment on this:

> When a Separatist movement begins to be accelerated with "prayers and counsels," the end is in sight. The leaders of the movement seemed to have been reluctant to become a separate denomination; partly, one may hope, through sentiment, partly because, being markedly independent, they feared any suggestion of denominational control, and partly (though this is mere surmise) they did not know exactly what to become or how with entire agreement to designate themselves.[37]

The forming of a Unitarian Association took place in 1825, thus effectively marking a permanent schism in New England Congregational ranks.

One distinction provokes another. When the Unitarian churches declared themselves, their sister churches of the Puritan tradition grew in self-awareness and in their sense of common cause in the orthodox Congregational mode. The sense of common cause expressed itself in renewed missionary zeal and in collaborative efforts to meet the needs of an expanding nation.

The *Plan of Union* of 1801 with the Presbyterians, probably because of its failure, can be credited with having set in motion a series of national gatherings that eventually gave the Congregational churches a denomination-like structure. As is often the case in developments of this kind, the outcome was unintended. The title of the agreement worked out between the General Association of Connecticut and the Presbyterian General Assembly did not imply a plan for uniting national bodies. Its intention was "to prevent alienation, and to promote union and harmony in those new settlements which are composed of inhabitants from these bodies."[38] Inaugurated with enthusiasm, the *Plan* actually resulted in "alienation" among these Presbyterians and Congregationalists who had a common Puritan heritage. That was the negative side of the unintended effect. The positive side was Congregational awareness of the need for the united action of their churches to abrogate the *Plan of Union*.

Although unhappiness with the *Plan of Union* had grown to much bitterness over the years, renunciation of it came slowly simply because there was no established organizational channel through which such unhappiness could produce action. Dissatisfaction was not all on one side; the Presbyterians—torn by doctrinal strife—were sufficiently displeased by 1837 to withdraw. Not until 1852 were the Congregational churches able to act in concert. The occasion was the Albany Convention in 1852.

Abrogation of the *Plan of Union*, although the immediate cause of the Albany Convention, was not the substantive cause. A much more significant agenda of concerns had been building over the years. These were announced in the call to the Convention issued by the General Association of New York and included items having to do with: relationships between churches in the various states, the American Home Missionary Association, building new churches, and common understanding of what Congregationalism is in respect to its theology and its practices. More than anything else, those agenda items reveal the growing influence of Congregational self-consciousness—the basic ingredient of denominational identification. Subsequent general conventions confirmed this by their steady testimony to reliance upon the Congregational mode of church life.

The experience of the Albany Convention, supplemented by a host of growing concerns, which again illustrate Congregational self-consciousness, led to a second national gathering. This one, held in Boston during June 1865, was noteworthy for the amount of discussion given to defining Congregationalism. An important element of that defining process was the concern to retain the advantages of local church independency, while responding in some united way to the crises brought on by the Civil War. Within that concern was also recognition of the need to "state the faith." Significantly, the most quoted product of the Boston Council was the *Burial Hill Declaration*.[39] This statement of faith occasioned lengthy debate. Its chief significance lies in explicit concern for "the union of all true believers"—disunity being "the shame and scandal of Christendom"—and in a commitment to work for "restoring unity to the divided Church." The inclusion of this concern for unity in a council moving toward denominational definition for Congregational churches is of significance for understanding later calls for unity.

A reiteration of polity principles reminiscent of the *Saybrook Platform*, except for substitution of hortatory for penal language, was also adopted in Boston. Its most striking sentence bears quotation:

That the ministry of the gospel by members of the churches who have been duly called and set apart to that work *implies in itself no power of government*, and that ministers of the gospel not elected to office in any church are not a hierarchy, nor are they invested with any official power in or over the churches.[40]

In that statement was a clear delimitation of the power of the office of ministry, which has ever since differentiated the Congregational from the Presbyterian understanding of the ordained minister's role in the churches of the Reformed tradition.

The Albany and Boston meetings had advanced the common cause of Congregational churches throughout the nation by giving them a sense of identity in their faith, history, and polity. However, no continuing general organization was anticipated or proposed in those meetings. That step was taken at Oberlin in 1871 when the National Council of Congregational Churches was organized. The heart of the agreement adopted was in the paragraph that declared:

The churches, therefore, while establishing this National Council for the furtherance of the common interests and work of all the churches, do maintain the Scriptural and inalienable right of each church to self-government and administration; and this National Council shall never exercise legislative or judicial authority, nor consent to act as a council of reference.[41]

Provisions were made for regular meetings on a triennial basis, for representation of the churches through delegates composed of both ministers and laity, for officers to serve from one triennial session to another, and for a provisional committee to make arrangements for succeeding sessions. Thus, the Congregational churches, after two hundred fifty years on the American scene, became a denomination by establishing a continuing organization to implement common purposes and to enhance the relationship of the churches to one another.

The 1871 Oberlin Council made history in yet another way. Adoption of a "Declaration on the Unity of the Church" gave the new denomination a sense of destiny. The words of the final paragraph of that declaration were expressive of the concern for Christian unity affirmed in all the Reformed tradition.

We believe in "the holy catholic church." It is our prayer and endeavor, that the unity of the church may be more and more apparent, and that the prayer of our Lord for his disciples may be speedily and completely answered, and all be one; that by consequence of this Christian unity in love, the world may believe in Christ as sent of the Father to save the world.[42]

CONGREGATIONALISM AND FREEDOM'S FERMENT

To recount the organizational development of the Congregational churches in the nineteenth century without recognition of their role in the Protestant shaping of the young nation is to pass over much of the story of the continuing Puritan impulse to which historians point. That impulse expressed itself in "freedom's ferment," particularly during the pre-Civil War years.[43] At that time its energies were thrown into evangelizing the new settlements of the West and into humanitarian endeavors to meet ever-increasing social problems, particularly slavery. Following the war that impulse exhibited itself in the evangelical liberalism which produced, on the one hand, the Social Gospel and, on the other, the extension of a Protestant empire through the denominational network.[44]

Evangelism and humanitarian endeavor were not confined to the Congregational churches in the early decades of the nineteenth century, but these churches were uniquely free to respond to the claims laid upon them by their faith and by the society. Unfettered by ecclesiastical structures, Congregationalists gave expression to their evangelistic and humanitarian impulses by organizing a vast array of voluntary societies. Inheritors of a Calvinist faith (translated in Edwardean categories) in which the sovereign rule of God implied

156

the restraint of evil and the transformation of individuals and the society, these Christians poured their energies into the voluntary agencies with a serene confidence in the rightness of their causes and in the possibility of achievement.

Although many causes attracted their concern, by the fourth decade one cause dominated: the antislavery movement. Abolitionist sentiment and activity flourished in New England, gradually overcoming antagonism and crystallizing public opinion. Even evangelization and missionary societies took up the cause as Christian awareness was heightened. This confluence of evangelizing energies and humanitarian concern in the antislavery movement issued in an organization whose history extended beyond the Civil War, through the Reconstruction, to the present. That organization is the American Missionary Association.

The story of this remarkable organization, which continues as a corporate entity within the United Church Board for Homeland Ministries, epitomizes the major strains of the religious humanitarian impulses of the Awakenings. Both its long history and the focus of its work, particularly in education, exemplify the special qualities of the voluntary societies of the nineteenth century. Organized in 1846, it brought together several other groups involved in the antislavery movement. Clara Merritt De Boer has called attention to the unique feature of its charter—directing its concern not simply to Blacks but to the "elimination of caste"—and to the fact that a large number of Afro-Americans were active supporters and workers in the association.[45] The educational focus of its work during the Reconstruction earned for it the commendation of being the "most effective of these church-oriented agencies for the freedman."[46]

Unlike the Presbyterians, Methodists, and Episcopalians, the Congregationalists were free of the severe strains of sectional division caused by the slavery issue and the Civil War. Few New England Congregationalists migrated southward. Their migration carried them across New York State into Ohio, Michigan, Illinois, and westward. They were a northern group, and, in addition, they lacked the connectional system that gave way under sectional conflict. The result was the direction of energies toward constructive service in the voluntary societies.

CONGREGATIONALISTS AND A CHRISTIAN AMERICA

The Protestant vision of a Christian civilization shaped by America was a major force in denominational activity and expansion following the Civil War. Congregationalists shared that vision widely and contributed some of the most influential voices to the interpretation of it. Horace Bushnell, whose name has been remembered longer than almost any other theologian of that period because of his book *Christian Nurture*, was one of the earlier Congregational theologian-pastors to hold aloft that vision. His words have been frequently quoted:

157

The wilderness shall bud and blossom as the rose before us; and we will not cease, till a christian nation throws up its temples of worship on every hill and plain; till knowledge, virtue and religion, blending their dignity and their healthful power, have filled our great country with a manly and happy race of people, and the bands of a complete christian commonwealth are seen to span the continent.[47]

In the post-Civil War period this theme was picked up in chauvinistic fashion by many denominational leaders as a way of giving focus to their ambitious programs. In such expressions the real spirit of evangelical liberalism was lost. Dreams of a "righteous empire" tended to be far removed from the spirit of the Christ.

Nevertheless, there were positive and constructive voices during the same period calling attention to Christian responsibility for dealing with the difficult issues of the society. What was known as the Social Gospel movement drew heavily upon the transformationist emphases of evangelical liberalism. Although the name of Walter Rauschenbusch, a Baptist, is most prominently identified with the Social Gospel, it was Josiah Strong, a Congregational minister, who provided creative leadership in the implementation of the vision. Strong was a disciple of Bushnell and reflected the latter's visionary stance. At the same time, however, he was a keen social analyst and a superior organization shaper. Along with others in the Congregational fellowship, he helped to focus the concern of the churches upon the growing urban crises brought on by industrialization. Other voices of national prominence on the scene of social concern were Washington Gladden and Graham Taylor.

Adding to the vision of a Christian America, so prominent among the Congregationalists of the period, was the consistent commitment to education, which over the years gave to the nation more than forty colleges and a dozen theological seminaries. The passion for education, the cultivation of reason, and the enlightenment of the mind were first in the service of the gospel. Education of ministers was the primary motive for the establishment of many schools, with Harvard leading the way in 1638, followed by Yale and many others as the years went on. Equally important, however, was the commitment to a vision of life in which the transformation of the person required intellectual nurture. Westward expansion of Congregational churches can be traced by the colleges and seminaries established along the way as far as the West Coast.

Perhaps some of the most severe testing of the vision of a Christian America came through the challenge to the churches posed by the vast immigration of peoples, particularly from Europe. Congregationalists intent upon their home missionary task did not neglect those who came from the Continent. Providing ministerial leadership for the large number of German- and Scandinavian-speaking immigrants who pushed westward from Chicago became a major objective of Chicago Theological Seminary, which had been founded in 1855.

Foreign-language programs were an essential part of the curriculum. Absorption of different ethnic peoples gave the Congregational churches an ever-increasing pluralistic character.

THE ERA OF DENOMINATIONAL CONSOLIDATION

One question that never failed of discussion through the years of denominational formation from 1852 onward was over the matter of polity. How is Congregationalism defined? Every step toward cooperative action and new relationships required review of whether and in what way the basic principle of local church independence could be accommodated to the new proposals. Two kinds of relationships became increasingly important from 1871 onward: those involving the National Council with the conferences and associations, and those that brought the various voluntary movements in missionary work, education, and publication into the purview of National Council concerns.

When the bylaws were written for the National Council in 1871, the voting membership was assigned to delegates from associations and conferences. This had the effect of enhancing particularly the role of the state conferences. As national organization assumed an ever larger place in the total denominational scene, and as the number of churches increased in far-flung parts of the nation, the state conference became a necessary link between the local churches and the National Council. In 1907 the National Council urged that state conferences take the initiative in the planting of new churches, thus supporting local churches in their extension concerns.[48] This action marked a significant shift of some aspects of missionary responsibility from the voluntary societies to structures created by and responsible to the churches.

As early as the Boston Council in 1865, concerns were being expressed about the channeling of local church support to the many voluntary societies engaged in missionary, educational, and humanitarian work. The major societies of concern to Congregationalists had at one time drawn their support from more than one denomination. As other denominations developed their own national structures and created agencies for their work, support of some of the voluntary groups was confined to Congregational churches. This was particularly true of the American Board of Commissioners for Foreign Missions, the American Missionary Association, the Congregational Home Missionary Society, and the Education Society.

While the 1871 National Council recognized one delegate from each of the "Congregational" societies,[49] voting privileges were not accorded to them until 1901. The major motivation for closer relationships between the societies and the National Council was a concern to ensure adequate support while also giving to the churches some "sense of ownership." The latter became the crux of the problem since legal ownership was already invested in the controlling boards of these societies. Nevertheless, if the churches were to have any claim laid upon them for supporting the work that was still important to them, a sense of ownership was essential. The Connecticut General Conference put the matter plainly, stating that the mission boards, "though vitally related to the Congregational churches in every point of *fact*, are nevertheless wholly *independent* of them in law and management; and that these facts not only discredit our polity, but threaten our peace."[50]

Matters of this kind were not easily concluded, and they continued to be the focus of attention in subsequent National Councils. The growing financial needs of the boards and societies added pressure for some resolution of the complicated issues. An advisory and consultative relationship lacked the essential ingredient of an administrative role with authority from the churches. One committee after another was assigned the task of finding a solution. The Committee of Fifteen, the Committee of Seven, the Commission of Nineteen, the Committee of Twelve, the Strategy Committee—all in succession over the years offered proposals that were accepted either in part or in whole. The Kansas City National Council, in 1917, took a step that at least identified the boards and societies with the council. *Voting members of the council were made voting members of the societies.*[51] While thus ensuring a relationship of common concerns, this did not give control to either the churches or the council. Control remained vested in the corporate boards of directors by law. Nevertheless, the relationship thus established gave the council more influence in the promotional and educational work of the boards.

Partly as a consequence of this new relationship and partly because of changing circumstances in which their work had to be carried out, there was a gradual process of consolidation of the societies working in the same general areas. The result was concentration of all foreign mission groups in the American Board of Commissioners for Foreign Missions and of several home mission and educational societies in the Board for Home Missions.

Recognition of the growing need for administrative services on the part of the National Council eventuated, after many hesitant steps, in assigning new responsibilities to an executive committee. When this was done in 1936, the Congregational churches had completed movements toward national organization begun sixty-five years earlier.

Tension between local church autonomy and the requirements of responsible fellowship remained. They were heightened whenever the requirements of the gospel led to a sense of responsibility for new undertakings. This came to a critical point in the union that moved the Congregationalists into the United Church of Christ in 1957.

AND THEY BECAME THE CONGREGATIONAL CHRISTIAN CHURCHES

In recounting the development of a denominational organization for the Congregational churches, no attention has been given thus far to efforts to imple-

160

ment the concern for Christian unity. That concern was expressed repeatedly as the denominational organization took shape. Atkins and Fagley comment that "no other religious body in America has made as many gestures toward union with other religious bodies as have the various National Councils."[52]

Denominational organization itself, of course, posed problems of a special kind for the Congregationalists with respect to the question of unity. Their voluntary "associational" relationship made it relatively easy for individual local churches to affiliate with a Congregational association.* However, the union of the national organs of the Congregational Churches with other national structures tended to be more complicated.

On two occasions the National Council acted to recognize other groups of churches as conferences on parity with state conferences. The effect was to give such conferences representation in the National Council. One such action, in 1925, was to recognize the Evangelical Protestant Conference. Made up of a small number of German "union" (Lutheran and Reformed) churches in western Pennsylvania, this conference later disappeared as the congregations were absorbed into the state conference.

In many respects a more important event of the same kind took place in 1927, when the General Conference of German Congregational Churches was given parity recognition. This group of churches is one of the best illustrations of the energetic missionary work carried on among German immigrants by Congregational churches and the American Home Missionary Society. George Eisenach has traced the history of the General Conference from its beginnings in Iowa, calling the State of Iowa "the cradle of German Congregationalism in the United States."[53]

It was the American Home Missionary Society that responded to the needs of the Germans there by bringing ministers and missionaries from Germany and Switzerland. As that effort among the Germans grew, they organized associations, sought twice to establish schools for the training of ministers in the German language, and became a conference in 1883. The role of the society was augmented in 1882, when Chicago Theological Seminary agreed to establish a German department to take over the theological training of ministers that had been started at Crete, Nebraska four years earlier. The positive influence of this department over the years is acknowledged again and again by Eisenach.[54] In 1936 there were 215 congregations scattered in the northwestern states. Many of them maintained their identity out of a later immigration of German-Russians after 1872. These German people had first migrated to the Odessa and Volga regions of Russia and then, after many generations, found life there too restrictive. They found freedom in the United States, settling in the Dakotas and other western states.

*This was the way some Congregational Methodist churches became part of the Congregational fellowship in 1892. Those churches had originally formed in Georgia before the Civil War.

161

The chief concern in this section of the chapter, however, is the union in 1931 of the National Council of Congregational Churches and the General Convention of Christian Churches. Discussions about the possibility of union had been undertaken in 1894. These were terminated in 1898, when some sections of the Christian Church expressed strong opposition. Conversations were reopened in 1923. A Plan of Union was drawn up and adopted by both bodies in 1929. Consummation came in 1931, when the National Council and the General Convention met concurrently in Seattle. The name of the newly formed church body was the General Council of the Congregational Christian Churches.

Several features of this union merit special consideration. First, it brought together a church body whose birthright had been established in the Second Great Awakening in frontier situations and a body whose birthright had been established in the first colonial settlements. Second, it was the only union for either group up to that time despite repeated declarations of unity intentions throughout their long histories. Third, it gave the new denomination a wider geographical distribution of churches.

The Christian Church was itself the result of a "flowing together" of three quite diverse groups, initially located in Virginia, New England, and Kentucky, and drawing from the Methodists, the Baptists, and the Presbyterians. James O'Kelly, a Methodist lay preacher in Virginia, rallied a group of Methodists who shared his convictions about democracy in church government. Known first as "Republican Methodists" because of their opposition to an episcopal system, these followers of O'Kelly assembled themselves in a general meeting in 1794. The name, Christian Church, was taken as a symbol of their noncreedal, New Testament, faith stance. The test of membership was simply "a Christian character." Most important was the insistence upon the parity of laity and clergy in all matters.

A few years later and several hundred miles to the northeast another "Christian" movement was born, when Abner Jones formed the first "free Christian Church" in New England.[55] Protesting standard New England church membership requirements—Calvinist doctrine, baptism, and a restricted communion table—Jones also insisted upon Christian character as the only requirement for membership. Known as the "Christian Connection," the churches following Jones' principles eventually organized the New England Christian Convention in 1845. Because of the noncreedal tenet some of these churches became Unitarian.

The origins of the third group that became a founding part of the Christian Church are less easily identified, except for the fact that, as in the case of the Abner Jones movement in New England, it shared a common frontier dissatisfaction with Calvinist theology. When Barton W. Stone, moved by the impulses of the Second Awakening, withdrew with a group of followers from the

Presbyterian Synod of Kentucky in 1803, they also took the simple name "Christian."* These churches spread into Ohio, Indiana, and Illinois.

What brought these three "Christian" movements together? Historians have pointed to two incidents that have undoubtedly played a part in their convergence. One of James O'Kelly's co-workers was Rice Haggard, a dedicated and untiring exponent of New Testament simplicity. Haggard is known to have worked among the Kentucky churches of the Stone movement, thus establishing common ground. Contact with the Jones group of churches in New England was given a boost when Haggard wrote an article addressed "To the Different Societies on the Sacred Import of the Name Christian." When this appeared in the *Herald of Gospel Liberty*, a paper published by the New England Christian Connection churches, the movement gained visibility. James O'Kelly likewise wrote an article for the *Herald of Gospel Liberty* in which he discussed "A Plan of Union Proposed," giving a long list of reasons for the union of all Christians. Some years passed before any formal meetings occurred, but in 1820 the United General Conference of Christians was held in Connecticut.

William T. Scott argues that the convergence of these groups, each with such different beginnings but with a common passion for Christian union, was the work of God.[56] Six principles were unanimously affirmed for the basis of their common venture as the Christian Church: (1) Christ as the only head of the church; (2) the name Christian so as to exclude party distinctions; (3) the holy scriptures as the only rule of faith and practice; (4) Christian character as the only requirement for membership; (5) the right of private judgment and liberty of conscience; (6) the union of all of Christ's followers.

There were in all three groups and in their subsequent development as a denomination the distinctive marks of the Awakening in the frontier settlements. The frontier tended to elevate and exaggerate traits of the Awakening, which in New England were muted by the tradition of a more settled social situation. They were the "levelling" tendencies that dominated the frontier spirit of democracy, the anticreedalism that moved toward biblical literalism, and the extreme individualism that issued from the claim to the right of private judgment and liberty of conscience. An egalitarian idealism emerged in the frontier conditions that affected the churches as well as the society generally. In the churches (in varying degrees according to the different traditions) it supplanted the authority of tradition.

All of this, however, continued to exhibit the primal Puritan rootage of so much of American Protestantism. Nurtured in the soil of frontier life, that root-

---

*Some of the churches of Stone's movement later entered into local unions with another group that was using the names "Christian" and "Disciples of Christ"—a group having its origins in the work of Alexander Campbell. The latter group eventually became the largest indigenous body of Protestants in the land. The connection in the 1830s has resulted in much confusion, especially for those churches under discussion in this chapter.

age produced an understanding of church life completely different from that of the New England "establishment." William T. Scott, for example, uses nontraditional terms to define the distinctive nature of the Christian Church: "a spiritual democracy, a religious brotherhood, a Christian fellowship."[57] New beginnings in family life, community building, and civil government on the frontier encouraged new beginnings in models of church life.

Two other marks of the New England Puritan roots of the Christian Church movement in its beginning years must be noted: a leadership drawn from the well-educated New England dominant social class and a humanitarian spirit. The frontier was rough and crude; life was marked by vice and violence. But at the same time the religious leadership generally represented the civility and compassion of educated people. Herein were the foundations of the concern for education that later involved this "frontier-formed" denomination to establish colleges, to enter missionary work with zeal, and to undertake humanitarian causes.

The concern for humanitarian reform was signaled in founder James O'Kelly's denunciation of slavery in 1789, long before the abolition movement gained public support.[58] That concern, linked with the revivalistic zeal of the Awakening, brought many Blacks into the Christian churches in the South. As early as 1848 the Christian Church ordained a Black to serve as a missionary in Liberia.[59] It appears, however, that Black churches as such were not organized until after the Civil War. As a matter of record, efforts to achieve a greater consolidation of the three sections of Christian Churches, which by that time had increased in number, were shattered in 1844 over the slavery issue. The New England Convention at that time produced a strong resolution against slavery which deeply offended the churches in the South. Formation of the Southern Christian Association was the result, thus keeping the New England and southern churches apart.[60]

Ruptured relationships resulting from the Civil War took many years to heal. Meanwhile, in the era of Reconstruction, the Christian Churches both north and south became more denominational in character. The evolving of a denomination from what was primarily a movement quite naturally brought changes that were not always easily accepted. In a time of rapid growth of other denominations, the Christian Churches became aware of their own limited growth. In the 1870s several steps were taken to give the Southern Convention more organization structure and more explicit identity. For the latter purpose a *Manual* was adopted, standardizing practices of worship and the rites and supplying a statement of "Principles."

In the postwar period Blacks withdrew from white churches and formed their own. By 1867 the North Carolina Colored Christian Conference was formed. Other conferences of Black churches followed. In 1892 the Afro-American Christian Convention was established in North Carolina. At that time sixty-nine churches with 3,395 members were reported.[61] By 1929 the Afro-American Convention reported to the General Convention of the Christian Church a total of one hundred sixty-five churches and over 30,000 members.[62]

From the beginning of the Christian Church movement, the theme of Christian unity was sounded repeatedly. When the General Convention assembled in 1874, the delegates adopted a *Manifesto* setting forth principles of unity. Prompted in part by the involvement of several leaders who had participated in the international Evangelical Alliance,[63] the *Manifesto* reflected the fundamental sense of the Christian Church movement that unity is primarily a matter of Christian spirit and character. No unity in doctrine or polity was considered possible; only that which springs from the love and forebearance of "true Christians." In that spirit the *Manifesto* concludes: "We are ready to form a corporate union with any body of Christians upon the basis of those great doctrines which underlie the religion of Christ. . . . We are ready to submit all minor matters to . . . the individual conscience."[64]

Unity, for all of such declarations, came no more easily for the Christian Church movement than it did for other denominations. Doctrine and polity are not the only things that divide the body of Christ; the spirit of love and forebearance that Christian character should manifest is always countered by human self-concern (thus defensiveness), prejudice, and the limits of understanding. Efforts to reunite the northern and southern groups of these churches were inhibited by these factors. Finally, however, in 1890, a Plan of Union was adopted, bringing the American Convention of Christian Churches (north) and the General Convention (south) into the new General Convention. No central organization was established, but a pattern of collaboration was begun, although not without friction.[65]

CONGREGATIONALISM LOOKING AHEAD

The 1931 union, which brought this convention with the National Council of Congregational Churches into the new body known as the General Council of Congregational Christian Churches, marked a watershed of denominational development of Congregationally organized churches. Church union was abroad in the land, and no church body was more concerned about it. In ten other nations Congregational churches as national bodies had entered into union with other communions between 1900 and 1950, with a consequent disappearance of the "congregational" name.

The process of church union challenged Congregational Christian Churches to reconsider their basic theology of the church—to go farther back into their tradition than simply the nineteenth century. In response to that challenge they discovered anew a point of view that guided their Puritan forebears. Whether separatist or nonseparatist, unity in Christ required expression. The church is one. If separation seemed necessary, it was only a step toward re-forming the church. In such a conception the church is understood as the Body of Christ. The one Head of the church is its reality as a unity even where the church is not all together in one place. Because the Lord gathers the church, the local church is, as Peter Forsyth said, "but the outcrop of the total and continuous Church. . . . People did not go to a meeting which was on its way to become a Church; they went to *the Church* at a certain place of meeting. . . . It is not *a* Church with sympathies with others, it was *the* Church, and there were no others—only similar outcrops of the one . . . Church."[66]

In this movement back toward their fundamental English Reformed tradition, the Congregational Christian Churches found church union in terms of denominational structures a real possibility. In that tradition the forms or organs of the church as an organization are always provisional—related to the realities of the society in which Christians live. The aim, however encumbered by limited human vision or circumstance, remains that of all who confess and know Christ: to live the life of discipleship. The church, then, is where Christ lives in the midst of the people.

CHAPTER 7

FROM THE CONTINENT OF EUROPE: THE EVANGELICAL AND REFORMED STORY

Immigration rather than colonization is the frame of reference for understanding the Evangelical and Reformed story in American church life. While that history does have a colonial phase, its formative elements are derived chiefly from a later period, when the nation was being molded by vast waves of immigration. The role of colonial influence gains significance when considered from the perspective of denominational development in the nineteenth century.

It was English colonization that made the Evangelical and Reformed story possible. The German people who formed the parent bodies of this denomination were among the vast numbers of emigrants from the Continent who used the "bridge" built between the Old World and the New by England's colonizing efforts. While they were already the largest group of non-English immigrants in colonial days, their numbers in the nineteenth century had an "exodus" dimension.*

The German experience in America is, therefore, the context of Evangelical and Reformed history.† This is paralleled, of course, by the Lutherans, Roman Catholics, and sectarian groups who comprised so large a proportion of the German immigrant population. While social historians have treated various aspects of this experience, it is important for the purposes of this book to call attention also to the special religious circumstances of the German migration. In many respects these provide a sharp contrast with the English situation and are, therefore, determinative of the German experience.

For most immigrants from the Continent, America was as much a land of

---

*Population in the English colonies is estimated at nearly three million by the time of Independence in 1776. Natural increase was augmented by a steady flow of immigrants from the British Isles and Germany. After 1800 the tide of immigrants swelled. It is estimated that more than thirty-six million came from the Continent between 1820 and 1970, with Germany supplying the largest number from any single country. That figure is nearly seven million.

†This does not overlook the fact that among the Reformed element in the Evangelical and Reformed Church there were also Swiss and Hungarian people. The Swiss, of course, were from the German cantons of Switzerland. Further, there were other national groups of the Reformed tradition—chiefly Dutch and French.

refuge as of opportunity. This was especially true for the Germans, who were literally refugees from war, poverty, and religious persecution in the early part of the eighteenth century. In later emigrations, particularly in the nineteenth century, the factor of war was less significant, but poverty, due chiefly to overpopulation, and religious persecution—although of lesser severity—continued to make America appear a haven of freedom and opportunity.

Religious conflict among the major church groups in Germany produced turmoil and fear if not outright persecution. The intimate ties between the churches and the civil governments of the several German states exacerbated all social and political issues, especially through the eighteenth century. Although the Peace of Westphalia, in 1648, had theoretically settled the traditional animosities of Lutheran, Reformed, and Catholic churches, the religious loyalties of rulers continued the struggles. The religious factor undoubtedly lay behind the ferocity of the armies of Louis XIV of France in the Rhineland in 1689 and again in 1701-14 in the War of the Spanish Succession. In the nineteenth century such religious strife was replaced by subtle political oppression in connection with the rising German national consciousness.

Because the German experience in America embraces two and one half centuries of this nation's history, the Evangelical and Reformed story may be viewed in three phases: the colonial, the national, and the church union phase. All three belong to the experience of the German Reformed people, while only the national and the union phases apply to the German Evangelical people. The Reformed group's colonial experience set them apart from the nineteenth-century German arrivals. At the same time the latter group, including both Reformed and Evangelical Germans, brought a new and significant dimension of the German experience into American church life.

THE COLONIAL PHASE: REFORMED

No national monument such as Plymouth Rock marks the location of the first contingent of German Reformed immigrants settling in this land. Early groups came in 1710 to the Carolinas, Virginia, Maryland, New Jersey, and New York. Some were Swiss Germans from northern Switzerland; others were known as Palatines from the upper Rhine area designated as the Rhenish-Palatinate, with Heidelberg as the center. Pennsylvania became the chief place of settlement after word of intolerable conditions in New York filtered back to Europe from some of the Palatinate Reformed people who had found a better situation in William Penn's colony.[1] From that time on the flow of German immigrants through the port of Philadelphia was almost continuous.

Who were these German Reformed people from the Palatinate? They were, first of all, refugees from intolerable living conditions in the fatherland, where grinding poverty, continually aggravated by wars, an unstable economy, and a period of severe climactic conditions, resulted in thousands (estimated at more

168

than 15,000) fleeing to England in 1709. There, because of the naturalization act which enabled foreign Protestants to become English citizens, these refugee Germans soon were the beneficiaries and sometimes victims of the colonization fever that was touching not only enterprising business interests but the Crown as well. In any case, the new colonies in America seemed a perfect solution to the refugee problem faced by the English government.

Great numbers of these people came to America as "redemptioners," that is, as people who had sold their time and service for a specified number of years in order to pay for their transportation across the ocean. Others came penniless, if not debt-free. All were laborers, farmers, tradespeople and artisans. Their hope for a better life lay in the promise of America's open spaces and uncrowded communities, where individual initiative, no matter what social class, was respected and rewarded.

Of greater significance for this account was the Reformed faith of a large portion of these Palatine emigres.[2] The Palatinate area of Germany was dominantly Reformed, but large numbers of Lutherans lived there as well and emigrated with their Reformed neighbors. Lutheran and Reformed relations, so strained and strife-filled in the Palatinate up through the middle of the seventeenth century, had become more peaceable in the latter half. This was due in part to the legal recognition accorded to the Reformed faith by the Treaty of Westphalia of 1648 but also in part to the unity produced by a common enemy—in this case the armies of Catholic France in the wars of the last two decades of the century. Religious differences receded in the common determination of these Palatines to escape the hopeless cycle of war, poverty, and oppression. They took their religious convictions and practices with them to the New World and demonstrated their common lot frequently by erecting church buildings that served both Reformed and Lutheran congregations.

These German Reformed forebears came, then, not primarily for religious reasons. They did not see themselves undertaking an "errand into the wilderness" as did their English Reformed cousins who had settled in New England almost one hundred years earlier. Consequently, they were not accompanied by clergy, in contrast with the Puritans, who from the beginning were helped by clergy to shape both the religious and civil life of the communities they established. They came, nevertheless, as Protestant Christians who had been nurtured in the Reformed faith for generations. Their chief religious distinction was that they were a people of the *Heidelberg Catechism*. Use of that devotional book in their families and in their corporate worship developed in them a piety characterized by fervent discipleship. Because of their Calvinist roots they too were as a people "possessed by God." This gave them a sense of security as well as of responsibility in the building of a new life in America.

Organization of church life in many of the new German Reformed settlements proceeded slowly in the absence of pastors and of any civil authorities to assume that responsibility. For many, family worship served as the means of sustaining the faith. Equipped with the *Catechism* and the *Bible*, they maintained their faith tradition until pastors were available. In this they exhibited the strength of the piety they had learned in their homeland.

Although some Dutch Reformed ministers served German settlements in adjacent states, Pennsylvania Germans had to wait for some time for pastoral care from their own number. James I. Good cites the work of the Rev. Paul Van Vlecq, a Dutch Reformed pastor at Neshaminy in Bucks County, who visited Skippack and White Marsh in 1710, where he organized a congregation and baptized children.[3] This congregation, which met in the house of a devout Dutch elder, later disbanded but then was reestablished in 1725. Samuel Guldin, a Swiss-German minister, is known to have preached and provided pastoral care among the German Reformed people, although he never served organized congregations.

The distinction of establishing and serving the first German Reformed churches in Pennsylvania apparently goes to two laymen, both trained schoolteachers. John Philip Boehm—most remembered for his lengthy and constructive service—and Conrad Templeman yielded to the religious needs of the people and began their "ministry" as lay readers. Thus, the "Church in Pennsylvania owes its origin to pious laymen."[4] Apparently Templeman was never ordained, but Boehm sought ordination after some years of pastoral service. The circumstances of this ordination had bearing upon the next sixty years of German Reformed church life; they were also significant in their exhibition of the principles of church organization that prevailed among these people.

Boehm's diligent and highly respected service as an unordained pastor became historically significant, when on October 15, 1725 he conducted the service of the Lord's Supper at the request of the members of the congregation he had organized at Falkner Swamp, a congregation continuing even now. He was not unconcerned about ordination, for as a Reformed church member he recognized that the authority to administer the sacraments came not from the individual congregation of laypeople but from the wider church composed of both clergy and laity. Circumstances, however, prevailed over his scruples.

Three years later Boehm sought and received ordination from the Dutch Reformed Church through the Classis of Amsterdam, which was then responsible for the Dutch churches in America. By that action the German Reformed churches established a relationship with the Dutch church that was to last for sixty-five years.[5] The relationship was more pastoral than governmental, partly because of the difficulties of communication at so great a distance and partly as a result of the less rigid and more irenic temper of the Palatinate Germans. Unquestionably the relationship was of great benefit to the German Reformed churches. At one point the Dutch Church in New Jersey encouraged the idea of making the German churches an integral part of their own Coetus.* The Germans in Pennsylvania, however, resisted the overture. The Holland churches, nevertheless, did care for their sister German churches in America by sending funds, maintaining procedures for regularizing the ministry, and receiving reports. When delays in communication hindered their efforts, they suggested that the German churches join the Presbyterians, but when that suggestion came to nought, they continued to help.

Perhaps the truly significant contribution of the Reformed Church in Holland to the German churches in America was the appeal made to the Palatinate Consistory for a German-speaking minister, which resulted in the sending of the Rev. Michael Schlatter to America. Schlatter, a German-Swiss minister, was deputized by the Holland synod to "organize the ministers and congregations into a coetus" and, in general, to supervise the German Reformed churches.[6] This action proved to be providential in every respect. While individual congregations had generally been well organized by Boehm after the Palatinate model, the absence of a higher body of authority had made these churches vulnerable to the work of the "sectaries" and "enthusiasts," who were especially active in the 1730s.

The arrival of Michael Schlatter in the summer of 1746 marked the beginning of a constructive period of church formation among German Reformed people. Within the year Schlatter had fulfilled one of his major assignments—the formation of the Coetus of the Reformed Ministerium of Congregations in Pennsylvania. Its model was that of the Dutch churches in New York, providing an organizational structure that enabled the churches to govern themselves while maintaining a proper ecclesiastical relationship with the church in the fatherland.

Schlatter's role in the organization of the Coetus was not so much that of a designer as it was of an organizer and administrator. Boehm also should receive credit since the Coetus used the organizational constitution that he had devised for the congregations. This was adopted in 1748. The document, the Kirchen-Ordnung of 1748, adapted from the constitution Boehm had prepared in 1725, sets forth an order of church life exhibiting the characteristic features of the Reformed tradition that had developed in the upper Rhineland of Germany and in Switzerland.

The care and discipline of the church as a spiritual community was in the hands of the elders and deacons along with the minister. Having been elected by the congregation, these individuals constituted the consistory, the official body to whom the members entrusted authority and responsibility. Upon the conscience of members and officers alike was laid the responsibility of "fraternal correction and mutual edification." Upon the minister was placed responsibility for preaching

*Coetus, a Latin word for a synod, but in the Dutch system not having the powers thereof.

171

the pure doctrine of the Reformed Church according to the Word of God and to administer *the holy seals* (sacraments) *of the Covenant* at their appointed time and place; always to adhere to the confession of faith of the Reformed churches and to the *Heidelberg Catechism,* to explain the same . . . , to hold catechetical instruction. . . . He shall give special attention to *church discipline and correct practice, together with those who have oversight of the congregation.* [7]

In adapting this order for use in the Coetus, the Reformed churches extended the principles of government by ministers and elders from the local congregation to the larger body of churches. This left undisturbed the internal life of the individual congregations that were under their own consistories. At the same time the extension of this form of government to the Coetus protected the local churches from unscrupulous religious entrepreneurs by regularizing admission and ordination to the ministry. Moreover, it provided desperately needed mutual support in common identity and faith practice. Undergirding it all was commitment to the shared responsibility of clergy and laity together in ordering the life of the church under Christ the Lord. It was democracy at work within the framework of a community of faith under a sovereign Lord. Recognition of that sovereignty was expressed in reliance upon Word and Sacrament and upon the responsibility for fraternal correction and mutual edification. [8]

The results of this organizational step for German Reformed churches in eastern Pennsylvania were salutary throughout the difficult years of religious turmoil engendered by the German sects and also by the disruptive circumstances of the American Revolution. Under such tumultuous conditions the nurture of faith and the Christian life was made possible by the "church" character of the faith experience in contrast to the individualistic exercises encouraged by the sects. The Coetus period of organization provided the organizational experience that led to denominational formation in 1793. [9]

Comparatively little is known of any significant theological and intellectual efforts of these people during the colonial period. In this the contrast to the Puritans in New England is pronounced. Several reasons are apparent: a less-educated lower class, a much smaller number of clergy, and less homogeneity in the total area. Penn's colony had drawn highly diverse groups, making common cause difficult. Whereas New England through the seventeenth and most of the eighteenth century was almost totally English, Pennsylvania drew the English, Dutch, Germans, and Scots-Irish. Religious identity inevitably required a parochial style of life, with its consequent absence of intellectual ferment. The relatively small number of clergy had overwhelming pastoral tasks and were not given to writing theological dissertations. Finally, the German Reformed people were not agitated by the same theological and ecclesiological issues facing their English cousins.

However, the effects of eighteenth-century Pietism in Europe were felt especially among these Reformed people from about 1770 onward. In part this was due to a number of new ministers arriving from Germany who had been trained in the pietistic centers of that country. Out of this tendency in Pennsylvania came the movement that prepared the way for the work of Philip William Otterbein and the eventual break that established the United Brethren Church.

Concern about education, however, prevailed among all these German people. Schoolmasters were among them, Boehm and Templeman being prominent examples. Parish schools were regularly conducted. Still there was not enough education. Their concern and plight stirred the English, who were aroused through the efforts of David Thomson, pastor of the English Reformed Church in Amsterdam, and organized "The Society for Propagation of the Knowledge of God among the Germans."[10] The generous response of the English churches to this need in their colonies resulted in the establishment of many charity schools in Pennsylvania. They were the forerunners of the public school system. Michael Schlatter, after dissociating himself from the Coetus, headed the charity school enterprise for a time and was called by one historian the "first superintendent of public instruction in Pennsylvania."[11]

German Reformed involvement in public affairs was limited both by the tradition of their homeland and by the language barrier. As settlers they had common cause with the English in their defense against Indian attacks. Pledges of loyalty to the Crown were given without question. At the same time they were cautious about the Crown's exercise of authority, and when Pennsylvania was considering a change from proprietary to Crown rule, they exercised their voting rights and came out against the Crown. By the time of the War of Independence they were thoroughgoing "Americans." In keeping with the Reformed tradition of public responsibility, they became increasingly involved in the welfare of the colonies, both in the war itself and in expressions of concern for the emerging new nation.[12] James I. Good cites a "memorial of congratulation to General Washington on his election as president."[13]

Independence for the nation created the atmosphere for the independence of the German Reformed churches from the Reformed Church in Holland. The difficulties of communication created continual frustration over the years but surprisingly little dissension. Nevertheless, the problems had an inhibiting effect. As the Coetus grew in its own self-awareness and self-confidence, reliance upon the Holland churches was less significant. In the postwar period, as the nation shaped its own government, the Reformed churches began to think of their responsibilities, in which the Dutch Church could have little part.

A formal relationship was maintained on two levels with the Holland ecclesiastical authorities: the ordination of ministers and the reporting of all actions to the Dutch church. By 1791 the German Reformed churches were ready to declare themselves on their own. The action to do this reflected no hostility but simply maturity. It was voted: "That the coetus has the right at all times to examine and ordain those who offer themselves as candidates for the ministry, without asking or waiting for permission to do so from the fathers in Holland."[14] It was not until 1793 that the formal ties were broken. At the gathering of that year, the Coetus was transformed into a synod by the adoption of a constitution or "Synodal Ordnung" and of a name, *The Synod of the German Reformed Church in the United States of America,* and the appointment of a committee to prepare a hymnbook.[15]

Thus, the German Reformed churches entered the denominational stream of American church life as the eighteenth century drew to a close. Both the church and the nation were entering a new era. It was a time of new beginnings, of learning the burden and the opportunity of self-government, of facing unanticipated responsibilities. As the new church body moved into the nineteenth century, it entered what Kenneth Scott Latourette called "The Great Century," which witnessed "the most extensive geographic spread of Christianity."[16]

THE NATIONAL PHASE: REFORMED

By all accounts the formation of denominational Protestantism through the nineteenth century in America was an exceedingly complex experience for most church bodies. This was no less true for the German Reformed people, who were entering that century with a new and untested synodical organization. Their experience of the national phase* of American Protestant development quite naturally exhibits the strains and challenges faced by all the churches as the nation developed. It was true of them as it was of others that the colonial period was largely a time of regrouping and reordering for tasks that were just beginning to loom over the horizon.[17] At the same time theirs was a very different experience from that of the Methodists, Baptists, Presbyterians, and Disciples particularly, for whom the national period was a time of unprecedented expansion.

Two circumstances of the general American religious scene of that period require concentrated attention in tracing the development of The Synod of the German Reformed Church. They are: first, the American religious temper, which had been shaped initially by the Great Awakening of the 1730s and 40s and which came to full maturity in the Second Awakening about 1792 to 1801; and second, church expansion and growth resulting partly from the Awakening impulses, but chiefly from the massive waves of immigration from 1830 to the end of the century. The responses of the German Reformed Church to these circumstances exhibit both the essence of the faith tradition it represented and the way in which the sociocultural ethos of the growing nation defined limits as well as opportunities for that tradition. Before discussing the impact of these

*The term national phase is used to designate the period in which the American people developed national character.

174

circumstances, however, attention should be given to some of the internal concerns faced by the new Synod.

It was a relatively small Synod that entered the ranks of American denominations at the turn of the century. J.H. Dubbs reported twenty-two ministers at that time, although only thirteen were present at the organization on April 27, 1793.[18] In another report it was estimated that there were one hundred seventy-eight churches with 15,000 communicants. In addition, there were many people of German Reformed background who counted themselves as such but apparently were not listed as communicant members.

Critical issues confronted the fledgling Synod, not least of which was the general spiritual malaise cited earlier. Related to that was anxiety among the clergy, especially concerning what was called "widespread infidelity," with Thomas Paine as the object of many charges of destroying the "faith." In addition, there were internal problems facing the Synod that tended to be very divisive. Two deserve attention at this point: the language issue and the seminary issue.

All immigrant churches have found the language question troublesome if not explosive. Ethnic identity in a foreign land requires use of the mother tongue. But that in itself retards and often prohibits the cultural accommodation that enables ethnic groups to participate in the life of the nation that has opened its space to them. In the closely knit life of the immigrant churches, where ethnicity tends to be a critical factor of religious devotion, the mother tongue is often defended with ferocity. The question became critical for the German Reformed churches at the beginning of the national phase of its development and at several stages later.

Although the Synod encountered the language question as early as 1804, it was the swelling of the immigrant tide toward the end of the second decade that resulted in split congregations. The Synod itself used the German language officially in its proceedings and minutes until 1825. David Dunn comments on the consequences:

> The conclusion can hardly be avoided that the tenacity with which large sections of the German Reformed Church clung to the language of their fathers had much to do with the slow pace at which consciousness of being an American denomination developed. It surely had something to do with the reluctance and opposition with which the more dyed-in-the-wool German sections of the church met the challenges to educational and missionary enterprise that the new century presented. The loss of congregations, families, and individuals to English-using denominations, while it cannot be measured in statistics, was undoubtedly very large.[19]

The continual dearth of ministers had plagued German Reformed churches from earliest days, and in the first decades of the Synod's life this led to the seminary issue. James I. Good gives considerable detailed information about

175

the personal as well as the organizational issues.[20] Underlying the whole matter were subtle concerns relating to ethnic identity and the perennial issue of authority in churches in a voluntary society. It is impossible to separate these concerns. Suffice it to say that the seminary issue, although of great importance for the future, was simply one aspect of the struggles that the German Reformed Church experienced in becoming an American denomination. The most obvious negative result was the synodical split in 1822, when a "Free Synod" was formed. The positive result, though much delayed by the controversy, was the establishment of the seminary in 1825 at Carlisle, Pennsylvania. As was the case with many denominational seminaries, this one moved several times: in 1829 to York, in 1837 to Mercersburg, and in 1853 to Lancaster, where it came to be known as Lancaster Theological Seminary.

Quite obviously, the organizational structure of the Synod underwent important changes in the years of dealing with such issues. Some of the changes, however, were of a developmental nature, reflecting simply the growth of the Synod in numbers of churches and ministers. In 1819 the Synod acted to establish area groups of churches known as classes (a term corresponding to presbyteries in a structural sense). A committee recommended that:

Because of the rapid growth of the population of the United States many Reformed congregations have been organized, and because it is our great desire that all regular ministers of our church in the United States shall be united by an inseparable bond of union, and because our church has spread far and wide, thus making synodical activities ever more difficult, and because some of the brethren have great distances to cover . . . Synod shall be divided into classes.[21]

Adoption of the recommendation also required a restructuring of the Synod, defining the responsibilities of the classes, their relationship to the Synod, and the manner of election of delegates to the same. Initially, eight classes were formed and others added as the years went by.

Of greater importance at this point of the discussion of the synodical organization are the divisions that took place in 1822 and in 1824. Reference was made above to the formation of the Free Synod over the seminary issue. That synod was, of course, within the same geographical area as the mother Synod. In 1824 the Ohio Classis, located chiefly west of the Allegheny River, separated from the Synod over the question of the right to ordain ministers. Although distance and communication problems were primary factors here, an underlying impulse was the growing self-consciousness of the "western" churches of the German Reformed tradition. The traditions inherited from the colonial period were more important to the churches in eastern Pennsylvania than they were to the newly formed churches in Ohio.

Actually, separating tendencies, whether exacerbated by local circumstances or a changing cultural ethos, are relatively insignificant in German Reformed

176

history generally.* First of all, they simply were not congruent with the Reformed understanding of the church. Thus, the Free Synod returned to the mother Synod in 1837, and the Ohio Synod (originally a classis, but then a synod as it organized other classes in expanding westward) in 1863 became a part of the General Synod. However, it is important to note that already in the 1840s there is a countervailing tendency to separation. Bard Thompson calls attention to a rising denominational self-consciousness as expressed in sermons delivered at the various Synod gatherings at that time.[22] One preacher declared that "the time for . . . union with any other denomination has passed away," and that the Reformed Church "wants no further Reformation." Strange statements indeed from those who belonged to the Calvinist tradition!

Denominational identity was the chief concern of almost all Protestant groups in that period. In one way or another religious diversity connected with religious vitality produced the need to be identified. In the German Reformed Church this led to the formation of the General Synod of the Reformed Church in the United States in 1863. The occasion was the Tercentenary Celebration of the *Heidelberg Catechism,* a most appropriate time from any point of view within the Reformed tradition. For the *Catechism* continued to be the primary molding agent of the Reformed expression of the Calvinist tradition among German people. Here its unifying power was at work, a point to remember when a scholastic tendency and a form of *Heidelberg Catechism* orthodoxy later became a divisive element.

The internal issues and organizational development of the German Reformed Church in the period from the first synodical organization in 1793 to the formation of the General Synod in 1863 are of considerable significance in themselves. At the same time they do not account for the clearer self-understanding, the increased commitment to the Reformed tradition, and the emerging sense of "place" in the American denominational picture that were exhibited in the years following the Civil War. That accounting requires a closer examination of the American religious temper of the times and the experience of growth resulting from immigration.

By the second decade of the nineteenth century the American religious temper was all-pervasive, quickly affecting newly arrived immigrant groups. Produced by the First and Second Great Awakenings, drawing its understanding of human nature as much from the Enlightenment as from the Reformation tradition, it had become at one and the same time the source of impressive religious vitality and the bane of organized religious life. That temper was characterized—and still is largely so in this twentieth century—by primary accent

*While the exceptions seem to be the United Brethren movement involving Philip William Otterbein and the Church of God movement involving John Winebrenner, both over revival measures, the fact is that small numbers were involved in each case.

177

upon the individual's religious experience and consciousness. The result was the absolute individual and a depreciation of the reality and place of the church in religious experience.

It was precisely at this point that American religious temper and German Reformed piety clashed. For although Reformed piety did involve an inward discipline in which the experience of grace became real in the transformation of life, that discipline and experience were always set in the context of the church where Word and Sacrament countered subjectivistic tendencies. The dilemma of the German Reformed church member in the early part of the nineteenth century was real and often painful. Should one seek reassurance from an "experience" generated by the intense excitement of revivalistic preaching, or from the promise of God expressed by the church in Word and Sacrament? It is not surprising that the earnestness of a people made devout over the years by disciplined living would be susceptible to the persuasions of those who made the experience of salvation the criterion of the Christian life.

The records of the German Reformed Church in the first half of the nineteenth century reveal the confusion and turmoil produced by revivalism. At the same time the countervailing tendencies inherent in the Reformed understanding of the church moved the churches in a direction opposite from the prevailing American religious mood and practice. That is the real significance of the development and strengthening of the synodical organization leading up to the General Synod in 1863. It is important to see this, however, in relation to parallel tendencies in other church bodies, where subjective, individualistic religious activity was also seen as continually divisive. A growing recognition of the need for a "well-organized and self-conscious church that possessed authority" lay behind the "church" reaction to revivalism in the second quarter of the century.[23]

One of the clearest examples and primary forces behind this renewed accent on the church was produced within the German Reformed Church. Known as the Mercersburg Theology, or Movement, since its exponents were the faculty of the seminary at Mercersburg, this theological perspective had an immeasurable influence on American Protestantism generally as well as on the German Reformed Church. Of special significance is the fact that it laid the foundations of evangelical catholicity and Christian unity, which became a focal concern of Protestant Christianity decades later. It was the German Reformed Church's first major contribution to the cause of unity in the struggle against sectarianism. Commenting generally about this and parallel perspectives in the midnineteenth century, Lefferts Loetscher asserts: "A more ultimate and far more constructive consequence of their churchly emphasis was the preservation of the classical Reformation and pre-Reformation heritages for a day when Christian unity could be explored in its larger dimensions."[24]

The moving spirits of the Mercersburg Theology were John Williamson

Nevin and Philip Schaff. Nevin, of Scots-Irish background, had come to Mercersburg in 1840 from the Presbyterian seminary at Pittsburgh. He was followed four years later by Schaff, a Swiss-German. Although both were of the Reformed tradition, neither was native to the German Reformed Church. Yet their theological initiative and creativity found a congenial response in a church body prepared for them by the Heidelberg Catechism. This is not to pass over the controversy and struggle engendered by their work. That controversy was an inevitable consequence of the clash between the American religious temper, which had left its mark on the Reformed churches, and the church theology of Nevin and Schaff, which exposed the real significance of the Catechism so widely used and long cherished.

When the heat of controversy had dissipated, it was clear that the Mercersburg Theology had made an impression. True, not all German Reformed people could accept the new perspective. They were the "Old Reformed," in whom the American religious temper had taken firm hold. But the Mercersburg heritage had been woven into the experience and the theological tradition of the Reformed Church in a way that would become evident in the commitment and "attitude toward Christian unity" so characteristic of that body in the twentieth century.[25] Nevin and Schaff had succeeded in their attempt

> to recover the Reformation in its catholic dimensions, the Reformed doctrine of the Eucharist, the stature of the Heidelberg Catechism, the liturgical basis of Reformed worship, the sense of Reformed churchmanship. To the American church as a whole, they opened a vast new historical perspective.[26]

The special significance of the Mercersburg Movement for gaining perspective upon the role of the German Reformed Church tradition in the shaping of the United Church of Christ lies in the convergence of three forces in American church life at that time. The first is represented in the Heidelberg Catechism ethos, which Nevin adopted and expounded. Schaff represents the second force as he brought to bear upon the issues of the churches in America the fruits of the "singular burst of scholarly and theological energy in nineteenth-century Germany."[27] The third force was the increased German-American consciousness brought on by the massive German immigration of the middle decades of the century.

Nevin's use of the Heidelberg Catechism ethos seemed to some an introduction of foreign elements, particularly a Romanizing tendency. Such charges came from those whose religious orientation had become highly individualistic and subjective. They reacted to Nevin's recovery of the organic nature of the church, his Calvinist interpretation of the eucharist, and his insistence upon the unbroken historical continuity of the church, including medieval catholicism. Whatever excesses Nevin's theology seemed to be for some, his recovery of the Catechism for the church was salutary in every way.

When Schaff came to America in 1844, he was already recognized in Europe as a most promising scholar. He had not only been trained in the vigorous German "church" theology of that time—including experiences that made him more cosmopolitan than many of his German theological contemporaries—but he also shared the emerging German theological self-confidence of the nineteenth century. This made Schaff an unusually acute observer of the American scene. Further, it equipped him to be an interpreter of the significance of the "German experience" in American church life at the very time that German immigration was changing the face of the American Midwest.

Schaff returned to Germany ten years later to give lectures on his American experience. The result was the publication of *America*, a classic interpretation not simply of America, but quite specifically of the mission of German (particularly Reformed) theology in American church life.[28] His words have been quoted often.

> Here now is the work of the German Church for America; not only of the Lutheran, but also of the German Reformed. . . . The German church, with its hearty enjoyment of Christianity, and direct intercourse with a personal Savior, its contemplative turn, its depth of inward view, its regard for history, and its spirited theology, might and should enter as a wholesome supplemental element into the development of American Protestantism.[29]

Thus Schaff conceived German theology's nineteenth-century "errand" into the wilderness of American individualistic and subjectivistic religious life. He saw. the special value in this of the "three most important and fundamental features of the Reformed type of Protestantism . . . absolute supremacy of the Holy Scriptures, absolute sovereignty of Divine grace, and radical moral reform on the basis of both."[30]

Of special note is the fact that the work of Schaff and Nevin represents the cosmopolitan and international aspects of the Protestant theological enterprise, which had been more characteristic generally of the eighteenth century than of the nineteenth, when national and sectarian specifics were prominent. Theirs was not the only movement of this kind in America, of course, but "in its breadth of theological horizon and its degree of interrelationship, the work of Nevin and Schaff was unparalleled in America and hardly matched in England and Germany."[31] While modern readers of *America* may discern in Schaff some of the same American chauvinism of Bushnell and others of the neo-Puritanism of the nineteenth century, the fusion of his German sense of historical development and his American sense of national destiny gave greater depth and profundity to America's growing national self-consciousness.

The third force converging in the Mercersburg Movement was the increasing German-American self-consciousness, which cherished the heritage from the fatherland but accepted responsibility for the newly adopted nation of so many thousands of German immigrants. This growing self-consciousness had negative and positive aspects. On the negative side were the tensions of cultural and language differences. On the positive side was the maintenance of identity so essential to societal development. This can be traced, of course, in the other German background churches, where the influence was usually felt in the same way. In the German Reformed Church it was a significant factor in the more intensive period of denominational formation that accompanied the westward movement of the immigrants.

In concluding this section on the national phase of Reformed Church development, it is necessary, then, to identify and interpret the emerging German Reformed self-consciousness in the churches of the West and to show the relationship to the churches of the East.* Differences and tension were inevitable. At the same time the unifying influence of the *Heidelberg Catechism* shows repeatedly.

The organizational setting of the following interpretation requires attention first however. Between 1840 and 1870 large numbers of Germans moved into the Midwest, chiefly via the major waterways: the Great Lakes and the Ohio and the Mississippi rivers. A great many of these were newly arrived immigrants, but many were of the American-born generation of Germans from Pennsylvania, New York, and New Jersey. The latter group settled heavily in Ohio, Indiana, Illinois, and Iowa; they were the English-speaking Germans. The newer, German-speaking groups were concentrated farther west in Wisconsin, Illinois, Iowa, and the Dakotas, many of them forming distinct communities of German Reformed people. The tensions between these two German Reformed groups determined much of the organizational expansion of the denomination through the remainder of the century and up to the post-World War I period.

Most noteworthy was the formation of so-called "German" synods. By holding to the German language, they felt some distance from the English-speaking church groups. In 1867, incidentally, the name German was dropped from the denominational title—a reflection of the stronger American spirit of the churches in the East. Ironically, eight years later the German Synod of the East was formed in the interest of those churches, largely of immigrant membership, who used the language. In 1867 the German Synod of the Northwest was formed at Fort Wayne, Indiana chiefly because the Ohio Synod (English-speaking) seemed not to understand the needs of the German Reformed settlements in Indiana, Illinois, Wisconsin, and Iowa. The dividing and re-forming of synods was for the most part a matter of difference over language. Such divisions in

---

*The liturgical controversy, which was an outgrowth of the Mercersburg Movement, is being passed over here, not because it is unimportant but because it did not *in itself* have a significant role in the subsequent development of the church among western immigrant churches. The liturgical controversy tore apart many of the churches and classes in the East. See David Dunn, et al., *A History of the Evangelical and Reformed Church* (Philadelphia: Christian Education Press, 1961), chapter 4.

many cases were not motivated by hostility; they were essentially a pragmatic solution to organizational problems.

Nevertheless, different theological accents prevailed as well. These were not as divisive as many have assumed. But they were significant in relation to the union developments of the twentieth century. Two distinctions must be kept in mind with respect to the synods west of Pittsburgh. First, the Ohio Synod tended to reflect the Americanizing that had been assailed in the Mercersburg Movement. As a result, newly arrived German immigrants were not comfortable there.[32] Second, the new German immigrants exhibited the influence of the dominant church theology of nineteenth-century Germany, in which there was a resurgence of confessionalism in some sections. Reinhard Ulrich has argued the significance of the conflict between the churches in Ohio particularly, which were attuned to what he calls the "Old Reformed" party in the East and the confessionalism of the churches among the new immigrants. He has called attention, further, to the fact that the shaping influence of nineteenth-century German theology in the churches of the West gave them a common heritage with the Mercersburg Movement.[33]

The new confessionalism was strongly oriented to the *Heidelberg Catechism*. Its institutional anchor and home for many decades was the Mission House, established by the Sheboygan Classis in 1862 in eastern Wisconsin.[34] That institution, modeled after similar institutions of Germany and Switzerland, later became a college and seminary. By supplying trained ministers for genuine mission efforts, the Mission House established the covenant theology of the *Heidelberg Catechism* in hundreds of churches. Although its *Heidelberg Catechism* covenant theology shared elements of a significant heritage with Mercersburg, it was distinguished from the latter by its appropriation of the older Reformed piety with its emphasis upon disciplined living as a sign of participation in the covenant and therefore the church. While this was hardly denied by the Mercersburg proponents, their emphasis was placed upon sacramental participation in the divine-human organism that is the church.

Extension of the Reformed Church among German immigrants in the upper Midwest throughout the last half of the nineteenth century testifies to the vitality of the churches for which the Mission House was the home base. As time went on, however, that vitality disappeared, largely as a result of the singular focus upon a mission to the German people. As German communities were steadily acclimated to American culture, the churches narrowed their concern to a defense of the Reformed faith; often that meant simply a defense of German language and culture.

By 1914 there were four German synods in the Reformed Church, all except one being located in the Midwest. Even as the last one was organized it was clear that there was no good reason for separate synodical organizations. Following World War I realignments took place which tended to eliminate such lines. The German Reformed Church was increasingly an American church body, except in portions of the Synod of the Northwest, where ethnic self-consciousness was hardening as late as the 1920s.

In the meantime the denominational organization developing under the General Synod could scarcely be distinguished from that of any other American denomination.* Boards were established for missions, ministerial pensions, Christian education, and publication. Organizations for men and women were promoted—all parallel to other denominations. Of special historical interest was the formation in 1838 of the Board of Foreign Missions, which participated in the work of the American Board of Commissioners for Foreign Missions, a nondenominational voluntary association that later became entirely Congregational. Those were the years when most missionary and humanitarian work was done by voluntary agencies, drawing from all denominations. But denominational development by the 1850s meant denominational mission boards. By 1866 the German Reformed Church had its own board program. Home missions were synodical efforts for many years until the General Synod, in 1886, established a board for this work. A special feature of this was work among Hungarian Reformed people, who were coming into the metropolitan areas of Cleveland, Chicago, and Pittsburgh. In 1921, after World War I had broken Hungarian ties with the homeland, about eighty congregations became organically related to the Reformed Church in the United States, being formed into four separate classes.[35]

THE NATIONAL PHASE: EVANGELICAL

A significantly different facet of the German experience in American church life is shown in the establishment and development of what came to be known as the Evangelical Synod of North America.† This portion of the Evangelical and Reformed Church story covers a shorter span of time, but its beginning on the American scene in the second quarter of the nineteenth century provides another perspective on denominational formation among German immigrants. The differences between the Evangelical Synod experience and that of the Reformed Church discussed above lie both in the European roots of these groups and in the circumstances they faced on the Western frontier.

Carl E. Schneider, in the preface of his definitive history of the German experience on the frontier, writes:

---

*In parallel with other Protestant denominations during the nineteenth century, the Reformed Church established many educational institutions. By the time of its union with the Evangelical Synod three seminaries, seven colleges, and three academies were listed in its higher education roster.

†The European background of this movement of German people was discussed in chapter 5.

183

Conditions prevailing in both Germany and America at the time favored the rise of a Germanism which in the isolation of the Western frontier frequently sought to further its cause independent not only of American influences but also of contacts with the older German culture of the East. We are here dealing with the rise of a unique German civilization which, sometimes divided against itself, did not begin to integrate with American culture until the national crisis of the Civil War.[36]*

The German Evangelical immigrants had no tradition of a colonial experience and no ties to any church body in the eastern part of the country. They were very much on their own in the frontier situation and thus dependent upon the culture and religious tradition of the fatherland. In the second decade many of the earlier settlers were of the peasant class, from Wuerttemberg. In succeeding decades people who were more educated and trained arrived from other parts of Germany. It is not surprising that German identity was critically important.

In the Protestant spectrum the immigrants of the period were chiefly Lutheran and Evangelical, with Reformed groups scattered among them. At the same time there was great diversity in religious understanding and loyalty as the result of the fragmented civil-political organization of Germany. Of particular interest for this chapter were the Evangelicals (known as the Evangelical Church), whose identity was drawn from the Church of the Prussian Union of 1817. They represented Lutheran and Reformed traditions in Germany, but even more the "unionistic" Protestantism that had emerged under the influence of Friedrich Schleiermacher and other religious leaders. These people found neither the Lutheran nor Reformed churches of America to their liking.

Without an established church organization and tradition in their new homeland, the German Evangelical settlers at first experienced what the German Reformed people had known a century earlier in the East—no pastoral leadership and no authority for church establishment. The forming of these Evangelicals into a church body that became a denomination resulted from three sets of circumstances.

First, was the inability of the established Reformed and Lutheran synods from the East to meet their needs and wants as a frontier people. The German consciousness of the immigrants reflected the vastly different cultural and religious situation of the fatherland in the nineteenth century, which made them seem utterly foreign to American-born Germans of the eastern synods. Even

---

*The point applies as well, of course, to the German Reformed people on the frontier with the qualification that they generally settled with an awareness of the presence of an already organized Reformed Synod in the nation. For those aware of that fact, the frontier experience was qualified by the colonial experience. In addition, many German Reformed people came with a profound commitment to the *Heidelberg Catechism*, which gave them a sense of identity even in frontier circumstances.

Samuel Schmucker's unionism in the Lutheran churches of Pennsylvania did not appeal to the Evangelicals who were unionists from Germany.

Second, a few German Evangelical churches were organized by devout laypeople, particularly schoolteachers. Some of these churches tended to remain independent, seeking no relationship with any synod. Occasionally also, a trained pastor who had emigrated with a group of settlers would take the initiative in establishing a church, as did Hermann Garlichs at Femme Osage and St. Charles, Missouri.[37]

Third and most important were the missionaries sent to America by the Basel and Barmen missionary societies specifically for work among German immigrants. One hundred fifty-eight of the Basel group served Evangelical churches. Many others worked among Reformed people and among the German immigrants who were gathered into the churches that eventually became part of the General Conference of German Congregational Churches. These missionary societies, with their training institutes at Basel and Barmen, were the fruit of the German Pietism that crossed Lutheran and Reformed confessional lines long before the union movement of the nineteenth century. Their role in the German churches on the American frontier was remarkable in every way. Because they represented the pietistic emphasis upon the experience of salvation rather than upon acceptance of a confession as the basis of church membership, they were especially effective in a situation where voluntary association was the model of church organization. Moreover, they identified readily with a people who were not antichurch nor antisacraments, but who were impatient with synodical ecclesiastical authoritarianism.

Basel missionaries, then, were most instrumental in the formation of Evangelical churches among German immigrants. A historic coincidence of singular importance in the affinity of the Evangelical people and the American Congregationalists is linked to the Basel missionaries. It was a group of Hartford, Connecticut laypeople—chiefly Congregationalists—who asked the Basel Missionary Society to send missionaries to serve among the German immigrants.[38] The first two sent were Joseph Rieger and George W. Wall, who, upon their arrival in America in May 1836, spent several months in Hartford and visited New York before going on to the West. Contacts were made then with the American Home Missionary Society and the American Board of Commissioners for Foreign Missions that were to prove valuable for the future. Other missionaries followed, with the result that an ever-increasing number of Evangelical churches were founded.

Although Rieger and Wall were not the first Basel missionaries among the German Evangelical people, Friedrich Schmid having preceded them, they became key individuals in the organization of the churches into a cohesive group. Rieger was away on a European trip at the time, but he may be included

185

with Hermann Garlichs, George Wall, Louis Nollau, Philip Heyer, Johann Riess, and Karl Daubert as founders of the *Kirchenverein des Westens** in October 1840 at Gravois Settlement. Not desiring to establish a synod, these founders laid the basis for future synodical organization. Carl E. Schneider suggests that one reason for the decision to organize at this time was the increasing effort of the Lutheran synods and the Episcopal Church to draw the German Evangelicals into their organizations.[39] Further, divisions among the Lutherans and the animosity of the Saxon Lutherans to unionism had been a source of irritation to Evangelical people.

The nature of the *Kirchenverein* organization itself suggests the uncertainties and ambivalent feelings among the group about ecclesiastical structures. Typical of the pietist tradition, there was reluctance to establish constitutional ecclesiastical authority. The result was a kind of pastoral conference with only pastors holding full membership. Nevertheless, congregations were invited to send lay delegates, who could vote, with the number restricted to the number of clergy. Further evidence of pietist influence from the mother country may be seen in the concern to admit for ordination only those of acceptable character, with apparently no concern about a theological position or doctrinal loyalty.[40] No careful confessional statement was included; only reference to the symbolic writings of the "Evangelical mother church in Germany." Other concerns before the organizing group related to missionary intentions, religious education of the youth, a catechism, a book of worship, and clerical dress. In every respect the concerns of the group reflected the models of German rather than American church life. This supports Schneider's claim that the frontier favored the rise of Germanism among the immigrant groups.

Nothing reveals the tumultuous circumstances of church life on the frontier as much as the controversy over the *Kirchenverein,* which broke out shortly thereafter among the Germans in Missouri. Attacks of a public nature exhibited features of the frontier that are sometimes overlooked in modern attempts to glorify the virtues of independence, courage, and adventuresomeness. Most vicious were attacks from the self-styled rationalists, whose anticlerical and anticonfessional attitudes were much a part of nineteenth-century Germany. Their attitude was akin to the infidelity of American rationalists, which had been cause for concern in the churches in the East.

Lutheran resistance to the *Kirchenverein* grew from the ultraconservative Lutheran stance against unionism in the mother country. There was fear that an organized body of Evangelical churches would succeed in drawing Lutheran churches away from pure Lutheran doctrine. Again, the evidence supports the

*Officially *Der Deutsche Evangelische Kirchenverein des Westens* (The German Evangelical Church Society of the West).

thesis that the frontier circumstances tended to reproduce in America the nineteenth-century patterns of religious life in Germany.

It is important at this point in the discussion to outline the salient features of Evangelical theology as it is exhibited both in the emerging denominational structure and in the style of church life that prevailed. Observers generally have agreed that Lutheran traditions and theological temper are more easily identified than the Calvinist in the Evangelical churches.[41] This was most pronounced in the order and organization of the life of the church, which, in the tradition of Luther's teaching and in marked contrast to Calvin, is of relatively little importance. Where Calvin saw the ordered life of the visible church as essential to the sustenance of faith and to the proclamation of the gospel through the example of a disciplined community of faith, Luther emphasized simply the preaching of the Word and the administration of the sacraments as *constitutive* of the church. Consequently, the *essential* element of the church is the pastoral office. Luther "conceived the Church as a *Pastorenkirche.*"[42]

From the formation of the *Kirchenverein,* in which only pastors had full membership, to the development of the synodical structure, the central role of the pastor was clear among Evangelical people. The movement in this direction was less a matter of choice than of the unconscious assumptions brought from Germany. In most districts from which Evangelical people had come, the Lutheran pattern prevailed. Moreover, a residue of bitterness toward the bureaucratic and authoritarian consistories in Germany, which had their origin in the Reformed system, undoubtedly inclined Evangelical pastors and laity toward the *Pastorenkirche* model. The consequence was a form of church life that accentuated worship, the sacraments, Christian nurture, and voluntary organization for Christian service, in all of which the pastoral function was the key. In view of this it is not surprising that very early in the life of the *Kirchenverein*— 1848—attention was given to establishing a seminary.

Theologically, *Kirchenverein* pastors were inclined toward the nonconfessional tradition in Germany, which had been nurtured by Pietism and strengthened by the formation of the Church of the Prussian Union. The heritage of Pietism, transmitted through the Basel and Barmen missionaries who comprised the majority of *Kirchenverein* pastors, provided the zeal for the gospel that invigorated the churches. Theophil W. Menzel characterized it as a "passionate concern for building, not a Lutheran or Reformed or Evangelical Zion, but a kingdom of God."[43]

"Indifference to matters of doctrine" was certainly a characteristic of the *Kirchenverein* in its early years.[44] However, as was noted in chapter 5, religious conditions on the frontier led the pastors to recognize the necessity of some substantive expression of the faith within the tradition of the Reformation. By 1847 there was not only a statement of the confessional traditions to be used within "the liberty of conscience prevailing in the Evangelical Church," but also a catechism for instruction in the faith.

The 1862 edition of the Evangelical Catechism, largely the product of Andreas Irion, represented a dogmatic trend in the *Kirchenverein* and later in the Synod, according to Carl Schneider.[45] Partly a result of narrowing denominational self-consciousness and partly a reflection of some trends in Germany—so often reflected among the German churches in America—the dogmatic tendency appeared from time to time and can be traced later in the history of the seminary. In general, however, the theological temper of the Evangelical Synod exhibited an American convergence of two theological trends. One has been cited earlier, in the discussion of the work of Philip Schaff, the Mercersburg theologian who saw creeds and confessions as part of the ongoing historical process of the church's use of revelation. Since "the actual church is a process, . . . always looking and pressing for completion," the theological task is unending yet must never allow itself to rest in what inevitably is the sectarian error of dogmatism.[46] The other trend was the focus upon the inward religious experience of the individual by the work of God in the Spirit. This combination gave rise to what became a familiar phrase in later church union efforts: "Creeds are testimonies, not tests, of the experience of faith."

Concern about substance of the faith expressed itself in another way. Its focus was provision for well-trained pastoral leadership. From the beginning days of the *Kirchenverein*, strong pastoral leadership showed its influence. To the initial group there were added a few years later several pastors who had been trained in some of the more prominent German universities. They brought to the Evangelical churches in America not only the best of nineteenth-century German Pietism but also an awareness of the importance of rigorous intellectual discipline for dealing with the issues of the time. From this came the early move to establish a seminary. In 1848, just eight years after the forming of the *Kirchenverein*, planning began. By 1850 the seminary, forerunner of the modern Eden Theological Seminary, opened at Marthasville, west of St. Louis. The names of Friedrich Birkner, William Binner, Andreas Irion, and Adolph Baltzer are firmly fixed in the solid foundations they gave to a seminary that later was to number among its graduates two of America's foremost theologians, Reinhold and Richard Niebuhr.

The synodical development of the *Kirchenverein* dates from 1866, when the name Synod was adopted at a General Conference of pastors and lay delegates. Thus, the German Evangelical Synod of the West moved these churches one more step along the road of American denominational development. The election of a full-time president was symbolic of the centralization of responsibility so characteristic of the Evangelical Synod all through its history. Along with the seminary, this office, filled first by Adolph Baltzer, became the primary unifying force for the German Evangelical churches. Although there was some resistance years later to the full-time presidency, that did not last.

Much of the German Evangelical story tends to be focused in Missouri and southern Illinois because of the large concentration there. But in other parts of the country, groups of churches had grown in much the same way among the immigrants, having pastoral leadership from the same sources and sharing common patterns of religious life. These groups formed synods at about the same time. In 1872 the three synods came together: the Synod of the West (two and one half times larger than the other two put together), the Synod of the East (western New York and Ohio), and the Synod of the Northwest (Illinois, Michigan, and Indiana). Thus, the German Evangelical Synod of North America came into being. The word German was dropped in 1927, although the German language continued to be used widely for another generation.

In closing this discussion of the national phase of Evangelical Synod development, brief attention should be given to the unique fruits of the pietist heritage in this church body. Educational concerns on parish as well as synodical levels were always in the forefront. But equally important and perhaps most distinctive was the home mission enterprise. Extended in typical German fashion, this included not only a vigorous program of establishing new churches but also organized ways of meeting the special needs of the sick, the handicapped, the orphaned, and the disadvantaged. The number of hospitals, institutions, and other enterprises established by the churches of this Evangelical tradition proportionately exceeds that of most Protestant bodies.

THE UNION PHASE: EVANGELICAL AND REFORMED

Denominational patterns of church life for both the Evangelical Synod of North America and the Reformed Church in the United States toward the end of the national period followed those of other American denominations. There were few distinctions of any importance. As the twentieth century opened, a wave of ecumenical concern enveloped the major church bodies. The result was concentrated attention on questions of church union as practical ways of implementing the increasingly important vision of Christian unity. The discussion of this in chapter 5 is pertinent to the following paragraphs concerning the union of the Evangelical Synod and the Reformed Church.

Ecumenical commitment in both of these church bodies was high. In the Mercersburg Movement the Reformed Church had gained a profound theological vision of "evangelical catholicity and the catholic unity of the church."[47] The Evangelical Synod had received "the choice legacy of the *Kirchenverein*," which was "its zeal for church union."[48] Intensive involvement, then, in the church union efforts of the twentieth century was inevitable. While leaders in both groups participated in ecumenical assemblies and conferences, official conversations and actions of significance did not begin until after World War I.

A Reformed "consensus" had been developing before the war, when *Articles of Agreement* were adopted by several bodies of that tradition, including the Reformed Church in the United States, in 1907 and 1908. At a Conference on Organic Union held after the war (1918), a *Plan of Federal Union* was proposed and was affirmed by the General Synod of the Reformed Church.[49] George W. Richards was the moving spirit behind this. In many ways he seemed to have inherited the mantle of Philip Schaff, who had done so much for a "Reformed consensus."

Similar concerns were being expressed in the general conferences of the Evangelical Synod, in 1925 and 1927. Here again, involvement in the great ecumenical assemblies of that era gave new vitality to long-held church union convictions. This was the case for Samuel Press, of the Evangelical Synod, as it was for George Richards, of the Reformed Church. Of equal importance was the strong response of the church bodies themselves. In 1925 the General Conference of the Evangelical Synod specifically instructed its officers to become active in "negotiations . . . looking toward organic union."[50]

Three years later there was concrete expression of such concerns in a series of negotiations involving the Evangelical Synod and the Reformed Church with the United Brethren and, for a time, the Evangelical Church.* The latter group never involved itself seriously in the meetings of these churches. The consultations, which began in 1928, resulted in a three-way plan of union that included the United Brethren. The name proposed was "United Church in America." By 1930 the negotiations involved only the Reformed Church and the Evangelical Synod.

Two observations about the negotiations up to this point will throw some light upon what appeared to be a time of confusion but also of growing maturity in the church union enterprise. First, on the Reformed Church side there were repeated expressions of concern about doctrinal matters, especially relating to the difference between Reformed Church Calvinism and United Brethren Arminianism. Most striking, however, was the absence of substantive discussions about such matters.[51] At the same time the Reformed Church rejected a Presbyterian overture lest it jeopardize the talks with the Evangelical Synod. Second, on the Evangelical Synod side there were informal contacts with the United Lutheran Church and the Moravians.[52] These never moved beyond the informal stage. In both cases the movement of the Evangelical Synod and the

---

*The Evangelical Church here named represented the union in 1922 of the United Evangelical Church (German, but not related to the Evangelical Synod) and the Evangelical Association churches, which were an offspring of the work of Jacob Albright among the Germans in Pennsylvania in 1796, and were Methodist in polity.

190

Reformed Church toward each other by exclusion of other interested parties reflected a deepened recognition of the shared elements of their own traditions. That shared tradition was the European rather than the American form of Christian piety, which was more firmly imbedded in the historical continuity of Reformation thought. The possibility of the union of these two groups became a matter of commitment as a result of that maturing recognition of a common heritage.

Approval of a *Plan of Union* by the General Synod of the Reformed Church in 1932 was followed in 1933 by its ratification at the quadrennial General Convention of the Evangelical Synod. When the day of union arrived on June 26, 1934, the Evangelical and Reformed Church was born. A scant six years had passed since the initial conversations, but the hope that such a union would take place had been expressed eighty years earlier by Philip Schaff.* Commentators of that time called attention to the most noteworthy feature of the act of union—the agreement to unite and then to create the constitutional and organizational arrangements for implementation. Samuel McCrea Cavert, of the Federal Council of Churches, said: "Your decision to *unite* and to trust to the future for the working out of the implications of the union sets a new precedent in the history of American churches."[53] The public commitment of these two church bodies to a life together in trust and in obedience to Christ led them on a journey of exploration in the difficult terrain of the institutional organization of the church. Another six years were required to design a constitution and organization consonant with the traditions represented but also adequate for the times. In the interim the two church bodies maintained their individual legal structures but at the same time proceeded to consolidation on all levels of denominational life.

With the adoption of a constitution in 1938 and its implementation in 1940, the Evangelical and Reformed Church entered the mainstream of American church life. At that point its total confirmed membership numbered 655,366, a small denomination by American standards but prepared to grow in the following decades at a comparable rate with other church bodies. The constitution represented a blend of polities rooted in the histories of the two churches. Ideally, this blend was designed to maintain a lively tension between *autonomy* and *authority*, a tension that is of the very essence of the Reformed ecclesiological tradition. George W. Richards characterized the Evangelical and Reformed polity as "essentially presbyterial," that is, a government by judicatories, with its

---

*George W. Richards asserted that in 1854 Schaff entered into correspondence with Prof. William Binner, of the seminary of the *Kirchenverein*, then located at Marthasville, Missouri. From that correspondence the conviction grew in Schaff's mind that these two German church bodies should unite. He urged his Mercersburg colleagues to work toward that. Cf. George W. Richards Collection, Archives, Lancaster Theological Seminary.

"fontal source of authority in the congregation acting through representatives in the congregational and the denominational judicatories."[54]

In the same connection Richards acknowledged that the presbyterial character of the new denominational organization was a concession made to the Reformed Church by the Evangelical Synod. That Synod was organized in the Congregationalist model of most Lutheran bodies in America. Perhaps the sharpest contrast between the Reformed and the Evangelical polities can be expressed by saying that in the former the connectionalism of the denomination lay in the office and role of the elder, whereas in the latter it lay in the office of the pastor. The provision for a system of judicatories—consistory (or church council), synod, and General Synod—introduced an explicit line of authority reaching from the General Synod to the local church through the latter's consistory. Moreover, it was a line of authority that balanced the roles of clergy and laity.

In the six years' work of building a denominational structure, the two groups made concessions to one another out of a spirit of growing trust based on commitment to the lordship of Christ. The concession Richards referred to, in the previous paragraph, was one. In a revealing letter, Louis W. Goebel, vice-president of the Evangelical Synod, wrote to C.W. Locher, Synod president, indicating a concession on the part of the Reformed Church to the Evangelical Synod:

I had a perfectly splendid time at Akron [site of the 1932 Reformed General Synod]. These good folk are so much like our own church that one feels perfectly at home with them. . . . The Evangelical Synod cannot fail to ratify this union if it wishes to remain true to its cardinal principles. *The agreement on the point of doctrine is certainly a concession on the part of the Reformed Church and amounts in fact to an acceptance of our position.*[55]

Both concessions reflected fundamental characteristics of the two churches. Carl E. Schneider, noting the "spirit of Luther" in the Evangelical Synod and the Calvinistic heritage of the Reformed Church, argued that such apparent diversity was not a hindrance to union.

The vital significance of this union, however, is not to be found in the doctrinal and ecclesiastical *rapprochement* of two antithetical bodies, but in the mutual appropriation of the religious values common to both. That the Evangelical Synod was . . . rooted in the . . . German Reformation has never been seriously questioned. It has not always been equally clear that the Reformed Church was congenial to the spiritual and religious message of the German movement. If, therefore, it can be shown that the genius of the Reformed Church . . . lies not in its Calvinistic predilections but in its vital committal to *the liberal heritage of German Protestantism*, then it may become . . . clear that the union with the Evangelical Synod was *consummated on a functional rather than an ecclesiastical basis.*[56]

The cogency of Schneider's point cannot be denied. The liberal* heritage of German Protestantism, particularly of the nineteenth-century variety, influenced both churches. Philip Schaff has already been identified as the most influential transmitter of that heritage from Germany to the Reformed Church and indirectly as a confirmer of it in the Evangelical Synod.

Nevertheless, the observation must be qualified by calling attention to elements of the Calvinistic heritage that can be identified not only in the Reformed Church before the union but also in the Evangelical and Reformed Church constitution. Two may be cited: the doctrine of the church as the reality of the kingdom of grace and the place of order and discipline in the church as witness to God's reign in the world. Both have their ground in the *Heidelberg Catechism*, which was one of the three confessional documents upon which the Evangelical and Reformed Church based its faith stance.

While there is widespread agreement that the *Heidelberg Catechism* was an effectual bridge between Calvinist and Lutheran traditions, it should be remembered that this refers more to its functional and devotional style than to its content. "It emphasized not the Calvinistic-theological but the Lutheran-experiential approach to religion."[57] At the same time its theological conceptual framework utilizes Calvin's understanding of the church in relation to the doctrine of election.[58] Bard Thompson, in discussing the question of assurance of election, makes the point that such assurance does not come by "some extraordinary perception into the hidden decrees of God, . . . [but] by what Calvin designates 'our inward calling,' namely our conscious awareness that the Word of God has come alive in our hearts through the action of the Holy Spirit and that we do indeed belong to Christ through faith."[59] That sense of inward calling is the work of the Word and the Spirit in the church, the called community, and results in the Christian's affirmation of God's election:

> I believe that, from the beginning to the end of the world, and from among the whole human race, the Son of God, by his Spirit and his Word, gathers, protects, and preserves for himself, in the unity of the true faith, a congregation chosen for eternal life. Moreover, I believe that I am and forever will remain a living member of it.[60]

The church, then, is the visible reality of the kingdom of grace, in which the Christian experiences both calling and assurance. As such, the church's form in the world is not a matter of indifference; its form must express the reality of the Christian's calling and assurance. In the Calvinist Reformed tradition that requires the ordered ministry of Word and Sacrament and the disciplined life of the believer. In the Evangelical and Reformed Church this tradition was incor-

---

*The word liberal as Schneider used it must be understood in its nineteenth-century *German* setting not in the twentieth-century American setting. It was characterized by an interconfessional, unionistic stance in all forms of church life.

porated in the office of elder and in the judicatories from the congregation on up to the General Synod, as provided in the constitution. The constitution began with words expressing a principle dear to the hearts of Reformed people: "For the maintenance of *truth* and *order* . . . the Evangelical and Reformed Church . . . ordains this constitution to be its fundamental law and declares the same to have authority over all its ministers, members, congregations and judicatories."

Although well expressed in constitutional form, it is clear from the experience of the succeeding years that this understanding of the church was acknowledged more in letter than in practice. The implicit expectations of discipline, whether in the local church or the synod, were rarely met. The proper use of the judicatory system fell by the wayside. Although many reasons may be cited, it is certainly true that the times were calling for a different form of church order and organization. The constitution had been prepared with much regard for the founding traditions; it did not reflect awareness of the changes taking place in American religious life. The implications of the long-developing accent upon the centrality of the faith experience in the formation of the church in American life was not given recognition in the constitution. At the same time the religious practice of both churches had reflected this for a long time in varying degrees. That is why George W. Richards could write, in 1942, about the spirit of the Evangelical and Reformed Church:

The article of the standing and falling Church is the experience contained in the confession: "I believe that Jesus Christ is my Saviour and Lord." When men have that conviction in the heart and make confession with the mouth, they have passed from the bondage of ordinances and the rudiments of the world into the liberty of the sons of God. *They are then free to work out statements of doctrine, forms of worship, and ways of life which are true to their experience, to the spirit of the glorified Christ, and to the conditions of the age in which they live.*[61]

The Evangelical and Reformed venture in the development of the institutional form of the church marked another step in the German experience in American church life. It was a significant transitional step in that it was a recognition of the limits of an ethnic tradition in church formation, but even more so in the recognition that through that tradition there were expressions of the Protestant faith to be preserved and conveyed to future generations. That is what lay behind the commitment to the cause of Christian unity through church union. It was a response of obedient faith, marked by the willingness to risk cherished forms and practices. It represented acknowledgment of the lordship of Jesus Christ in the church and in the world.

As a singular denominational body the Evangelical and Reformed Church had a short life of only twenty-three years. Its contributions to American Christianity are, therefore, difficult to assess. In the union negotiations both churches

194

displayed some self-consciousness about the contributions of their respective heritages. For the Evangelical Synod this meant a concern to extend the inter-confessional, unionistic, and liberal evangelical stance, which it had developed from its German roots, into the mainstream of Protestant life. For the Reformed Church it meant an opportunity to extend the witness of its Calvinist heritage, as expressed in its order of church life and passion for evangelical catholicity, in a new organizational form.

The concessions noted earlier resulted in some ambiguities. However, in the process of developing the constitution, the fundamental affinities of the two groups tended either to overcome or brush aside such ambiguities in a spirit of commitment to unity. The words of Richards quoted above exhibit this; but in another connection even more, when he said: "Without the Christlike spirit no constitution will ever be effective; *with that spirit one will need only a minimum of law for the administration of the affairs of the fellowship of men and women.*"[62] This last quotation is in many respects a singular example of the flowing together of the spirit of both Calvin and Luther in a man who, in his lifetime, was a foremost ecumenical leader. In the first half of the quotation, Calvin's passion for the rule of Christ shines through; in the last half, Luther's diffidence toward administration in the church is accentuated.

That spirit seemed to be characteristic of the new denomination as it found itself needing to be responsive to the needs of the world as it moved into times of catastrophic war and social change. The three presidents who served during those years—George W. Richards, Louis W. Goebel, and James E. Wagner—represented styles of leadership sensitive both to the traditions and to the times. It was characteristic of James E. Wagner to say: "The new church, to justify its validity as a church of the Reformation tradition, had to demonstrate that it was not only a Reformed but also a reforming church, responding to the ever-changing needs of man and to the never-changing imperatives of the church's Lord."[63]

Perhaps the essential character of the Evangelical and Reformed Church lay in its commitment to "the liberty of conscience inherent in the Gospel" and in its passion to respond to the mandate for unity. That character meant the eventual surrender of its own life for the sake of the formation of the United Church of Christ.

CHAPTER 8

ASSESSMENT
AND FORECAST

The temptation to romanticize the story of the past subtly intrudes on almost every account of individual and group achievement. This is especially true when faith and dedication beyond the ordinary can be identified in what was accomplished in response to a vision.

At the same time the evidence of what such faith and dedication produced is really the essence of any historical account. It becomes a testimony to succeeding generations. In receiving such testimony from the past, the church must learn to overcome the sin of pride with the grace of gratitude. "Liturgies of self-esteem" seldom include prayers of thanksgiving to God. The fact is, as John T. McNeill has stated so well: "In the total record of any church, there is much to be repented of rather than defended; there is always a danger that in approving our peculiar traditions we shall glory in our very shame."[1]

The formation of the United Church of Christ was a venture of faith, a response to a vision created out of the heritage of the past and in the context of new responsibilities. Whether as a church it has "the authenticity of those that have been sculpted in history"[2] is a judgment that only the divine wisdom and future generations have the right to make. As the foregoing chapters show, the United Church *has* been "sculpted in history"—not merely the history of the recent past but also of many generations long gone. To know the beliefs, movements, and events comprising that history is to begin to accept ownership and to be shaped by it. Assessment and reassessment in the context of new circumstances is the continual task of those who would own the history of the United Church and thus come to understand it. In that process insights are gained, perspectives brought into focus, and visions renewed.

The story of the United Church has been recounted here as "a case study of the reconfiguration of American church life" in the midtwentieth century as it was reflected in church union.* Along with many other American Protestant church bodies, the two communions forming this new denomination saw union as an appropriate response to the mandate of Christian unity. It was a union that took place in an era of organizational revolution and of shifting accents in religious and cultural pluralism.

*The reader is referred to the Introduction, p. 16, for a statement of this theme.

In any union there is considerable ambivalence about the necessary break with the past. While the need for such a break may be affirmed, the steps to accomplish it produce anxiety and engender significant risks. Lukas Vischer, director of Faith and Order Studies for the World Council of Churches, called attention to the risks: "The experience of this break can . . . cause the united church to lose consciousness of its own origins, . . . and to lose sight of the fellowship with the generations which preceded it in faith. . . . It succumbs more easily to the spirit of a particular age."[3] For the United Church of Christ this possibility of losing a sense of origins and of fellowship with preceding generations constitutes a real danger. With a large portion of its total membership drawn from diverse backgrounds, the sense of the church's continuity is difficult to maintain. A minimal sense of the particularities of the United Church's progenitors is a serious limitation in the experience of "owning" a history. It is even more difficult when the common heritage of American Protestants is misunderstood and discounted.

The problem has been a persistent one in much of American Christianity. In the nineteenth century Philip Schaff and John Williamson Nevin devoted their theological energies toward recapturing the sense of the organic continuity of the church. That sense was high in the 1940s and 1950s, as the union moved toward completion; now, three decades later, it is hardly discernible. A sense of the transcendent ground of faith in the being of God, of being part of God's redemptive activity on behalf of the world, of sharing the fellowship of the divine community—all that sense tends to be forgotten as human beings turn inward to find authentication for life.

To charge that the United Church has succumbed to "this spirit of the age" would be arrogant; but to fail to see the danger and to identify it would be irresponsible. The special danger for the United Church lies in the absence of significant and recognized symbols of its continuity with a distinctive past, which has been identified in these pages as a constructive element in the shaping of American Christianity. Religious traditions can be the "embrace of death" unless transformed by that transcendent vision of God's sovereignty and Christ's lordship.

Those who have participated in the United Church experience, especially in the two decades of its official existence, can testify nevertheless to times of a special Providence. In the context of conflict and testing, when repentance and obedience are the fundamental expressions of faith, the ambiguities attendant upon all religious institutional effort were indeed exposed and, in principle, overcome. Such times have given witness to Paul Tillich's point about the churches:

The Spiritual Community as the dynamic essence of the churches makes them existing communities of faith and love in which the ambiguities of religion are not eliminated but are conquered in principle. The phrase "in principle" does not mean *in abstracto* but means the power of beginning, which remains the controlling power in a whole process. . . . The ambiguities of the religious life are conquered in principle in the churches' life; their self-destructive force is broken.[4]

For United Church people to "own their history" and to acknowledge the organic continuity of the community of faith is to *see* "the power of beginning" and the breaking of "self-destructive" forces in the church's life as the evidence of God's continuing work with God's people.

Although a young denomination, the United Church's experience in developing a new institutional form for the community of faith has already underlined the need to be alert to self-destructive forces in its life. Not least among these forces is what Daniel Jenkins called "the characteristic ecclesiastical danger, that of subordinating Christ to the Church."[5] Obedience to Christ the Lord can be subtly changed into obedience to an image of Christ conjured by minds and hearts not subject to the discipline of the Word and the Spirit through scripture and tradition.

The inevitable process of formation followed by deformation has been written large in the history of the church as an institution.[6] Two responses are possible when the deformation of an original vision is perceived: either reformation or transformation. Reformation as a touching again of the "power of beginning" has had a transformative effect in the church, as history eloquently testifies. Nevertheless, reformation narrowly conceived in a *restorationist* sense can be and usually is simply a new way of absolutizing a particular form of the church. History has shown the new rigidities produced under the name of the Reformation.

The crucial insight of the sixteenth-century Reformation was not "restoration" but continual renewal: the church re-formed and always re-forming. It is this understanding of reformation that results in *transformation*, the capability of renewal expressed in an internal dynamic as well as an external re-formation. Transformation represents not only a hope but also a commitment in the twentieth-century ecumenical movement. For churches accepting that commitment by their ventures in church union, the theme of renewal has been especially prominent.

This was true of the United Church as it sought to create an organizational form expressive of the presence of the living Lord in the community of faith. Initial steps were tentative, as seen in chapter 3. New structures could not be created ex nihilo; there were given elements and long-established patterns of thought. Nevertheless, the uniting communions did reach beyond old models to new arrangements, which some saw as a combination of traditional Congregational and presbyterian-synodical forms. This may very well have been an appropriate description except for what emerged from the testing of the "system" in the late Sixties, as church structures everywhere came under attack in a wrenching social struggle.

In that time of testing the original vision of a "new polity and plan of organization for the United Church," to some extent blurred and, more implicit than explicit in the Constitution and By-Laws, showed its power. As the changes proposed by the Committee on Structure, in 1967 and 1969, were considered, some latent elements in the organizational arrangement framed in 1959 and 1960 emerged as possibilities for meeting the challenges of new circumstances in the church's mission. Perhaps more than many people realized, the structure of the United Church did possess a remarkable flexibility. What appeared to be a fragile structure of relationships among autonomous units turned out to be an opportunity to demonstrate that "the purpose of church order is to ensure that the people of God are kept moving toward their true destination rather than to perfect the organization and to define the limits of the temporary camps of their earthly pilgrimage."[7] The significance of the United Church can be said to lie in an implicit recognition that the organic model of unity does not require a uniform polity. What is affirmed is the liberty to develop structures that facilitate mission and open the door to obedience to Christ.

A structure capable of facilitating the mission of God's people is never designed once-and-for-all-time. What emerged in the late 1960s as an effective response to the tasks God laid upon the church in a time of great human need can be easily wrapped in protective layers of self-satisfaction. Organizational structures are human creations, sharing in all the ambiguities of the religious life. Only the sense of being God's people, claimed and sustained by God, can make structure functional. Generations of faithful discipleship are needed to make full use of the gifts of God for the church.

In retrospect it is clear that the built-in flexibility of United Church structure has been exploited most effectively in the present decade by new styles of decision-making on all levels. A slow but steady enhancement of a sense of responsibility through participation—not simply contrived activity—has had important consequences in many aspects of the church's life. Nevertheless, it is also clear that as an organization the United Church is subject to the same degenerative forces at work in all society. Participational decision-making as exercised on behalf of self-serving concerns is displayed in the churches even as it is in the wider society. The only corrective to the misuse of participational decision-making lies in the recognition that in the church responsible relationships among the people are under the discipline of the lordship of Christ. The church's distinctive characteristic is concern that the form of the church may demonstrate a new community rooted in a new covenant mediated between God and God's people through Jesus Christ.

On still another level the experience of the United Church illustrates the

200

ambiguities of the institutional forms of the religious life and the need to be alert to their destructive power. Committed to the work of the transformation of the society as well as the individual, it has sought to stand on the side of justice and mercy, with the oppressed and disadvantaged. Along with sister denominations sharing that commitment, it has sought to make clear that the reign of God in the world means the redemption of other human communities as well as the community of faith. Even in this commitment, however, the human propensity for religionizing the gospel results in muting the prophetic voice of the church, making it uncritical and blind to the ambiguities of its own life as well as of the society generally. At such times prophetic concern becomes self-serving and is used to promote ecclesiastical images of importance. The difficulty of discriminating among the levels of good and evil exhibited in social movements and issues cannot be overcome simply by intensified zeal and effort. What is required of the institutional church at all times is a confession of participation in the structures of evil as well as a courageous standing against them. *Repentance* and *obedience* are the requisite disciplines of faith.

The formation of the United Church came at a time of massive organizational development in American church life. This has posed many problems and has placed a special burden upon the church. In such circumstances commitment to the functional or instrumental model of church organization is difficult to maintain. Some critical aspects of this were discussed in chapter 4. Again, in retrospect it seems clear that for the most part there is an appropriate dynamic tension between the self-conserving energies of organizational bureaucracy and the creative energies flowing from the commitment to instrumental models of institutional life.

There are, nevertheless, continuing organizational problems rooted in some treasures of the heritage of the past. The two long-established and recognized program agencies for the mission of the church, the Board for Homeland Ministries and the Board for World Ministries, have a relationship to the denominational structure rooted in their own histories, which is never easily interpreted to the church at large. The details of this, particularly relating to the homeland board, have been discussed in earlier chapters. But any assessment of the present United Church situation must take into account that the *relationship* of these boards to the denomination needs continual review and reconsideration. There are two quite obvious reasons.

The first reason is surely the most obvious: They are United Church boards by both mutual commitment and constitutional provision. As national agencies with an assured but responsible autonomy of operation, however, they tend to be far removed from the experience of many local churches. Sensitivity to this remoteness is accentuated as individual members and congregations seek to participate responsibly in the wider mission of the denomination. They search for but do not easily find ways to influence the policies and programs of the boards. At the same time staff personnel of the boards also feel some frustration in their efforts to develop programs that do meet the needs and expectations of the churches. An effective means of communication between the rank-and-file church members and the professionally trained staff personnel of national agencies constitutes a continual and largely unresolved problem in the bureaucratic organizational life of the denomination.* The inhibiting effect this has upon the United Church is parallel to the experience of other American Protestant denominations.

The second reason is related. In every denomination there is a tendency to respond to difficult structural problems by creating parallel or complementary structures. In its own restructuring experience, begun in 1969 and culminating in 1973 with the establishment of the Office for Church Life and Leadership, the United Church sought to close the gap between national-level resources and local church needs. This new agency was designed to be a "resource for Conferences and Associations for their leadership development needs, particularly as they relate to the leadership needs of the local churches," and was intended to be "available to provide leadership development training for, and on behalf of, Instrumentalities." Both the charge given to this new agency and the design of its organization place it in a relatively close relationship with local churches. While this agency's responsibility to the two major program boards is clearly defined in the bylaws, the impact it will have upon their relationship to the conferences, associations, and churches is still unclear. It is clear, however, that the establishment of the Office for Church Life and Leadership could have the unintentional effect of complicating the relationship of the Board for Homeland Ministries to the denomination as a whole.

There is no easy resolution of these problems. The needs that called for the creation of the Office for Church Life and Leadership certainly justify its place in the United Church. What is required at the same time is recognition throughout the denomination that the major program boards represent areas of the church's mission in which national and international perspectives are critically important. They are indispensable resources for a church body committed to the life of mission. In their long histories, so interwoven with the major strands of American Christianity, they have consistently represented the central thrust of ecumenicity to which the United Church is committed.

The very flexibility that characterized United Church organizational structure can be a source of frustration. At times the organization will appear to be a conglomerate of autonomies, as it did to many in the testing time of the Sixties. However, the restructuring of that time underlined a fundamental feature of the denomination's capability. It is instructive for the future that it was possible to

*Paul Harrison's discussion of this general problem of American denominational life is especially pertinent here. See *Authority and Power in the Free Church Tradition* (Princeton: Princeton University Press, 1959), chapters VI-IX.

rearrange the relationships of autonomous units so as to make the whole a more effective expression of the energies of its parts. Reassignment of responsibilities among the autonomous units is one of the most promising signs of institutional vitality. It is this function that must remain a chief concern of the General Synod. The synod is the meeting place where the concerns and aims of the various units of denominational organization can be considered together.

And what of the future? Has the story of the shaping of the United Church given any hints about its future in God's mission? President Robert V. Moss, speaking to the 1973 General Synod, reminded the delegates that "our history would seem to indicate that denominations like persons have life-cycles. Indeed, if the history of our tradition is any sign, the life expectancy for denominations is decreasing while human life expectancy is increasing."[8] While it is not likely that the denominational form of church life will disappear in the near future, the form itself will continue to undergo modifications, as it has ever since its appearance on the American scene.

Insofar as the United Church is concerned, however, it is well to remember that it came into being on a Basis of Union which affirmed that "denominations exist not for themselves but as parts of that Church, within which each denomination is to live and labor and, if need be, die." Although that may be interpreted simply as a commitment to further church union—as indeed it is—it is expressive of an even more fundamental faith conviction, namely, that the church is not simply a human institution; it is God's instrument for mission. Through the power of God's Word in Christ and by the working of the Spirit, the church in its human and institutional form is continually reshaped. While human sin may seem to frustrate the divine purpose, the history of the church must also be understood as the working out of that purpose. In the end the church is where Christ is and history testifies to his presence in uncounted ways.

For this reason the church "flies in the face" of so much of human history. It counters the ancient cynical wisdom of Childe Harold:

There is a moral to all human tales;
'Tis but the same rehearsal of the past;
First freedom, and then glory—when that fails,
Wealth, vice, corruption—barbarism at last.

It is not by its own determination, however, that the church as an institution can counter the effects of human sin. It is the faith of the church that God shapes the church for the divine redemptive purpose and uses the occasions of human failure and corruption to bring forth structures appropriate to God's redemptive work.

Exactly how God will shape the church for redemptive work in the coming age, with its awesome prospects, is not now understood. For humankind to live as one family on a planet of limited resources requires more vision than is ordinarily found in any individual or group. It is possible, however, in the faith

203

that it is God who is at work through the church, to say that the history of God's work in the past gives intimations of God's intentions. One cannot read the history of the United Church, for example, without seeing those intimations. An illustration very much to the point is the catalytic experience of the work of Black men and women, whose witness to their white brothers and sisters in the Sixties helped the United Church face the realities of the gospel's claim on all human life. That experience was salutary but not complete. Blacks and whites are still learning; and that learning will include Native American brothers and sisters.

The church as a human institution, under a divine mandate and infused by the divine presence, lives by the vision God creates continually in the human heart and mind. The seer in the book of Revelation expressed this in words cherished and believed (21:1, 5, KJV): "And I saw a new heaven and a new earth" and God who "sat upon the throne said, Behold, I make all things new."

CHAPTER 9

SHAPED AND BEING SHAPED

The motto of the United Church of Christ, "United and Uniting," refers both to an event in time and to a dynamic, ongoing process. Similarly, the entire UCC national culture can be described as "shaped and being shaped." For instance, the UCC national structure was established when the Constitution and By-Laws were adopted by the 1959 General Synod and the Constitution was ratified thereafter by the Conferences. That structure has been modified constantly through the years, however, by both historical developments and sharpened insight. This chapter recounts five major passions that shaped and continue to shape the United Church of Christ national setting. It especially spotlights their refinement since 1977, the original publication date of this book. The undertakings are: (1) faith and theological clarity; (2) church unity and ecumenical relationships; (3) governance and polity; (4) mission structure and philosophy; and (5) justice and witness activities.

FAITH AND THEOLOGICAL CLARITY

At its dawning, the United Church of Christ exhibited immense clarity about the presence of God. In the initial address for the 1957 Uniting Synod, Co-President Fred Hoskins declared: "We come to this union in and with faith that God had [God's] hand in it all and that we shall bear a stronger and better witness to Christ than either of us has done separately." Co-President James Wagoner echoed that theme: "The words 'Hitherto hath the Lord helped us' reflect an assurance without which our being together would be an empty and pathetic masquerade. That assurance is that this union is of God's making and it is God who brought us to this hour." Co-Moderator George Hastings agreed: "As we measure the significance of this moment, we marvel at the mysterious power of the Holy Spirit. To [God] to whom a thousand years are but as yesterday when it is past we come, after 15 years of exploration, study and common counseling. Out of the background of that experience we now believe and we know that this union is the will of God."[1]

The hearty faith of delegates and officers of the Uniting Synod was anchored in at least three noteworthy theological ideas: God was fully present in the act of union; the authority for uniting was the love and sacrifice of Jesus Christ; and, through the Holy Spirit, God would be present with the United Church of Christ forever. The basic shape of the delegates' theology was highly orthodox, therefore, and decidedly trinitarian. Its roots could be found in Article II, "Faith of the Basis of Union" (see "Basis of Union of the Congregational Christian Churches and the Evangelical and Reformed Church with the Interpretations" in the appendixes). That article became the basis for the Constitution and By-Laws and the Statement of Faith, each adopted by the 1959 General Synod.[2]

Unfortunately, the theological clarity of the first two synods was short-lived. It was overwhelmed almost instantly by national and international events. Throughout the United Church of Christ's entire existence since 1957, the United States has been besieged by a succession of tragic challenges. Racial conflict, war in Vietnam, assassinations of a president and other national heroes, drugs, an explosion in the numbers of homeless and hungry people—all these and more shadowed our landscape. It was a time when every human institution—government, business, churches—struggled to survive amidst the wash of cynical floods. Over and over again, each setting of the United Church of Church was compelled to search "the faith of the historic Church" to "make [Christian] faith its own," as Paragraph 2 of the Preamble to the UCC Constitution advocates. Efforts to stem the tide frequently failed, followed sometimes by clergy depression as well as declining membership and income.

The quest for theological clarity in the United Church of Christ national setting was at once formal and informal. Formal faith exploration in this context refers here to official procedures and processes established by the General Synod. Informal inquiry refers to activities by individuals or entities in the national setting with or without specific General Synod approval. In this definition, the initial United Church of Christ search for theological clarity was decidedly formal. An early vote of the 1957 Uniting Synod, its sixteenth actual decision, established a commission to prepare a Statement of Faith. The commission completed its work by the 1959 General Synod, which enthusiastically adopted the Statement of Faith recommended to it. A theological commission was then created as a separate unit of national life. The intention was to establish a forum to reflect upon faith concerns, to inform United Church of Christ members about the church's historic faith, and to formulate official responses to internal and external theological inquiries. Among other things, the commission published several notable pamphlets interpreting the sacraments, the rites of the church, and other theological themes. By 1970, the commission was discontinued, hampered by lack of staff, the inability to meet more than once a year, and declining funds. The Office for Church Life and Leadership, created provisionally by the 1973 General Synod, eventually assumed its responsibilities.

Another synodical attempt to develop theological clarity was introduced at the 1977 General Synod when a series of theological lectures was launched. President Joseph Evans's hope was that General Synod delegates and visitors would be equipped with biblical and theological insights to undergird their decisions about major issues and concerns. The first lecturer in the series was Barbara Brown Zikmund, then dean of the Pacific School of Religion. Her lecture, "A Theology of the Laity,"[3] coincided with the establishment of the Office of Church Life and Leadership as a "permanent" agency of the United Church of Christ. These lectures continued similarly for the next seven synods, and involved distinguished seminary professors. They were discontinued in 1991, after which extended sermons during worship became the primary locus of synodical theological lecturing.

Discussions on faith and theology at General Synod have also arisen during consideration of resolutions, usually called pronouncements, and in Christian unity documents. Both types of document begin with a foundational faith statement usually labeled a theological and biblical call, affirmation, or rationale. Uneven and sometimes minimal in content, such testimonies often fail to realize their potential for developing theological knowledge and clarity. Nevertheless, they remind each synod that theology must undergird everything the synod sets out to accomplish.

Widespread and varied informal theological activity by UCC instrumentalities and other national bodies has accompanied formal General Synod theological work. During the 1980s virtually every unit in the national setting gave extensive attention to what came to be called the faith crisis. The Office for Church Life and Leadership (OCLL) and the United Church Board for Homeland Ministries (UCBHM) each committed major resources and energy to that dilemma, with OCLL stretching its resources virtually to the limit. In 1988, for example, OCLL attempted to engage the entire UCC in conversations about the theological character and work of the denomination. Following a Family Thank Offering project entitled "Theology and the United Church of Christ," OCLL concluded there is a need for:

intentional theological work by different parts of the church;
increased communication, interaction and coordination among the
    different settings of the church;
greater knowledge about the theological heritage of the UCC;
expanded sharing of the theological resources of the Church;
substantive study, reflection and dialogue on theological issues.[4]

These conclusions envisioned unprecedented theological activity, which unfortunately never developed principally because of severe budgetary limitations. Nonetheless, significant new resources to nurture faith were created after 1977. Notable among them are a *Manual on the Ministry* (1977) and the *Book of Worship, United Church of Christ* (1986), published by OCLL; a lectionary-based curriculum, *The Inviting Word* (1994), an inclusive-language hymnal, *The New Century Hymnal (1995),* and *The New Century Hymnal Companion* (1998) created by the UCBHM; the *Ecclesiology* Paper (1991) and the *Missio Dei* Paper (1992), produced by the General Synod Committee on Structure; and *The Living Theological Heritage* series, seven volumes reproducing historic theological documents of the UCC and its predecessors, sponsored by OCLL and the UCBHM.[5]

There is not space to enumerate all the theological documents and discussions produced by national setting units during the last two decades. Suffice it to say that widespread attention has focused upon UCC faith and theology. It must be noted, however, that no systematic or comprehensive theology evolved from this attention. In *United and Uniting*, Gunnemann laments the absence of discussion about ecclesiology, i.e., theological deliberation about the nature and purpose of the church. It is an appropriate lament, but it is only one example of missing theological discussion. The principal characteristic of the UCC theological vocation may be its unusually strong tie to action. Biblical and theological reflection sometimes seems linked almost exclusively to issues the denomination is addressing in the church or in the world. Doctrinal, confessional, and creedal integrity is not the ordinary goal for synodical theological discourse except when ecumenical relationships force clarifying responses. Important theological soil has undoubtedly been tilled by the UCC during the last forty years, but much ground has not yet been explored.

CHURCH UNITY AND ECUMENICAL RELATIONSHIPS

The United Church of Christ began its existence with a formidable vision: the UCC would be the stimulus for a generation of major mergers among U.S. Protestants. If it did not become the chief inspiration, surely it would participate eagerly in all such ventures. The Uniting Synod shaped that vision, first, by deliberately choosing a name, United Church of Christ, free from doctrinal controversy and prior denominational ownership. No mere name could ever be allowed to impede additional mergers. The vision was shaped, second, when the motto "United and Uniting" was adopted to express the fundamental UCC ecumenical hope.[6] The vision was shaped, third, with the adoption by the 1959 Synod of Paragraph 1 of the Preamble to the UCC Constitution, stating forthrightly that the UCC ecumenical vocation is to express "more fully the oneness [of Christians] with Christ."[7] One defining characteristic of the UCC is its singular ecumenical commitment, expressed and shaped for all time by these three major decisions regarding its name, motto, and vocation.

At least four circumstances made it difficult to sustain the early passion for church unity, however. First, throughout the 1960s and 1970s, pervasive social and political problems made discussion regarding denominational mergers difficult. Christians were hard pressed to expend energy and resources on ecumenical relationships while U.S. cities burned, its citizens were dying in Vietnam, and many of its masses were homeless and hungry. The attention of compassionate Christians turned from discussions of church unity to the tragedy and suffering afflicting so many Americans.

Second, Christians in other communions pursued their own objectives. A major goal of Methodists, for instance, was the reunion of previously separated members of that denominational family. The Evangelical United Brethren participation in the 1968 organization of the United Methodist Church completed a process begun in 1939 by the reunion of three branches of Methodist churches. The 1983 organization of the Presbyterian Church (USA) healed the Civil War rift between northern and southern Presbyterians. Unitarians and Universalists consolidated in 1961. Several major branches of Lutherans did likewise in 1988. The consequence of all this activity was that some of the UCC's most promising prospective partners, preoccupied with achieving their own purposes, had little interest in other institutional merger conversations except for the Consultation on Church Union.

Third, the UCC was itself absorbed with completing the union on which it had embarked in 1957. Many clergy and members were apprehensive even about conversations regarding additional mergers. The 1977–79 exploratory conversations between the United Church of Christ and the Christian Church (Disciples of Christ) are a case in point. Despite a rather lengthy history of negotiations, the joint working group reported to the 1979 synod that "the interest of congregations, regions/conferences, and national organizations [about merging the two denominations] . . . was mixed. Some were apathetic or indifferent, others expressed strong enthusiasm for continuing the conversations."[8]

Despite indications of uneasiness, the 1979 synod agreed to embark upon a six-year "covenant" of continued conversations. By 1985, however, negative feelings toward institutional merger had heightened. The steering committee on the Covenant Between the United Church of Christ and the Christian Church (Disciples of Christ) described the following opinions for the General Synod:

Fear of a hidden plan of union already in existence.

Apathy toward union.

The cost of corporate union and organizational change would be too high.

False stereotyping within each of the parties about the other.

Trauma left over from previous unions (UCC) and previous separations (Disciples).

Differing views and practices of ministry, the Lord's Supper and baptism.[9]

Nonetheless, the 1985 General Synod reasserted the original UCC ecumenical vision. It voted to continue church unity discussions with the Christian Church (Disciples of Christ), as well as with the Consultation on Church Union (refer to the appendixes) and other configurations.

Fourth, insufficient annual income caused the near collapse of ecumenical activity. Every president of the denomination, from Robert Moss to Paul Sherry, found it necessary to address the General Synods about dwindling financial resources. While the national setting share of Our Church's Wider Mission normally rose slightly during each biennium, it rarely kept even with inflation. Limited financial resources eventually meant insufficient staff support for church unity discussions, responses to ecumenical documents, or UCC Ecumenical Commission deliberations. Anxious about this situation, the 1973 General Synod adopted a resolution entitled "The Ecumenical Stance of the United Church of Christ." It contained a paragraph directing the Executive Council to give serious consideration to "appoint[ing] an administrative secretary [to] assist in the coordination of ecumenical participation by the United Church of Christ; gather data concerning ecumenical development; [and] assist the Commission on Christian Unity in fulfilling its constitutional requirements."[10] Nonetheless, it was not until 1991, eighteen years later, that agreement within the Council of Instrumentality Executives produced the needed budget allocations. The position of administrative secretary was then filled in early 1992.

210

Regardless of these and other difficulties, the UCC ecumenical commitment was being shaped annually by a broad spectrum of church unity discussions in which it was heavily involved. Gunnemann having described most of those activities up to 1986 in *United and Uniting,* additional discussion is not required here. Let it suffice simply to list some of the more notable ecumenical episodes:

•Adoption of a Covenant of Mission and Faith between the UCC and the Evangelical Church of the Union in Germany. The UCC journey toward this covenant dates back to a visit to Germany in 1960 by Professors Roger Hazelton and John Dillenberger. It was crowned when the 1981 General Synod adopted the covenant.[11]

•Creation of an ecumenical partnership between the UCC and the Christian Church (Disciples of Christ). Conversations about merging these denominations began before the formation of the UCC. The partnership was voted by the 1985 Synod as a continuing process of sharing life rather than an institutional merger.[12] One strong affirmation of this partnership is the merger of the United Church Board for World Ministries with the Disciples Division of World Ministries under a unified board of directors named the Common Global Ministries Board.

•Participation in the Consultation on Church Union.[13] The UCC was an original COCU member, and it provided significant early COCU leadership. The 1995 General Synod declared its willingness "to enter into a relationship of covenant communion with member churches of the Consultation on Church Union," and to begin the steps needed to be a Church in Covenant Communion.[14]

•Participation in the Lutheran–Reformed Dialogue which led to adoption of the resolution "Full Communion with the Evangelical Lutheran Church in America, the Presbyterian Church (USA) and the Reformed Church in America" by the 1997 General Synod.[15] (In the Covenant of Mission and Faith with the Evangelical Church of the Union, the ecumenical partnership with the Christian Church [Disciples of Christ], the Churches in Covenanted Communion of the Consultation on Church Union, and the Full Communion relationships with Reformed and Lutheran bodies, major new alternatives to merger are being explored that seem to have much wider approval and appeal. The patterns of "shared life" which those arrangements now test could become the most viable church unity prototype for the emerging millennium.)

•Membership in the World Alliance of Reformed Churches, the International Council of Congregational Churches, the World Council of Churches, and the National Council of Churches in the USA.

•The development of important UCC/Partner Church relationships with

211

churches around the world under policies and initiatives of the United Church Board for World Ministries after approval by the General Synod. At the end of four decades, the UCC ecumenical vision is as strong as it has ever been. Internal UCC volunteer structures, plus professional staff to support and develop ecumenical activity, have been strengthened immeasurably. The president continues to be "the official representative of the Church in ecumenical and interdenominational relations." Today, an assistant to the president for ecumenical concerns carries forward the mountain of day-to-day work required. A strong and effective Council for Ecumenism supplants earlier committees and commissions. And the budget for ecumenical activity is more clearly defined and committed.

GOVERNANCE AND POLITY

The essential contours of United Church of Christ governance and polity were shaped when the 1959 General Synod adopted the Constitution and By-Laws. Two years earlier, delegates and officers of the Uniting Synod had hoped something new and creative in ecclesial governance would eventually emanate from the union. In its "Message to the Churches," that synod declared:

> Now . . . two classical polities of Christian history have adjusted themselves to each other through union in such a way as to leave intact and effective the excellence of each. Differences in ecclesiastical procedure . . . are appointed their secondary place and divested of evil effect. . . . Our union brings forth treasures old and new. The old treasures we intend to conserve; we turn toward the new in limitless anticipation.[16]

Both major parties brought very different systems of church government to the union. One form of governance was congregational, the other presbyterian. (See Gunnemann's discussion in chapter 2, especially pages 42–44.) One of the smaller partners, the Calvin Synod of the Hungarian Reformed Church, also brought a special history of episcopal polity complete with a bishop. No one expected any of these three contrasting patterns to become the UCC norm. Instead, the early dream was that a completely original structure would eventually emerge. For that reason, every decade in UCC history has witnessed a search for a creative form of denominational governance.

In chapter 3, Gunnemann describes the first effort, the work of the 1965–69 Committee on Structure (pp. 79–81). A nationally known management consulting firm was employed, and a sizable budget expended. Yet the 1969 General Synod never adopted the report and recommendations of this blue

212

ribbon committee. It was doomed by strong, unanimous opposition from executives of national bodies. Each of the next two decades witnessed more limited discussions on restructure. Professional management consulting firms were utilized on each occasion, although with much smaller expenditures. In both instances, recommendations received negative responses and were never put in place.

Finally, in 1987, the Executive Council felt compelled to try again. It voted to appoint a special advisory commission on structure to guide the council's thinking about what to do. This action was taken because of (1) widespread dissatisfaction throughout the UCC over the failure of previous structure processes; (2) the continuing decline in the percentage of Our Church's Wider Mission Basic Support received by national entities; (3) significant disparities between the permanent fiscal resources available to the various national units; (4) an apparent proliferation of national bodies created for specific purposes; (5) ambiguity about the authority and power of the Office of the President and the Executive Council to coordinate and evaluate the work of national bodies; (6) divergent and unclear beliefs in the UCC about the nature and purpose of the church; and (7) lack of staff and fiscal resources to support the UCC ecumenical commitment.

Three important Executive Council decisions accompanied the appointment of the advisory commission. First, the commission could utilize only staff and resources internal to the UCC. Second, the broad spectrum of voting members on the commission would include chief executives from national bodies. Third, staff and budget for the commission would be provided by the budget of the General Synod. Only very limited supplementary resources would ever be assigned. Behind these prerequisites was a paucity of available funding, of course. The more compelling motivation by far, however, was history. In each prior restructure attempt, professional management consultants had insisted upon complete secrecy while recommendations were formulated. When the analyses concluded, the recommendations were unveiled in highly dramatic fashion, followed quickly by disastrous reactions from those whose life and work were affected. Armed with that experience, the Executive Council sought to create a different, more highly inclusive restructure process. The three stipulations guaranteed that the deliberations would be lengthy, but they proved critical to eventual success. Also critical was the work of the board of directors and staff of the UCBHM, which ferreted out the significant legal and ecclesiastical difficulties posed by restructure and led the way in resolving them. Gratified by the commission's discussions during the 1987–89 biennium, the Executive Council requested that the 1989 General Synod reestablish the commission as a General Synod Committee on Structure to endow the investigations with even greater status, authority, and credibility.

The committee's report, adopted by the 1995 General Synod, addressed two crucial interests. The first interest was theological. Clarity about ecclesiology (the nature and purpose of the church) and polity (theological, biblical, and historical foundations for church governance) was required before structure could be devised. In 1991 and 1992 the committee responded to these questions by producing two exceptional papers about the nature, purpose, and mission of the church: "United Church of Christ: An Ecclesiology" and "A Mission Framework for the General Synod Committee on Structure."[17] These papers provoked lively discussion within the committee, and indeed across the UCC, as Gunnemann had hoped in *United and Uniting*. They were never adopted in such a way as to become the definitive UCC theology, but they did forge the "foundational principles" for the committee's structural recommendations.

The second concern was obviously organizational. If the dreams of the founders were to be realized, the national setting of the UCC required significant restructuring. Notable changes in the UCC national organization voted by the 1985 General Synod include the following:

•A new Article III for the UCC Constitution, "Covenantal Relationships," that points toward broader horizons of mutually responsible relationships within an ecclesial structure, especially one committed to important autonomies. Covenant theology is not new, but this application of the concept launches the good ship UCC in waters only minimally charted.

•Four "covenanted ministries" that consolidate the work of nine national agencies: Office of General Ministries, plus Local Church Ministries, Justice and Witness Ministries, and Wider Church Ministries. A considerable structural contraction occurs, but, since former programs have largely been moved from one place to another, there has not been significant reduction of mandates and program expectations.

•Two additionally defined ministries for the national setting, affiliated ministries and associated ministries, that address special realities of the Pension Boards and the United Church Foundation.

•Two new bodies—the Collegium of Officers and the Mission Planning Council—to provide leadership for planning and implementing mission programming.

•A greatly expanded General Synod that, in addition to delegates from the conferences, will include as members for the first time the full director-

214

ates of Local Church Ministries, Justice and Witness Ministries, and Wider Church Ministries. The intention is to create a forum where all the major players in the national setting can participate in discussions about the UCC mission and design covenants needed to fulfill it.

•A compact design for officers of the UCC, with five new titles and assignments designated therefor: a general minister and president; an associate general minister to be the associate of the president and chief operating officer for the Office of General Ministries; and three executive ministers for the covenanted ministries other than the Office of General Ministries. All five are officers of the UCC elected by the General Synod. Each executive minister is also chief operating officer of a covenanted ministry who is elected to that post by its board of directors. The secretary and treasurer of the UCC will no longer be elected by the General Synod, their duties having been assigned to the Office of General Ministries.

By June 30, 1998, thirty-one of the thirty-seven Conferences, more than the two-thirds required, had ratified the constitutional amendments to implement the new structure. The 1999 General Synod will elect the persons and budget required to effect the restructure and move it to completion in 2001. The original hope for innovative UCC governance and polity will thus be thoroughly tested in the new millennium of Christian history.

One felicitous corollary to the discussions on structure was the decision by the 1989 General Synod to move the national offices of the UCC to Cleveland, Ohio. In prior years the UCC executive offices and those of other national agencies were housed in at least three New York City locations. Still other offices were located in Boston, Philadelphia, and St. Louis. The boards of directors of the United Church Board for Homeland Ministries and the United Church Board for World Ministries voted jointly to set aside substantial portions of their capital resources as security for UCC mortgages on property to house the national units in Cleveland. Each board also directly invested $2.65 million in the property. For persuasive reasons, however, the Pension Boards, the United Church Foundation, and a portion of the United Church Board for World Ministries continued to maintain offices at 475 Riverside Drive in New York City. The move from New York to Cleveland was completed in 1990. In 1998 the UCC constructed a hotel, the Radisson Inn at Gateway, on what had been the parking lot for this property. The inn, a franchise of the Radisson Hotels Corporation, is wholly owned by a corporation organized by the UCBHM which pledged the necessary securities to cover the loan for construction costs. A major reason for the decision to construct a hotel on UCC property is to contain costs for ongoing UCC meetings. The eventual dream is to fashion a UCC national church center, complete with offices for national bodies, a hotel, and an attractive worship center. Such a center could serve the church in a variety of important ways.

MISSION STRUCTURE AND PHILOSOPHY

Formation of the United Church of Christ joined two vigorous and distinguished histories of pursuing God's mission that reach back to Colonial America. Profound hopes about mission were expressed at the Uniting Synod. Co-President Fred Hoskins proclaimed this optimistic word:

> We are impatient to press forward to prosecute the mission of the Church. It is the mission of the Church to be a tool for a divine penetration of the world. The Church is under orders to confront and penetrate with the gospel of Jesus Christ every dimension of life. Overseas ministry, homeland witness, social action, religious education, evangelism, stewardship, divide the mission as you will, call the parts what you may, there still is but one mission for the Church. It is the mission which God endorsed by the resurrection, the same one upon which God sent Jesus Christ.[18]

Seeing the UCC as standing on twentieth-century frontiers of faith and mission, Purd Dietz declared:

> It is a tremendous mission which awaits us on America's new frontier. The United Church of Christ is confronted by fast-moving situations which call for unusual faith and daring. Our mission is with the souls of people—people caught up in the swift currents of modern life—people desperately in need of God. Our mission is to proclaim our Christian faith boldly and effectively, to make it relevant to mid-twentieth century Americans.[19]

In the years after those rousing words were spoken at the Uniting Synod, UCC mission activities experienced two pivotal transformations.

One transformation was structural. The UCC began with a mission system dominated by independent corporations which were granted complete authority to plan, control, and conduct God's mission *for* the church. Now, in its fourth decade, the General Synod has adopted a system in which the church itself is the mission vehicle, creating and utilizing entities it establishes and controls. The initial mission structure described in the 1959 UCC Constitution contained two species of national bodies: established instrumentalities and recognized instrumentalities. Article VIII *established* five councils: Higher Education, Institutional Benevolences, Social Action and Education, Church and Ministry, and Stewardship. An Office of Communication was also established. These six national bodies were expected "to discharge the responsibilities of the General Synod." The same article *recognized* the American Board of Commissioners for Foreign Missions "to plan and con-

216

duct programs of missions and service abroad"; and the Board for Home Missions of the United Church of Christ "to plan and conduct the homeland mission not otherwise assigned." This language suggests that the established instrumentalities, created by the General Synod, were charged with UCC national ecclesial responsibilities, and that the two recognized mission boards, autonomous corporations descended in large measure from nineteenth-century Congregational Christian voluntary societies, were given responsibility for conducting UCC participation in God's mission at home and abroad. Whether or not the initial intention was to separate UCC ecclesiastical and mission responsibilities, it wasn't long before the self-perception of both recognized and established instrumentalities was that they were all engaged substantially in mission. There was one highly important difference, however: between them the recognized mission boards possessed and controlled all the permanent fiscal assets the UCC and its predecessor bodies had accumulated for mission programs. With the exception of the Pension Boards and the United Church Foundation, other national bodies had only current income to utilize. This fact, more than any other, caused continual friction and became a major reason for the structural shifts that eventually came about.

Adoption of the report of the Committee on Structure by the 1995 General Synod launched the UCC in an unprecedented direction. Three distinct "mission" ministries were established, plus a sharply delineated "general" ministry. All four share equal footing. For the first time, each is incorporated so that it may legally possess and administer fiscal resources and enter into contractual agreements. As creatures of the UCC, these covenanted ministries are integral to it. In the 1995 structure report, organizational devices such as boards of directors for the covenanted ministries retain appropriate independence, but all four are in fact ministries of the United Church of Christ, rather than simply ministries related to it. That is accomplished with the consent of the participating instrumentalities. It is also consistent with a major principle in the *Missio Dei* Paper of the General Synod Committee on Structure: "It is no longer theologically appropriate to continue a dichotomy between ecclesiological and mission structure. All ecclesiological entities exist because of mission, and mission bodies need the nurture of the spiritual life, and the ordering of the Church as the body of Christ."[20]

This radical change was accomplished because the previous recognized mission boards, and especially the UCBHM, agreed, first, to redistribute their mandates and assets among the new covenanted ministries; and, second, to continue their historic identities by becoming the nuclei of the new corporations created to manage the covenanted ministries. Their remarkable allegiance to the UCC is demonstrated by their affirmative votes on both actions. The General Synod Committee on Structure hoped initially that the covenanted ministries would have equal fiscal resources available to them. That did not prove possible once program mandates were finally established, and existing finances followed the mandates to their new location. Nonetheless, it is a remarkable transition.

The other transformation relates to the nature and purpose of mission. Two elements are involved. In one of the elements, UCC ideas about *mission* are changed by a broadened concept about *ministry*. In the other, UCC mission styles change from *paternalism* to *partnership*.

The very names of the two recognized mission boards provide a clue to the conceptual change embedded in moving from the idea of mission to an expanded concept of ministry. At the Uniting Synod one board bore a historic label, the American Board of Commissioners for Foreign *Missions* (ABCFM), its name since 1810. The other was named the Board for Home *Missions* of the United Church of Christ. At the 1961 General Synod, they became, respectively, the United Church Board for World *Ministries* and the United Church Board for Homeland *Ministries*. The shift from the word "missions" to the word "ministries" may seem overly subtle and semantic, two aspects of a single task. On the other hand, for some Christians the word "ministry" is a more overarching concept than the idea of "missions," an expanded understanding about the scope of God's work in the world. That is the change to which the new title refers. The mission of God, "Missio Dei," about which the General Synod committee wrote so passionately, is ministry in the fullest and broadest sense.[21] It concerns every aspect of human life, secular as well as theological. The essence of this concept is contained in the memorable Statement of Mission adopted by the 1987 General Synod. The United Church of Christ is called:

to proclaim the Gospel of Jesus Christ in our suffering world;
to embody God's love for all people;
to hear and give voice to creation's cry for justice and peace;
to name and confront the powers of evil within and among us;
to repent our silence and complicity with the powers of chaos and
   death;
to join oppressed and troubled people in the struggle for liberation;
to work for justice, healing and wholeness of life;
to embrace the unity of Christ's church;
to discern and celebrate the present and coming reign of God.[22]

These are some dimensions of the transition from missions to ministries. It is a more consequential transformation than it may appear at first.

218

The transition from *paternalism* to *partnership* may be even more substantial. Church historian John von Rohr has a brief passage which provides a clue to this shift. He reports that, during the nineteenth century, the ABCFM conceptualized missions aimed at four distinct groups: (1) peoples of ancient civilizations; (2) peoples of primitive cultures; (3) peoples of ancient Christian churches; and (4) peoples of Islamic faith.[23] The very choice of descriptive words has paternalistic overtones. The goal among these four kinds of people was not only to save their souls from damnation, but to transform them into a North American version of the ideal Christian. ABCFM agents always knew best and always maintained control. When political colonialism died around the world during the 1960s and 1970s, newly independent nations determined for themselves what foreign missionaries could do. The situation had changed radically. Eventually the idea of partnerships as a viable methodology for ministry emerged. For more than twenty years the United Church Board for World Ministries, the successor to the ABCFM, has built partnerships with churches across the earth. In the new scheme, each partner brings knowledge, experience, and resources to the endeavors—the ministries—in which they engage together. Often, partners outside the United States offer impressive resources to the UCC, not just vice versa. That is a remarkable change from an era in which peoples of the world were UCC mission targets rather than partners with it in God's mission in the world.

The issue was similar in the homeland. Local churches, associations, and conferences sometimes felt alienated by the perception that the best UCC knowledge and expertise, as well as most of its financial resources, would be found only in its New York offices. The new UCC structure insists upon covenantal relationships between all the church's settings. Note the language of the new Article III in the UCC Constitution:

Within the United Church of Christ, the various expressions of the church relate to each other in a covenantal manner. Each expression of the church has responsibilities and rights in relation to the others, to the end that the whole church will seek God's will and be faithful to God's mission. Decisions are made in consultation and collaboration among the various parts of the structure. As members of the Body of Christ, each expression of the church is called to honor and respect the work and ministry of each other part. Each expression of the church listens, hears, and carefully considers the advice, counsel and requests of others. In this covenant, the various expressions of the United Church of Christ seek to walk together in all God's ways.

The concept and language of this article are not new in UCC history, but their constitutional garb gives them significantly higher prominence and expectation.

It should be apparent from this brief discussion that mission theology and governance have already undergone considerable reshaping. UCC participation in the Missio Dei will continue to be shaped as restructuring proceeds.

JUSTICE AND WITNESS ACTIVITIES

One defining characteristic of the United Church of Christ is its ecumenical vision. The other is its unwavering determination to pursue justice for all people. The roots of this devotion go far back in United States history, but the UCC has established its own version of the obligation. At the Uniting General Synod, Ray Gibbons, executive director of the Council for Christian Social Action, sketched the basic shape for the UCC social justice initiative. The frontier facing the UCC is human relationships, he declared. To conquer that frontier

the Church has the faith; it needs the answers. To secure the answers it must establish and support agencies of social action—church committees to consider the issues, discuss and speak up when the outcome really counts. With the courage to confront controversy, with access to information and guidance for cooperative action, church members can face the new frontiers in family, community, school, government and communication.[24]

The UCC justice and witness commitment was shaped further when the 1959 General Synod adopted "The Call to Christian Action in Society," recommended by the Council for Christian Social Action. The preamble to that call states the basic theological foundations for UCC justice and witness:

(1) God as revealed in Jesus Christ is the ruler of all human affairs— nations, social orders, institutions. To [God] belong our souls and bodies, our possessions and cultures, our churches and communities.

(2) God has made us to live together in community. Without love of neighbor there is no love of God. Without service to [people] there is no service to God. We live, we rise, we fall as members of one family under God.

(3) We confess the pride and greed which separate us from God and from each other. Before God we repent of our smugness and sloth, our absorption with self and neglect of neighbor. The judgment of God lies upon us and all our affairs.

(4) We rejoice in many signs of the power and grace of God. We are grateful that people everywhere are demanding recognition of their God-given worth and that barriers between races, classes and nations are being brought down. We are grateful that God is stirring [God's] people against injustice and oppression.[25]

220

Therein lies the key to understanding the militant UCC commitment to social justice and witness. Gibbons rightly discerned the frontier for the church as human relationships. Paragraph 2 of "The Call" declares unequivocally that without love of neighbor there can be no love of God.

From 1959 onward, each General Synod was challenged to expand the understanding of UCC people about the horizons and content of God's demand for human love. People who had never previously been envisioned as neighbors suddenly began to insist upon inclusion. For example, the 1963 General Synod met in Denver with cities still burning across the nation. The March on Washington and Martin Luther King Jr.'s "I Have a Dream" speech were less than two months away. Confronted by urgent demands from UCC African Americans, synod delegates responded to the racial crisis in the nation by establishing the Committee for Racial Justice Now, and approved the substance of its program. During the debate about appointing the committee, President Ben Herbster told the delegates:

Two years ago I stood before you when you committed unto me the responsibility of the office of the President and said, "I pledge to all of you that we shall not be content as long as there are any disadvantaged people. We shall work, pray and strive that all [people] shall have a decent chance at life." . . . To fulfill this determination we must constantly rely upon the strength which comes alone from God. In [God's] Spirit let us make our decision.[26]

The words of Gibbons and Herbster, "The Call," and the extraordinarily prophetic demands from its African American members launched the United Church of Christ upon a stirring, two-part future.

On one hand, the UCC would be driven to exemplify love for neighbor internally. Getting its own house in order, albeit sometimes with reluctance, synod after synod demanded that the entire UCC examine, and change, employment and membership practices. As a result, the UCC leads the way among U.S. denominations in insisting that the church itself must provide volunteer, ministerial, and other staff opportunities for women, persons of diverse racial and ethnic backgrounds, people with disabilities, and those of a gay/lesbian/bisexual/transgender orientation. The theological premise is simple: the church is not a community of those who are instantly compatible. Instead, the church of Jesus Christ is a community, ordained by God, where all God's children are loved as much as we love ourselves, if not more. The 1993 General Synod expanded upon this idea of community by adopting a pronouncement calling upon all settings of the United Church of Christ to make it a "Multiracial and Multicultural Church," so that it "embodies these diversities as gifts to the human family and rejoices in the variety of God's grace."[27] It is a doctrine of inclusion that permits no one to be finally excluded.

On the other hand, the UCC would continually urge the nation and the world to reconsider all barriers erected against human beings. United Church of Christ national entities have been unusually persistent in seeking social justice in the United States and throughout the world, even in relation to controversial and contentious questions. Sometimes these advocacy activities have caused loss of membership and income, but the denomination has been steadfast in its convictions about what is contained in God's requirements for love between people. Here are three examples among many of General Synod actions in response to human cries for justice:

• The 1973 General Synod formally commissioned a portion of its members to be pilgrims on a chartered flight from St. Louis to Coachella Valley, California, in support of farmworkers.

• Delegates and officers at the 1977 General Synod marched down Connecticut Avenue to the White House to protest the continued imprisonment of the Wilmington 10.

• At the 1987 General Synod all of the Hispanic delegates and visitors walked out of the synod and returned only after the synod confronted and adopted a far-reaching proposal for "The Hispanic Ministry of the United Church of Christ."

Similar experiences occur not just at synods, but during meetings throughout the UCC national setting.

This UCC characteristic is so crucial that the report of the 1995 General Synod Committee on Structure decided to recommend a covenanted ministries unit named Justice and Witness. There was protracted and sometimes passionate debate in the committee about whether to do that. Some members felt this commitment could be fulfilled by including a precise justice mandate in each of the covenanted ministries. Others believed a separate unit was required since everybody's duty eventually becomes no one's. In the end the committee and the 1995 General Synod were convinced that a distinct national body, focusing upon justice, would symbolize this heartbeat of UCC life, and be an appropriate means for pursuing it.

At the 1977 General Synod President Joseph Evans captured the significance of UCC justice and witness activities in these words:

I love the United Church of Christ because it has been bold in its witness—and will be bold again. I love it because it has been true to its calling to proclaim the Good News that every man and woman is the daughter or son of a loving God, each equal in rights to be enjoyed, each equally precious. I love this Church because it has fed the hungry; it has clothed the naked and housed the homeless in countless earthquakes, hurricanes, floods, wars and revolution; it has tried to strike off the fetters of the oppressed; it has stood for an orderly and just "Civil Body Politic." But I love this Church most of all because I believe that in our fellowship we understand, better than most, that the love of God in Christ cannot ever be fully expressed except in a just society.[28]

There is no stronger United Church of Christ passion than its commitment to justice—justice for every human being, justice even for society's most unwanted and despised. That rich, red blood flows in UCC veins everywhere.

The United Church of Christ is a Christian community that understands itself never to be finally shaped. It is always and forever *being* shaped. This chapter summarizes five major commitments to which the UCC has clung energetically throughout its life. Obviously, these brief words do not exhaust knowledge about the UCC story during the past twenty years. They may uncover the essence of this church, however, for this and generations yet unborn.

APPENDIXES

A CHRONOLOGY OF UNION STEPS

Informal Steps

1937   Informal conversations in St. Louis, involving among others Samuel Press of Eden Seminary (Evangelical and Reformed) and Truman Douglass of Pilgrim Congregational Church.

1938   Telegram from Samuel Press to Dr. Douglass at the sessions of the 1938 General Council of Congregational Christian Churches.

1940-41   Correspondence between George W. Richards and Douglas Horton.

Formal Steps

1941   Authorization by the General Council (E&R) for conversations between the Committee on Closer Relations with Other Churches and the Congregational Christian Commission on Interchurch Relations and Christian Unity.

1942   Endorsements for union negotiations given by General Council (E&R) and steps toward preparation of a Basis of Union.

1943-47   Preparation of eight drafts of the Basis of Union.

1947   General Synod (E&R) approved the Basis of Union and sent it to the synods for ratification. The General Council (CC) sent it to the conferences and associations for study and transmission to the local churches.

1948   General Council (CC) at Oberlin added a set of *Interpretations* to the Basis of Union, thus making it necessary for the General Synod (E&R) to vote again and once more secure approval from the synods.

1949   General Council (CC) met in February to vote on the *Basis of Union with Interpretations*, which had been ratified by 72.8 percent of churches voting.

General Synod (E&R) approved and sent the *Basis of Union with Interpretations* to the synods for ratification. Approval was given in May.

A lawsuit was filed in Brooklyn, New York by the Cadman Memorial Church and the Cadman Memorial Congregational Society to test the right of the General Council to unite the churches.

1950   The union was enjoined in January by court order.

The General Council (CC) appealed the injunction.

1952   The 1950 New York injunction was reversed by the Appellate Division of the New York Supreme Court.

The General Council (CC) at Claremont, California voted to continue union negotiations.

1953   The New York Court of Appeals removed the last legal barrier to union.

1954   Joint meetings of the General Council (E&R) and the Executive Committee (CC) began the work of consummating the union.

1957   Uniting General Synod was held in Cleveland, Ohio, and the union achieved on June 25.

BASIS OF UNION OF THE CONGREGATIONAL CHRISTIAN CHURCHES AND THE EVANGELICAL AND REFORMED CHURCH WITH THE INTERPRETATIONS

PREAMBLE

We, the regularly constituted representatives of the Congregational Christian Churches and of the Evangelical and Reformed Church, moved by the conviction that we are united in spirit and purpose and are in agreement on the substance of the Christian faith and the essential character of the Christian life;

Affirming our devotion to one God, the Father of our Lord Jesus Christ, and our membership in the holy catholic Church, which is greater than any single Church and than all the Churches together;

Believing that denominations exist not for themselves but as parts of that Church, within which each denomination is to live and labor and, if need be, die; and

Confronting the divisions and hostilities of our world, and hearing with a deepened sense of responsibility the prayer of our Lord "that they all may be one";

Do now declare ourselves to be one body, and do set forth the following articles of agreement as the basis of our life, fellowship, witness, and proclamation of the Gospel to all nations.

I. NAME

The name of the Church formed by this union shall be UNITED CHURCH OF CHRIST.[1]

This name expresses a fact: it stands for the accomplished union of two church bodies each of which has arisen from a similar union of two church

[1] If the name "United Church of Christ" seems presumptuous, it should be remembered that any good general name must seem so, since it would apply equally well to other groups. A name, however, quickly becomes a mere means of classification, and it is hoped that the world will soon come to know that the Churches uniting under this name do not pretend to be more than they actually are.

(The purpose of this and other footnotes in this instrument is purely explanatory. They are designed to throw light on the text, but are not part of the Basis of Union.)

bodies.[2] It also expresses a hope: that in time soon to come, by further union between this Church and other bodies, there shall arise a more inclusive United Church.

II. FAITH

The faith which unites us and to which we bear witness is that faith in God which the Scriptures of the Old and New Testaments set forth, which the ancient Church expressed in the ecumenical creeds, to which our own spiritual fathers gave utterance in the evangelical confessions of the Reformation, and which we are in duty bound to express in the words of our time as God Himself gives us light. In all our expressions of that faith we seek to preserve unity of heart and spirit with those who have gone before us as well as those who now labor with us.

In token of that faith we unite in the following confession[3], as embodying those things most surely believed and taught among us:

We believe in God the Father Almighty, Creator and Sustainer of heaven and earth and in Jesus Christ, His Son, our Lord and Saviour, who for us and our salvation lived and died and rose again and lives for evermore; and in the Holy Spirit, who takes of the things of Christ and shows them to us, renewing, comforting, and inspiring the souls of men.

We acknowledge one holy catholic Church, the innumerable company of those who, in every age and nation, are united by the Holy Spirit to God in Christ, are one body in Christ, and have communion with Him and with one another.

We acknowledge as part of this universal fellowship all throughout the world who profess this faith in Jesus Christ and follow Him as Lord and Saviour.

We hold the Church to be established for calling men to repentance and faith, for the public worship of God, for the confession of His name by word and deed, for the administration of the sacraments, for witnessing to the saving grace of God in Christ, for the upbuilding of the saints, and for the universal propagation of the Gospel; and in the power of the love of God in Christ we labor for the progress of knowledge, the promotion of justice, the reign of peace, and the realization of human brotherhood.

Depending, as did our fathers, upon the continued guidance of the Holy Spirit to lead us into all truth, we work and pray for the consummation of the

[2]A brief history of the two communions is planned for publication as soon as possible.
[3]This confession expresses the content and meaning of the faith held generally by the members of the two uniting communions. It is not to be considered a substitute for any confession of faith which may be used in any congregation today. Like the ampler statement called for in Article IV, Section F, it is designed to be a testimony, and not a test, of faith.

228

Kingdom of God; and we look with faith for the triumph of righteousness and for the life everlasting.

III. PRACTICE

A. The basic unit of organization of the United Church of Christ is the Congregation; that is, the local church.

B. The Congregations, through their ministers and through delegates elected from their membership, may organize Associations for fellowship, mutual encouragement, inspiration, and such other functions as may be desired.

C. The Congregations, through their ministers and through delegates elected from their membership, constitute Conferences for fellowship, counsel, and cooperation in all matters of common concern. The Conferences exist to make cooperation effective (a) among their Congregations and (b) between their Congregations and the General Synod, the Boards, commissions, agencies, and instrumentalities[4] of the Church.

D. The Conferences, through delegates elected by them from the membership and ministers of the Congregations located within their respective bounds, constitute the General Synod.

E. Officers, Boards, councils, commissions, committees, departments, agencies, and instrumentalities are responsible to the bodies that elect them.

F. The government of the United Church is exercised through Congregations, Associations, Conferences, and the General Synod in such wise that the autonomy of each is respected in its own sphere, each having its own rights and responsibilities. This Basis of Union defines those rights and responsibilities in principle and the constitution which will be drafted after the consummation of the union shall further define them but shall in no wise abridge the rights now enjoyed by Congregations.

G. Individual communicants have the right of appeal, complaint, or reference to their Congregations, Associations, Conferences, and ultimately to the General Synod. Ministers, Congregations, Associations, and Conferences have similar rights of appeal, complaint, or reference. Decisions rendered in consequence of such appeals, complaints, or references are advisory, not mandatory.

H. Each Congregation, Association, and Conference has the right of retaining or adopting its own charter, constitution, by-laws, and other regulations which it deems essential and proper to its own welfare. This right includes the holding and operation of its own property.

I. The freedom of worship and of education at present enjoyed by the

---

[4]The Basis of Union employs both the word "agencies" and "instrumentalities" in order to meet legal requirements.

Congregations of the negotiating communions will be preserved in the United Church. Other freedoms at present enjoyed are not hereby abridged.

J. Men and women enjoy the same rights and privileges in the United Church. It is recommended that at least one third of the members of the national administrative bodies be women.

K. Baptism and the Lord's Supper are the recognized sacraments of the Church.

IV. FUNCTIONS OF THE GENERAL SYNOD

A. The General Synod shall initiate action for the preparation of a constitution of the United Church. This constitution shall be based upon the principles set forth in this Basis of Union. When prepared, it shall be submitted to the General Synod; and the General Synod shall declare it in force when it shall have been ratified by not less than two thirds of the former Congregational Christian churches voting, and by not less than two thirds of the former Evangelical and Reformed Synods.

B. The General Synod shall elect its officers and assign them their duties.

C. The General Synod, directly or through an executive committee, commissions, and other committees, shall carry on the general work of the Church which is now conducted by the General Council of the Congregational Christian Churches and the General Synod of the Evangelical and Reformed Church; and through the instrumentality of Boards, commissions, and other organizations as needed, shall meet the responsibilities of the Church for foreign missions, home missions, education, publication, the ministry and ministerial relief, evangelism, stewardship, social action, and institutional benevolence.

D. The General Synod shall have power to receive overtures and petitions; to give counsel in regard to cases referred to it; and to maintain correspondence with other communions.

E. The General Synod shall promote the reorganization of Conferences, Associations, and Synods into Conferences and Associations which shall be constituted on a territorial basis and enjoy a status similar to that of the former Conferences, Associations, and Synods. This reorganization shall be effected by the Conferences, Associations, and Synods concerned, with the counsel and confirmation of the General Synod.[5]

F. If and when the Basis of Union is regularly adopted, the General Synod shall appoint a commission composed of an equal number of representatives of the two uniting communions to prepare a statement of faith based in principle

[5]It is expected that the Conferences and Synods will take the first steps necessary to this reorganization as soon as practicable after the consummation of the union, forming noncompetitive units without overlapping boundaries capable of continuing all the work carried on by the present Conferences and Synods, together with such other work as may prove to be desirable. The formation of Associations, as deemed advisable, would follow.

upon Article II of this document, which shall be submitted for approval to the General Synod, Conferences, Associations, and Congregations. This statement shall be regarded as a testimony, and not as a test, of faith.

G. The General Synod shall meet in regular sessions, determine their time, place, frequency, and program, and provide for extraordinary sessions as may be necessary.

H. The executive committee of the General Synod shall be called the Executive Council. Its functions shall correspond to those of the present Executive Committee of the Congregational Christian General Council and of the present General Council of the Evangelical and Reformed General Synod. While it shall not be charged with the administration of the Boards and other agencies and instrumentalities of the communion, it shall be its duty to consider their work, to prevent duplication of activities, to effect all possible economies of administration, to correlate the work of the several organizations, including their publicity and promotional activities, so as to secure the maximum of efficiency with the minimum of expense. It shall have the right to examine the annual budgets of the several national organizations and have access to their books and records. It shall make report of its actions to the General Synod at each stated meeting of that body and present to that Synod such recommendations as it may deem wise for the furtherance of the efficiency and economical administration of the several organizations. It shall study the relative needs of these organizations, including the Conferences, and recommend the apportionment percentages for the distribution of benevolent contributions.

I. For the interim between the effecting of the union and the adoption of the constitution, the membership of the Executive Council shall be twenty-four, with equal representation of the uniting communions.[6]

J. This Executive Council shall have a budget under its control, with income for it derived from the present sources of revenue of the General Council of the Evangelical and Reformed Church and the Executive Committee of the General Council of the Congregational Christian Churches. It shall carry out faithfully all obligations of both of these bodies and conserve as separate funds all funds of both bodies until otherwise provided.

K. There shall be a central receiving treasury for all funds contributed to the General Synod and all the national agencies and instrumentalities. Each Conference will decide whether its Congregations shall be encouraged to send their moneys for these organizations direct to the central treasury or through the Conference treasurers.

[6]Paragraphs describing arrangements for the interim between the consummation of the union and the adoption of the constitution, while constituting part of the Basis of Union, are [set off by rules] to distinguish them from the rest of the text.

L. No attempt will be made to set up a detailed plan for the solicitation, collection, and disbursement of missionary, benevolent, and administrative funds before the union is effected, but the General Synod shall be requested at its first meeting to appoint a special committee adequately representing all interests to deal with these matters and to report at a later date. In any plan it is understood:

1. That all property rights and trust funds shall be scrupulously protected as provided in Article IX, Sections A and C, of the Basis of Union.
2. That an adequate budgetary system will be established which will be voluntary in character on the part of the Congregations, Associations, Conferences, and Synods but in which due emphasis will be placed on the moral responsibility of all to support the general work of the Church.

M. Pending the report of the committee to be appointed by the General Synod and until new policies are adopted, present practices in apportionment allocations, per capita assignments, and kindred matters shall be maintained.

N. The choice of location of headquarters for the United Church of Christ shall be left until after the union is effected.

V. CONFERENCES, ASSOCIATIONS, AND SYNODS

Until, according to Article IV, Section E, it is otherwise determined, the Conferences, Associations, and Synods shall continue; and each shall conduct its business in its own way. Whatever action is submitted to them by the General Synod shall be disposed of in the same way as these bodies respectively disposed of such action by the General Council of the Congregational Christian Churches or the General Synod of the Evangelical and Reformed Church prior to the union.

VI. MINISTERS AND CONGREGATIONS

A. The ministers of the two communions shall be enrolled as ministers of the United Church. Candidates for the ministry, after the union, and until a standard method is provided by the constitution, shall have the same status, and be licensed or ordained as ministers by the Associations or Conferences and Synods in the same way, as before the union. The standard method shall provide for ordination by authorization of the Conference or Association and normally upon the call to a Congregation. Similarly the formal induction of a minister into his parish, which is recommended as normal procedure, shall be by authority of the Conference or Association at the request of the Congregation.

B. A minister of another denomination shall not be accepted by any body of the United Church in which ministerial standing is held without recommendation from the body to which he belongs; if, however, a denomination refuses to recommend a minister in good and regular standing, he may be accepted after proper examination by the Conference or Association in which his standing would be held.

C. The calling of a minister to a Congregation is a concern of the Church at large, represented in the Association or Conference, as well as of the minister and the Congregation. Ministers and churches desiring to maintain a system of pastoral placement in which the Conference or Association shall have little or no part, shall be free to do so; but the recommended standard of denominational procedure shall be one in which the minister, Congregation, and Conference or Association cooperate, the Conference or Association approving candidates, the Congregation extending and the minister accepting the call. The new communion will appeal to all Congregations not to call or dismiss their ministers, and to all ministers not to respond to calls or resign, until the Association or Conference shall have given approval. In all relationships between minister and local church or Congregation, the freedom of the minister and the autonomy of the church are presupposed.

VII. MEMBERS.

All persons who are members of either communion at the time of the union shall be members of the United Church. Men, women, and children shall be admitted into the fellowship of the United Church through baptism and profession of faith according to the custom and usage of each congregation prior to the union. When they shall have been admitted they shall be recognized as members of the United Church.

VIII. ORGANIZATION OF BOARDS

[This article has been ratified (subject to the adoption of the entire Basis of Union by the negotiating communions) by the Executive Committee of the Congregational Christian General Council, by the Evangelical and Reformed General Council, and severally by the governing authorities of all Boards, agencies, and instrumentalities involved.]

A. The Boards, commissions, and other agencies and instrumentalities shall proceed to correlate their work under the General Synod as rapidly as their charters, constitutions, property rights, the effectiveness of their program, and the laws of the State will permit. In the original personnel of the Boards, commissions, and other agencies and instrumentalities, when consolidated, due representation shall be given to each of the consolidating communions.

B. At each regular meeting of the General Synod each Board and commission shall submit for review a report of its operations during the time elapsed since the last regular meeting of the General Synod.

C. Except in the case of the Pension Board, the members of the Boards shall be nominated and elected by the General Synod. They shall be represented through corresponding members, with voice but without vote, in the General

233

Synod itself. They shall elect their own officers. The executive committees or other governing groups of the Boards shall have a sufficient number of members to provide for geographical distribution, representation of both of the uniting Churches (*see Section A above*), and the inclusion of persons qualified to render specific services, as for example in the field of investment, medicine, education, etc., as the Boards may require.

D. The American Board of Commissioners for Foreign Missions and the Board of International Missions shall be united under the name of the AMERICAN BOARD OF COMMISSIONERS FOR FOREIGN MISSIONS.[7]

1. The Board thus constituted shall from the time of the consummation of the union until the adoption of a constitutional plan of organization consist of two hundred and twenty-five members, one hundred and thirteen of whom shall be chosen from the Evangelical and Reformed Church and one hundred and twelve from the Congregational Christian Churches, all to be elected by the General Synod of the United Church. One third of these members shall be women.

2. This body is smaller than the present Congregational Christian Board and larger than the present Evangelical and Reformed Board. Through its members its work will be related to the Conferences and Congregations. The traveling expenses of members incurred in connection with meetings will be borne in part by the Board and in part by the members themselves. It is believed that the additional interest and effectiveness in promoting the program resulting from these large group meetings will immeasurably outweigh the cost involved in the proposed plan of organization.

3. On the adoption of a constitution and by-laws for the United Church, the term of office of all Board members elected under these provisions shall terminate on the date designated by the General Synod for their successors to take office under the permanent plan of organization of the Boards.

4. Among the duties of this Board shall be the following:
   a. To receive and consider the reports of the board of directors (*see Paragraph 5 following*) and the executive officers and to give them any necessary directives.
   b. To determine long-range policies to be adopted by the Board.
   c. To nominate and elect the general officers of the Board, the members of the board of directors, and the executive officers.
   d. To report fully to the General Synod of the United Church concerning operations and finances of the Board (*see Section B above*).

[7]It is the intention of the present American Board to amend its Charter and By-laws to conform to those of the Board of the United Church.

5. The Board shall elect forty-five members who, with five persons ex officio, shall serve as a board of directors. The members ex officio shall be the President and the two Vice-Presidents of the Board and the two highest administrative officers of the General Synod of the United Church.

E. The homeland Boards, agencies, and instrumentalities of the Congregational Christian Churches and of the Evangelical and Reformed Church, exclusive of the Pension Board and the agencies for social action, from the time of the consummation of the union until the adoption of a constitutional plan for their organization, shall function by means of a single corporate body. The name of this corporate body shall be the BOARD FOR HOME MISSIONS OF THE UNITED CHURCH OF CHRIST. In order to provide the appropriate corporate structure for this enlarged and consolidated work, the charter of The Board of Home Missions of the Congregational and Christian Churches shall be amended so that it may be used for this purpose.

CORPORATE MEMBERSHIP

1. There shall be two hundred and twenty-five corporate members of the Board for Home Missions of the United Church of Christ elected by the General Synod of the Church.[8]
2. These corporate members shall represent the United Church of Christ in the promotion and administration of the work of home missions. The term "home missions" as here used shall include the founding, support, and building of churches, education, educational institutions, publication, ministerial relief, evangelism, stewardship, institutional benevolence, and other home services.
3. They shall elect a board of directors as hereinafter provided.
4. They shall meet periodically, but at least annually, to review the proceedings of the board of directors, to study the status of the work of home missions, and to plan for its further development. In the interim between meetings they shall be alert to inform themselves as to the progress of the work and shall individually seek opportunity to bring the work to the attention of the Congregations and members of the United Church of Christ.
5. The corporate members shall give careful consideration to all recommendations from the General Synod or its Executive Council, and in the field of home missions, as defined above, shall have responsibility for determining matters of promotion, administration, and policy.
6. The terms of these corporate members shall be six years and they shall

[8]Note that this Board, in size and structure, parallels and complements the American Board of Commissioners for Foreign Missions (see Article VIII, Section D, Paragraph 1).

235

be elected in three classes of seventy-five each, one class being elected every second year at the regular biennial meeting of the General Synod of the United Church of Christ. At the first meeting of the General Synod of the United Church, the two hundred and twenty-five persons shall be divided into three classes of seventy-five each, one class designated to serve two years, one class designated to serve four years, and one class designated to serve six years; provided however that, on the adoption of a constitution and by-laws for the United Church, the term of office of all Board members elected under these provisions shall terminate on the date designated by the General Synod for their successors to take office under the permanent plan of organization of the Boards. This paragraph is subject to amendment if it is decided that the General Synod shall meet otherwise than biennially.

7. In order that there may be continuity of operation during the years of reorganization the first list of corporate members shall include persons who are members of the Boards, agencies, and instrumentalities of the two uniting bodies at the time the union is consummated, as follows:

Members of the Board of National Missions of the Evangelical and Reformed Church 14

Members of the Board of Christian Education and Publication of the Evangelical and Reformed Church 12

Members of the Commission on Evangelism of the Evangelical and Reformed Church 10

Members of the Board of Business Management of the Evangelical and Reformed Church 12

Members of the Commission on Benevolent Institutions of the Evangelical and Reformed Church (excepting the representatives appointed by the institutions) 4

Members of the Commission on Higher Education of the Evangelical and Reformed Church (excepting the Presidents of Colleges) 12

Forty-eight persons elected at large from the membership of the Evangelical and Reformed Church 48

Sub-total 112

The President, three Vice-Presidents and thirty-six other members of the Board of Directors of The Board of Home Missions of the Congregational and Christian Churches 40

Members of the Commission on Evangelism of the Congregational Christian Churches (excluding the four persons elected to the Commission by The Board of Home Missions) 12

Three persons designated by the association of Congregational
Christian Colleges 3
Fifty-eight persons elected at large from the membership of the
Congregational Christian Churches 58
                                                                                                       ———
        Sub-total 113
                                                                                                       ———
        TOTAL 225

8. The particular class to which each individual belongs will be indicated by
   the General Synod at the time of election.

BOARD OF DIRECTORS

9. The board of directors, as constituted at the time of union, shall consist
   of the Chairman and the two Vice-Chairmen of the Board for Home
   Missions of the United Church of Christ, the two highest administrative
   officers of the General Synod of the United Church of Christ, and
   forty-five members who shall be chosen from and elected by the corporate members of the Board for Home Missions. At least one third of
   those elected shall be women.
10. In order that all interests may be represented, the first board of directors
    shall be nominated by a joint committee composed of an equal number
    of persons to be designated in advance by the appropriate bodies of the
    two uniting communions.
11. Of the first board of directors, twenty-four shall be chosen from the
    Evangelical and Reformed Church and twenty-four from the Congrega-
    tional Christian Churches.
12. The board of directors shall immediately elect committees as follows:
    a. An executive committee composed of thirteen persons, among
       whom shall be the chairman of the board of directors and the chair-
       men of the divisional committees. At least four of this committee shall
       be women.
           This executive committee shall exercise such powers as are con-
       ferred upon it from time to time by the board of directors.
    b. An investment committee consisting of five members, including the
       Treasurer, at least three of whom shall be members of the board of
       directors, who shall have power to invest and reinvest the funds of
       the corporation, or trust funds held by them, and to select invest-
       ments and reinvestments of the said funds, and to change the in-

237

vestments of such funds, and such other powers as may be given them by the Board.

c. Such divisional committees[9] which specialize in the founding, support, and building of churches, education, educational institutions, publication, ministerial relief, evangelism, stewardship, institutional benevolence, and other home services, as the interests of the work require, who shall have such powers as may be given them by the directors.

d. Such other standing committees as the interests of the work require, who shall have such powers as may be given them by the directors.

[9]It is at present believed that the Board for Home Missions will require the following Divisions in order to care for all the interests involved:

Division of Christian Education—*continuing*
CC   Division of Christian Education
ER   Board of Christian Education and Publication (education and curricular editorial functions only)
ER   Commission on Higher Education
ER   College and Seminary interests
CC   College and Seminary interests
       Certain aspects of the higher education interests to be lodged with a College Seminary Council composed of representatives of the Division of Christian Education, the American Missionary Association Division, and of the Colleges and Seminaries.

Division of Ministerial Relief—*continuing*
ER   Relief functions of the Board of Pensions and Relief
CC   Division of Ministerial Relief

Division of Evangelism and Church Extension—*continuing*
CC   Church Extension Division
CC   Commission on Evangelism
ER   Board of National Missions
ER   Commission on Evangelism

American Missionary Association Division—*continuing*
CC   American Missionary Association Division

Division of Publication—*continuing*
CC   Pilgrim Press Division
ER   Board of Business Management
       The Division of Publication (*continuing the Pilgrim Press Division and the Board of Business Management*) will proceed forthwith to develop and recommend particularly to the board of directors of the Board for Home Missions a plan for consolidating and unifying the publication and merchandising interests of the United Church.

238

F. The Commission on Christian Social Action of the Evangelical and Reformed Church and the Council for Social Action of the Congregational Christian Churches shall be united under the name, the COUNCIL FOR CHRISTIAN SOCIAL ACTION.

MEMBERSHIP

1. From the time of the consummation of the union of the communions until the adoption of a constitutional plan of organization, there shall be twenty-four members of the Council for Christian Social Action elected by the General Synod of the United Church of Christ. Of the first members of the Council, twelve shall be chosen from the Evangelical and Reformed Church and twelve from the Congregational Christian Churches. The terms of these members shall be six years and they shall be elected in classes of eight each, one class being elected every second year at the regular biennial meeting of the General Synod of the United Church of Christ. At the first meeting of the General Synod of the United Church, the twenty-four persons shall be divided into three classes of eight each, one class designated to serve two years, one class designated to serve four years and one class designated to serve six years. On the adoption of a constitution and by-laws for the United Church, the term of office of all Council members elected under these provisions shall terminate on the date designated by the General Synod for their successors to take office under the permanent plan of organization. This paragraph is subject to amendment, if it is decided that the General Synod shall meet otherwise than biennially.

2. The Council for Christian Social Action may choose as advisory members, with voice but not vote, representatives of other Boards, agencies and conferences, and of the men's, women's and youth fellowships.

COMMITTEES

3. The Council for Christian Social Action shall immediately elect such standing committees as the interests of the work require. They shall have such powers as shall be given to them by the Council.

FUNCTIONS

4. The Council for Christian Social Action shall be an agency under the General Synod of the United Church of Christ, and shall have power to take over, unify, and operate the activities carried on by the Council for Social Action of the Congregational Christian Churches and the Commission on Christian Social Action of the Evangelical and Reformed Church.

239

STAFF

5. The Director and other staff members shall be elected by the Council for Christian Social Action.

‎‎G. The pension activities of the United Church shall be administered by one corporation, the name of which shall be left for later decision by mutual agreement. It is here referred to as the MERGED FUND.

1. Provision shall be made in the by-laws of the Merged Fund whereby the General Synod of the United Church shall from time to time make examinations of the practices and developments of the Merged Fund.
2. The Trustees shall be chosen from eligible persons whose names have been presented to and approved by the General Synod of the United Church.
3. The Merged Fund shall be a non-profit membership corporation in which control lies in the members of the Fund through a Board of Trustees, elected by the members. Congregations and other employing agencies shall be included as participating members.
4. The maximum annuity[10] provided by the Pension Fund of the Evangelical Synod, the Sustentation Fund of the Reformed Church, and the Original Plan of the Annuity Fund for Congregational Ministers (hereafter referred to in this statement as the three "original plans") shall be in each case $500.00.
5. The liability of the Merged Fund to the members of the three "original plans" shall be set up on the books of the new corporation for the funded portion of their respective annuities only.
6. Sufficient money shall be designated in advance by the United Church as a prior claim upon apportionment to meet the indicated annual requirements for the unfunded portion of the annuities under all three "original plans" and to make cumulative provision for their funding.
7. This prior claim upon the apportionment[11] shall be for not less than

[10]By "maximum annuity" is meant the annuity paid to a member who has completed the full term of service or membership defined by the rules of the fund to which he belongs. The annuity of a member who has completed less than the full term of service or membership is a percentage of the maximum, stipulated by the rules of the fund in question. The annuity of the widow of a member of any of the "original plans" shall be 60% of the annuity to which her husband would be entitled.

[11]In 1945 the amounts received from the apportionment of the two denominations for similar purposes were as follows:

From the Evangelical and Reformed Churches	$210,741
From the Congregational Christian Churches	117,025
Total	$327,766

This amount does not include $176,846 contributed by the Congregational Christian Churches through the Unit Plan.

240

$500,000 in each year in which the apportionment giving of the United Church for the year immediately preceding equals or exceeds $3,300,000. The prior claim may be proportionately reduced in any year in which the apportionment giving for the preceding year is less than $3,300,000, but the prior claim shall in no case be for less than an amount sufficient to meet the requirements of the year in question for the unfunded portion of the annuities under all three "original plans" plus the necessary expense of promotion and administration. The prior claim upon the apportionment shall continue until the total liabilities of the three "original plans" are completely funded.[12]

8. Liability for payment of the unfunded portion of "original plan" annuities in any year shall be limited to the money received as applicable to such unfunded portion. In the event that in any year there shall not be sufficient money to pay the annuities which the denomination has designated, the legal liability of the Merged Fund shall be completely satisfied and fulfilled when such applicable money as is available has been disbursed to the "original plan" annuitants.

9. The assets and liabilities in the Merged Fund pertaining to members of the Ministers' Retirement Annuity Fund of the Evangelical and Reformed Church and of the Expanded Plan of the Annuity Fund for Congregational Ministers shall be consolidated as completely as legal requirements and considerations of equity permit.

10. Ministers enrolling in the Merged Fund other than those who are members of one of the present plans at the time of the union, shall be received under a new form of certificate.

11. The assets received by the Merged Fund from the present funds shall all be pooled into a common unit of investment and, together with investment of future receipts, shall be collectively available from time to time to meet the liabilities of the various Departments of the Merged Fund. No particular assets shall be segregated against the balance in any particular fund, except for conditional gift accounts and other accounts which may be required to be segregated by law.

PILGRIM MEMORIAL FUND INCOME

12. In the operation of the Merged Fund the Pilgrim Memorial Fund[13] In-

[12]It is estimated that the time required to fund the "Original Plan" annuities upon the above basis will be approximately thirty years.

[13]The Pilgrim Memorial Fund, consisting of about $5,500,000, is an endowment fund held for the benefit of The Annuity Fund for Congregational Ministers, the income of which is at present used for the administrative expenses of the Annuity Fund and the benefit of its members.

come received in any year shall be allocated in the succeeding year in the following manner:

a. A specific sum determined before the merger shall be allocated to the Original Plan of the Annuity Fund.

b. A further specific sum determined before the merger shall be allocated to the Merged Fund to meet the expenses incurred in the operation of the Original Plan of the Annuity Fund.

c. An amount determined from year to year shall be allocated to the Merged Fund to meet the expenses incurred on account of Congregational Christian members of the consolidated "expanded plan."

d. Such an amount shall be allocated for the benefit of the members of the Expanded Plan of the Annuity Fund as shall provide $45 for each unit sharer among the members of such Expanded Plan, according to the rules of the Annuity Fund, or as nearly this amount as can be provided after allocations a, b, and c have been made.

e. Any balance after the above four allocations shall be used for the strengthening of the whole Merged Fund, or in such manner as the Trustees believe most beneficial for the benefit of ministerial members of the Merged Fund and their families who do not fall within the four following categories:

I. Congregational Original Plan members

II. Evangelical Pension Fund members

III. Reformed Sustentation Fund members

IV. Congregational Christian Expanded Plan members

f. If allocations under heading e shall exceed $45.00 per member, members under heading d shall be entitled to further allocation.

13. The pension boards of the two denominations shall give careful attention to the continuance and extension of a plan to provide retirement income for lay workers of the churches and other organizations of the United Church.

IX. LEGAL OBLIGATIONS

A. The property rights of all bodies such as Congregations, Associations, Conferences, Synods, and corporations shall be scrupulously observed.

B. The theological seminaries, colleges, academies, denominational boards, benevolent institutions, and other corporations shall be controlled under the terms of their respective charters and other governing documents. Those institutions, however, which were under the supervision of the national bodies of the uniting communions shall, at least until the constitution is adopted, pass under the supervision of the General Synod. While they are under the supervision of the General Synod, the interests of the previously supervising groups shall be properly recognized.

C. Due protection shall be given all trust funds, including pension funds.

242

X. APPROVAL AND IMPLEMENTATION OF THE BASIS OF UNION

A. The Basis of Union shall be submitted to the General Council of the Congregational Christian Churches and the General Synod of the Evangelical and Reformed Church. Each shall proceed according to its own polity in the approval or disapproval of the Basis of Union. When the Basis has been approved by the regular action of the two bodies, each shall designate an equal number of its membership, approximately three hundred, with power to represent it at a joint meeting which shall constitute the first meeting of the General Synod of the United Church of Christ.

B. The joint meeting being duly called and assembled, to it the final report of the action of the communions upon the Basis of Union shall be made; and by joint resolution it shall be declared that the union of the communions is effected at that time, the General Synod of the United Church of Christ being the successor to the General Council of the Congregational Christian Churches and the General Synod of the Evangelical and Reformed Church, the joint meeting becoming the first meeting of the General Synod of the United Church. Then the delegates shall be led in a constituting prayer, effect an organization by the election of officers, and proceed to the transaction of business. From the time of the organization of the General Synod of the United Church until a constitution of the United Church has been adopted, this Basis of Union shall regulate the business and affairs of the United Church.

C. At the joint session referred to in the foregoing paragraph when the Union shall be formally effected, such action shall be taken as will unite the General Council of the Congregational Christian Churches and the General Synod of the Evangelical and Reformed Church: the further union of Conferences, Associations, Synods, and other bodies within the uniting communions shall proceed with the approval of the groups concerned, according to the principles laid down in this Basis of Union.

D. The General Synod of the United Church of Christ at its first meeting shall also take any and all appropriate steps necessary to insure the continuity and to effect the consolidation of the Boards, commissions, and other agencies and instrumentalities as described in Article IV, Section C, and to make effective an interim plan for their consolidation and operation, as more explicitly set forth in Article VIII.

E. The General Synod at its first meeting shall be made up of representatives elected as set forth in Article X, Section A; but at subsequent meetings, until a constitution shall have been adopted, the General Synod shall be composed of delegates elected by the present Conferences and Synods, or their successors, one delegate representing each three thousand communicants or major fraction thereof, so that the total number will be about six hundred.

F. Upon the consummation of the union the general officers of the former

243

Congregational Christian General Council and the former Evangelical and Reformed General Synod not connected with the Boards shall become the staff of the General Synod of the United Church of Christ until other arrangements are perfected by the General Synod.

G. Revisions and amendments of the constitution shall be made by the General Synod and ratified by the Conferences in collaboration with the Associations and Congregations.

XI. REVISIONS AND AMENDMENTS

Revisions and amendments of the Basis of Union while it is in force before the adoption of a constitution may be made by consent of ninety per cent of the members of the General Synod of the United Church of Christ duly assembled.

THE INTERPRETATIONS OF THE BASIS OF UNION

(a) The Basis of Union calls for a union of the General Council of Congregational Christian Churches and the General Synod of the Evangelical and Reformed Church to form the General Synod of the United Church of Christ.

(b) The constitution for the United Church of Christ provided for in Article IV-A of the Basis of Union: (1) will not come into force until it has been ratified by two-thirds of our churches voting; (2) is to be based on the principles set forth in the Basis of Union; (3) is in no wise to abridge the rights now enjoyed by the churches; (4) will define and regulate as regards the General Synod but describe the free and voluntary relationships which the churches, associations, and conferences shall sustain with the General Synod and with each other.

(c) The Basis of Union calls for a union of the Boards of Home Missions, the Boards of Foreign Missions, the Annuity Boards, the Councils for Social Action, and similarly all related Boards, commissions, agencies, and instrumentalities of the two denominations.

(d) Churches, associations, conferences and the General Synod, being self-governing fellowships, possess autonomy in their own spheres, which autonomy is acknowledged and will be respected.

(e) Synods, conferences, associations and churches are to retain their present status until they are united by their own action and when mutually agreeable.

(f) Congregational Christian churches do not go out of existence at the time of the union of the two communions. In consummating this union the Congregational Christian Churches and the Evangelical and Reformed Church are uniting without break in their respective historic continuities.

(g) The United Church of Christ will be a union of two denominations joined in fellowship and cooperation without involving any invasion of the rights now enjoyed by local churches or congregations.

244

(h) With the constituting of the General Synod of the United Church of Christ, the General Council of the Congregational Christian Churches [and the General Synod of the Evangelical and Reformed Church] will remain in existence in order to fulfil necessary legal functions, but shall transfer to the General Synod all of its functions which do not for legal reasons need to be retained.

COMMISSION TO PREPARE A CONSTITUTION

Congregational Christian
Mrs. Howard Stone Anderson
Mrs. Edgar A. Bark
John T. Beach—Vice Chairman
Ashby E. Bladen
William C. Dixon
Mrs. Judson E. Fiebiger
Roscoe W. Graves
Arthur D. Gray
George Hastings
William Maltbie
Frederick M. Meek
Henry E. Robinson
Frank J. Scribner
Hugh Vernon White
Richard A. Wolff

Evangelical and Reformed
Mrs. Guy A. Benchoff
*Mrs. E. Roy Corman
Louis H. Goebel
Gerhard W. Grauer—Chairman
Donald L. Helfferich
Ben M. Herbster
Mrs. Ralph Legeman
John G. Mueller
John W. Mueller
Arthur W. Newell
Paul R. Pontius
Ernst Press
Paul J. Schlueter
Mrs. Henderson L. V. Shinn
Daniel J. Snyder, Jr.
*Alternate for Mrs. Benchoff

COMMISSION TO PREPARE A STATEMENT OF FAITH

Congregational Christian
John C. Bennett
Mrs. W. Bayard Buckham
Loring DuBois Chase
Nels F. S. Ferre
Laurance K. Hall
Roger Hazelton
Douglas Horton—Vice Chairman
Walter M. Horton
Mary Ely Lyman
Edward F. Manthei
Richard R. Niebuhr
Oliver Powell
Helen Huntington Smith
Daniel D. Williams

Evangelical and Reformed
Elmer J. F. Arndt—Chairman
Edward W. Brueseke
Bernice A. Buehler
Alfred L. Creager
Louis H. Gunnemann
Robert G. Herrmann
Frederick L. Herzog
Beatrice Weaver McConnell
Allen O. Miller
Robert V. Moss, Jr.
John L. Schmidt
Roger L. Shinn
Morris D. Slifer
Bela Vassady

N.B. These lists are from the Second General Synod minutes, 1959.

NOTES

INTRODUCTION

1. Represented among the fraternal delegates were five overseas church bodies from Europe and Asia; three international interchurch bodies, including the World Council of Churches; and nineteen American denominations. Certified voting delegates from the two uniting bodies numbered 714.

2. "A Message to the Churches," *The Messenger*, July 30, 1957.

3. Reinhold Niebuhr, "A Landmark in American Religious History," *The Messenger*, June 18, 1957, pp. 11-23.

4. *The Christian Century*, July 17, 1957, p. 863.

5. *Minutes*, Uniting General Synod, June 25-27, 1957, pp. 81-82.

6. Ibid., pp. 86-89.

7. Robert Lee, *The Social Sources of Church Unity* (Nashville: Abingdon Press, 1960), p. 100.

8. Cf. Gibson Winter, *Religious Identity* (New York: Macmillan, 1968), and Paul Harrison, *Authority and Power in the Free Church Tradition* (Princeton: Princeton University Press, 1959).

9. H. Richard Niebuhr, *The Social Sources of Denominationalism* (New York: Henry Holt, 1929; Meridian, 1959), p. 21.

CHAPTER 1 TOWARD UNION: BEGINNINGS

1. *Minutes*, Uniting General Synod, June 25-27, 1957, p. 58.

2. Ibid., p. 10.

3. H. Paul Douglass, *Church Unity Movements in the United States* (New York: Institute for Social and Religious Research, 1934), p. 465.

4. Truman B. Douglass, *The Messenger*, June 18, 1957, p. 4. The original letter to Samuel Press is on file in the Evangelical and Reformed Archives at Eden Theological Seminary, Webster Groves, Missouri. Additional correspondence of Truman B. Douglass interpreting the event is in the George Arents Research Library, Syracuse University, Syracuse, New York.

5. *United Church Herald*, July 1965, p. 21.

6. Pres. George W. Richards reported to the Evangelical and Reformed General Council in January 1941 receipt of a letter from Douglas Horton

suggesting the exploration of union possibilities between the two denominations. In response the General Council authorized the Committee on Closer Relations with Other Churches to meet with the Congregational Christian Commission on Interchurch Relations and Christian Unity (CIRCU). Cf. *Minutes*, General Council (E&R), January 14-15, 1941.

7. Preliminary meetings of the two commissions were held March 18, 1941 and October 13, 1941 to draw up concurrent recommendations for the national bodies.

8. In this connection the works of Perry Miller, Alan Heimert, Edmund S. Morgan, Richard Bushman, and many others are important resources.

9. Thomas A. Tripp, "The United Church in America," *Advance*, May 1944, pp. 20-21.

10. Reinhold Niebuhr, "A Landmark in American Religious History," *The Messenger*, June 18, 1957, p. 12.

11. Thomas A. Tripp showed that "Evangelical and Reformed churches are practically four times more efficient in enlisting members under thirteen years of age than are Congregational Christian churches. Their practice of instructing and confirming children accounts for much of this favorable balance for the former group. It is probable that Evangelical and Reformed Churches have maintained family group participation to a stronger degree than Congregational Christian Churches." Tripp, op. cit., p. 22.

12. *The Messenger*, March 16, 1943, p. 4.

13. Amos N. Wilder, *Advance*, January 1938, p. 7.

14. Between meetings in late 1942 and June of 1943 the CIRCU inquired of several other church bodies concerning their possible interest in joining the union effort. Cf. *Minutes*, CIRCU, June 21-23, 1943.

15. Joint Meeting of the Committees on Union of the Congregational Christian Churches and the Evangelical and Reformed Church, September 28-October 1, 1942.

16. Joint Meeting of the Superintendents of the Congregational Christian Churches and Presidents of the Synods of the Evangelical and Reformed Church, Cleveland, Ohio, January 27, 1944.

17. Louis W. Goebel files, 55 (1), folder 48-6. Archives, Eden Theological Seminary Library, Webster Groves, Missouri.

18. *Minutes*, General Council Executive Committee, January 1946, p. 33.

19. "A Communication to the Synods," February 5, 1948, in the Louis W. Goebel files, op. cit.

20. Louis W. Goebel files, op. cit. (Italics added for emphasis.)

21. James E. Wagner, *The Messenger*, July 10, 1945, p. 7.

22. Although there are many discussions of this, see John A. Mackay, *God's Order: The Ephesian Letter and This Present Time* (New York: Macmillan, 1953), pp. 128-55, for an extended biblical interpretation of order.

23. Special characteristics arising from the histories of the two church bodies are discussed in later chapters, particularly with reference to both common rootage and divergent development.

24. See John Scotford in *Advance*, August 1948, p. 27, and the comments of Douglas Horton as reported by opposition groups. See *Merger Materials*, Congregational Library, Boston.

25. *Minutes*, General Council (E&R), September 30-October 2, 1948. (Italics added for emphasis.)

26. Louis W. Goebel files, op. cit.

27. George Warren Richards, *History of the Theological Seminary of the Evangelical and Reformed Church at Lancaster, Pennsylvania* (Lancaster: Theological Seminary of the Evangelical and Reformed Church, 1952), p. 294.

28. *Merger Materials*, op. cit.

29. *Advance*, January 1949, p. 1.

CHAPTER 2 TOWARD UNION: FACING THE ISSUES

1. The assumption here is that the development of a purposive national organization (a denomination), which dates from 1913, was preceded by events that heightened the national consciousness of the fellowship, the first being the Albany meeting in 1852. In a later chapter this development is described in greater detail.

2. The case was known as Cadman vs. Kenyon, since the suit was undertaken by the Cadman Memorial Congregational Society and the Cadman Memorial Congregational Church of Brooklyn, New York, against the General Council of the Congregational Christian Churches, Helen Kenyon, moderator.

3. *Minutes*, National Council of Congregational Churches, 1913.

4. See *Minutes*, General Council (CC), 1950, pp. 66-67, the address titled "Of Equability and Perseverance in Well-Doing."

5. Douglas Horton, *Congregationalism: A Study in Church Polity* (London: Independent Press, 1952), pp. 33-34.

6. Ibid., p. 42.

7. *Acts and Proceedings*, General Synod (E&R), 1950, pp. 29-34.

8. The appeal process meant a moratorium on all talks with Evangelical and Reformed leaders. Since the appeal could not be heard by the Appellate Division until January 14, 1952, the Executive Committee had considerable time to work at "in house" matters.

9. *Minutes*, General Council (CC), 1950, p. 19.

10. The Appellate Division of the New York courts had overturned the lower court's findings upon appeal by the General Council's Executive Committee, April 14, 1952. Anti-union forces immediately filed notice of appeal to the Court of Appeals (New York's Supreme Court); hence the December 3, 1953 finding.

11. This discussion of authority and power draws upon the exceptionally

important interpretation of such issues by Paul Harrison in his book *Authority and Power in the Free Church Tradition* (Princeton: Princeton University Press, 1959), especially chapters IV and V.

12. Established by action of the 1913 National (General) Council. See Chas. C. Merrill, *The Fulfillment of Congregationalism*, Southworth Lectures, 1951, Andover Theological Seminary, for a full discussion of the development of the council.

13. A full discussion of the *denominational* development of the Congregational Christian Churches is given in chapter 6.

14. Carl E. Schneider, "Journey into Union" in *A History of the Evangelical and Reformed Church*, ed., David Dunn (Philadelphia: Christian Education Press, 1961), p. 290.

15. Cf. James E. Wagner, "The New Witness," ibid., pp. 296 ff.

16. *Minutes*, General Council (CC), 1952, p. 22.

17. *Acts and Proceedings*, General Synod (E&R), 1950, p. 315.

18. L. Wendell Fifield, "An Open Letter," *Advance*, January 1955, pp. 22-24.

19. James E. Wagner, *The Messenger*, December 29, 1953.

20. *Minutes*, Joint Meeting of the Administrative Committee (E&R) and the Advisory Committee of the Executive Committee of the General Council (CC), February 9, 1954, Cleveland, Ohio, in *Merger Materials*, Congregational Library, Boston.

21. *Merger Materials*, op. cit.

22. *Minutes*, General Council (E&R), February 16-18, 1954, pp. 17-18.

23. *Minutes*, General Council (CC), June 23-30, 1954, pp. 21-22.

24. *Minutes*, Joint Meeting of the General Council (E&R) and the Executive Committee of the General Council (CC), October 12-13, 1954, p. 2.

25. Statement attached to the *Minutes*, Joint Meeting, October 12-13, 1954.

26. Ibid., p. 9.

27. Ibid., p. 5. (Italics not in the original but provided here for emphasis.)

28. Raymond Walker, "Report and Reflections Concerning the Joint Meeting," October 12-13, 1954, *Merger Materials*, op. cit.

29. This is evident in all the literature distributed by anti-union groups. It is particularly striking in *Destiny for Congregationalism* by Malcolm K. Burton, one of the most committed and vocal opponents of the union (Oklahoma City: Modern Publishers, 1953), which treats the issues in purely secular terms.

30. James M. Gustafson, *A Study in the Problem of Authority in Congregational Church Order*. Unpublished paper in the *Merger Materials*, op. cit., no date.

31. James E. Wagner, *Looking Forward to the United Church of Christ*, April 1955 (pamphlet).

32. *Minutes*, General Council (CC), 1956, p. 36. *Acts and Proceedings*, General Synod (E&R), 1956, p. 164.

33. *Minutes*, General Council (CC), 1956, Appendix G, pp. 89-90.

34. *Acts and Proceedings*, General Synod (E&R), 1956, pp. 164-65.

35. A *Complaint* was filed on behalf of four churches in the Midwest and a number of individual members of other Congregational Christian churches in the early part of 1957. The *Complaint* was dismissed by the court, March 28, 1958.

36. *Minutes*, Uniting General Synod, June 25-27, 1957, p. 47.

37. Ruth Rouse and Stephen C. Neill, eds., *A History of the Ecumenical Movement, 1517-1948* (2d ed.; Philadelphia: Westminster Press, 1967), p. 490.

CHAPTER 3   CONSUMMATION AND FORMATION

1. The phrase "actualizing a church union" is part of the title of an essay by James M. Gustafson concerning the United Church of Christ in *Institutionalism and Church Unity*, ed. Nils Ehrenstrom and Walter G. Muelder (New York: Association Press, 1963), p. 325. This perceptive essay gives important detail concerning the issues of institutionalization in church union.

2. Sydney E. Ahlstrom, *A Religious History of the American People* (New Haven: Yale University Press, 1972), p. 1080.

3. Gustafson, op. cit., p. 332.

4. Mary D. Fiebiger, "General Synod Sets Timetable for Action on Constitution," *United Church Herald*, August 6, 1959, p. 10.

5. See *The Yearbook for American Churches*, 1959 and 1963, showing figures for 1956 and 1960 respectively.

6. The formation of the United Student Fellowship in 1949 is sometimes cited as the first organizational development of the United Church of Christ. However, since it preceded the union by eight years, it was not a fruit of the union but a sign of things to come.

7. Combining the Evangelical and Reformed *Messenger* and the Congregational Christian *Advance*, the *United Church Herald* (hereafter cited as *Herald*) was the product of a Joint Publication Committee—an interim cooperative arrangement between the Pilgrim Press Division of the Congregational Christian Board for Home Missions and the General Council of the Evangelical and Reformed Church. Co-editors Theodore C. Braun and Andrew Vance Mc-Crackon had previously edited *The Messenger* and *Advance*, respectively.

8. *Herald*, October 9, 1958, pp. 2-3.

9. Ibid., p. 2. (Italics added for emphasis.)

10. *Herald*, March 31, 1960, pp. 4 ff.

11. Evangelical and Reformed readers of the *Herald* numbered 110,000 in 1959, while 40,000 Congregational Christians were on the subscription list,

reflecting again the somewhat disparate understandings of the meaning of the denomination as a church that prevailed in the two bodies.

12. *Minutes*, Second General Synod, July 5-9, 1959, Oberlin, Ohio, p. 32.

13. Robert W. Spike, *Herald*, August 18, 1960, p. 22. (Italics added for emphasis.)

14. *Minutes*, Adjourned Meeting of the Second General Synod, July 6-8, 1960, pp. 75-78. (Italics added for emphasis.)

15. Douglas Horton, *The United Church of Christ* (New York: Thomas Nelson & Sons, 1962), p. 22. Dr. Horton's book, written out of his experience in helping bring the United Church into being, is a rhapsodic and stirring interpretation of the new constitution as he saw it upon its completion. It deserves wider attention than it has received in the United Church fellowship.

16. Cf. Oliver Powell, "Homeland Mission Reviewed and United Agency Proposed," *Herald*, August 6, 1959, pp. 16 ff.

17. Harold E. Fey, "United Church Uniting," *The Christian Century*, July 22, 1959, p. 845.

18. Spike, op. cit.

19. *Minutes*, Adjourned Meeting of the Second General Synod, p. 86.

20. *Herald*, June 23, 1960, p. 31.

21. *Herald*, February 4, 1960, p. 31.

22. *Herald*, September 3, 1959, pp. 8-9.

23. Interpretive articles by Loring D. Chase and Elmer J.F. Arndt concerning the Statement of Faith appeared in the *Herald*, March 26, 1959 and October 29, 1959.

24. *Minutes*, Adjourned Meeting of the Second General Synod, p. 86.

25. *Minutes*, Second General Synod, p. 171.

26. Letter from William L. Rest, "To the Members of the North Illinois Synod," dated March 8, 1961 and mailed to all Evangelical and Reformed ministers and certain leaders of the CC churches, in the *Anti-merger Materials*, Archives, Eden Seminary Library, 48-6, Me 46 (2).

27. *Minutes*, Third General Synod, July 3-7, 1961, p. 240.

28. An interpretation of the distinctive character of the new organization is given in chapter 4.

29. Kyle Haselden, "Confirming Unity," *The Christian Century*, July 19, 1961, p. 871.

30. *Minutes*, Third General Synod, p. 38. (Italics added to original for emphasis.)

31. *Minutes*, Second General Synod, p. 175.

32. Cf. reference on pages 102-5.

33. *Minutes*, Third General Synod, p. 129.

34. Ibid., p. 84.

35. *Minutes*, Uniting General Synod, June 25-27, 1957, p. 41.

36. *Minutes*, Third General Synod, p. 57.

37. See the opening presentation at the Fourth General Synod, *Minutes*, General Synod, July 4-11, 1963, pp. 11-13.

38. Ibid., pp. 132-35.

39. *Minutes*, Fifth General Synod, July 1-7, 1965, p. 232.

40. Ibid., p. 221. Mr. Ayers was president of the Commonwealth Edison Company and of the Chicago Missionary Society.

41. *Minutes*, Sixth General Synod, June 22-29, 1967, p. 175.

42. Ibid., p. 176. (Italics added here for emphasis.)

43. The mimeographed memorandum is on file in the Archives, Eden Theological Seminary, Folder 41-2C2, Min 66 (1).

44. Gibson Winter, *Religious Identity* (New York: Macmillan, 1968), p. 10. (It is noteworthy that this book was published at the very time of the debate within the United Church.)

45. Ibid., p. 35. (Italics added here for emphasis.)

46. Ibid., p. 42.

47. Ibid., p. 3. It should also be noted that in 1968 the Methodist Church and the Evangelical United Brethren Church were merged as the United Methodist Church and developed a pattern of organization bearing out Winter's contention.

48. *Report of the Committee on Structure*, February 1, 1969, p. 16.

49. Ibid., pp. 17-18.

50. *Minutes*, Fourth General Synod, p. 39. (Italics added for emphasis.)

51. Papers of Ben Mohr Herbster, George Arents Research Library, Syracuse University, Syracuse, New York, M70-260.

52. This consultation, headed for four years by Benjamin R. Andrews, Jr., chairman of the Hymnal Committee (UCC), produced a list of ecumenical hymns, which were published as such for the first time in the new *Hymnal of the United Church of Christ* in 1974.

CHAPTER 4 IN SEARCH OF IDENTITY

1. The Committee for Racial Justice Now was replaced by the Commission for Racial Justice in the reorganization following the 1969 General Synod.

2. Ben M. Herbster was the choice of the Nominating Committee in 1961. Many Evangelical and Reformed people felt that two candidates should be named, while the Congregational Christian practice had been in the manner of calling a minister, that is, presenting one name for election. As a result, James E. Wagner, who had served as co-president for four years with Fred Hoskins, was nominated from the floor.

3. At the 1969 General Synod the Colorado Conference delegates introduced a resolution asking the synod's attention to the plight of Mexican Amer-

icans, Puerto Ricans, and Indians—all groups that became militant in succeeding years. Cf. *Minutes*, Seventh General Synod, 1969, p. 127.

4. For helpful discussions of these losses two writers are important. Concerning "loss of place," see Martin E. Marty, *Second Chance for American Protestants* (New York: Harper & Row, 1963); "loss of certainty" is discussed in Sydney E. Ahlstrom's essay "The 1960's: Radicalism in Theology and Ethics," in James M. Gustafson, ed., *The Annals* (Philadelphia: American Academy of Political and Social Science, January 1970).

5. *Herald*, editorial report, August 1969, p. 7.

6. No fewer than ten concerns were introduced by the Council for Social Action and included South Africa, the Portuguese Colonies, the Biafran-Nigerian War, Vietnam, housing, homosexuals, Selective Service System, cost of government, amnesty, and gun control. Cf. *Advance Reports*, Seventh General Synod, 1969, pp. 237-59.

7. *Herald*, August 1969, p. 20.

8. *Minutes*, Seventh General Synod, 1969, pp. 177-80.

9. The phrase "conglomerate of autonomies" was attributed to a conference executive in remarks to the 1971 General Synod by Francis X. Pirazzini, minister of Central Atlantic Conference. See *Minutes*, Eighth General Synod, 1971, p. 47.

10. See *Report of the Committee on Structure*, United Church of Christ, New York, February 1, 1969.

11. See reference to letter of William L. Rest addressed to North Illinois Synod, note #26, chapter 3.

12. *Report of the Committee on Structure*, p. 17. Unless otherwise indicated, other quotations in this section are taken from the same page of the *Report*.

13. Ibid., p. 28.

14. Gibson Winter, *Religious Identity* (New York: Macmillan, 1968), p. 12.

15. These figures were taken from the Treasurer's Reports in the *Minutes* of the General Synod (UCC) for 1963 through 1975.

16. An aspect of the increasing financial needs of the Executive Council was the growing ecumenical involvement of the church in COCU, the World Council, and the National Council.

17. See papers of Truman B. Douglass, George Arents Research Library, Syracuse University, Syracuse, New York.

18. Robert V. Moss brought comparatively different qualifications to the presidency. He was not out of the parish but the academic community. He had a Ph.D. in New Testament studies and had served as president of Lancaster Theological Seminary and of the American Association of Theological Schools. Although active in denominational concerns, he had not held any position near the top echelons of the church.

19. *Minutes*, Seventh General Synod, p. 253.
20. Ibid., p. 253. (Italics added for emphasis.)
21. *Minutes*, Eighth General Synod, 1971, p. 18.
22. Avery Dulles, S.J., *Models of the Church* (Garden City, N.Y.: Doubleday, 1974), p. 57.
23. *Minutes*, Eighth General Synod, p. 17.
24. The Review Committee procedure had been standard practice in the Evangelical and Reformed Church and represented the principle that all agencies of the church were subordinate to the General Synod.
25. *Minutes*, Eighth General Synod, p. 19.
26. Ibid., pp. 20-21.
27. Ibid., p. 73.
28. The AMA was a corporate entity within the Board for Homeland Ministries and handled trust funds for six Black colleges.
29. *Minutes*, Eighth General Synod, p. 60.
30. Ibid., pp. 208-9.
31. Ibid., p. 212.
32. *Herald*, December 1971, p. 45, quoted by J. Martin Bailey.
33. Ibid.
34. Ibid., p. 51.
35. *Minutes*, Ninth General Synod, 1973, p. 37.
36. The term "Office" to designate agencies of specific responsibility represented an effort to give a more explicit indication of the agency relationship to the General Synod and the Executive Council. It underplays autonomy and accentuates activity coordinated with the major objectives of the denomination.
37. *Minutes*, Tenth General Synod, 1975, p. 45.
38. Ibid., p. 76.
39. "Research Summary, Survey of UCC National and Conference Leadership," *Advance Materials*, Section II, Tenth General Synod, 1975.
40. *Minutes*, Eighth General Synod, pp. 129-30. The force of General Synod pronouncements varied. They were defined by the 1963 General Synod: "A pronouncement is a declaration of Christian conviction on a matter of social principle, approved by the General Synod and directed to the churches and the public." (See *Advance Reports*, Fourth General Synod, 1963, p. 38.)
41. *Minutes*, Ninth General Synod, pp. 45-46.
42. Ibid., p. 46.
43. Ibid., p. 57.
44. Ibid., p. 19.
45. See *Herald*, December 1971, p. 45.
46. Letter of July 7, 1975, addressed to all "Congregations and Ministers of the United Church of Christ." (Italics added for emphasis.)
47. *Minutes*, Tenth General Synod, p. 124.

48. Ibid., pp. 124-25.
49. Winter, op. cit., p. 9.
50. See Dean M. Kelley, *Why Conservative Churches Are Growing* (New York: Harper & Row, 1972).
51. Ibid., p. 10.
52. *Herald*, May 1972, p. 7.
53. Ibid., p. 44. (Italics added for emphasis.)
54. *Advance Materials*, Section II, Tenth General Synod, p. 51.
55. Ibid., p. 52. (Italics added for emphasis.)
56. Thomas C. Campbell and Yoshio Fukuyama, *The Fragmented Layman* (Philadelphia: United Church Press, 1970), p. 194. Further use of this important book is made in chapter 5, "Why the United Church of Christ?"
57. *The UCC Directory of Black Churches and Ministers*, prepared in 1976 by the Black Church Development Program (a collaboration effort of the Commission for Racial Justice, the Office for Church Life and Leadership, and the Board for Homeland Ministries) lists 249 Black UCC churches and sixteen Congregational Christian churches.
58. The 1971 General Assembly of the United Presbyterian Church voted to withdraw from the Consultation. The 1973 Assembly reversed the decision.
59. Memorandum, *Minutes*, Executive Council, March 1972.
60. See *Herald*, July-August 1972, pp. 46-47.

CHAPTER 5   WHY THE UNITED CHURCH OF CHRIST?

1. Roger Shinn, *Unity and Diversity in the United Church of Christ* (Royal Oak, Mich.: Cathedral Publishers, 1972), p. 1.
2. H. Richard Niebuhr, *The Social Sources of Denominationalism* (New York: Henry Holt, 1929; Meridian, 1959).
3. Robert Lee, *The Social Sources of Church Unity* (Nashville: Abingdon Press, 1960), p. 17. (Italics added for emphasis.)
4. Douglas Horton, "Now the United Church of Christ," *The Christian Century*, June 12, 1957, p. 131.
5. Thomas C. Campbell and Yoshio Fukuyama, *The Fragmented Layman* (Philadelphia: United Church Press, 1970).
6. Ibid., p. 4.
7. Ibid., pp. 17-18.
8. Ibid., p. 197.
9. Ibid., pp. 96-97.
10. Ibid., p. 47. "More than half of the respondents are not 'birthright' members of the United Church of Christ."
11. John T. McNeill and James H. Nichols, *Ecumenical Testimony* (Philadelphia: Westminster Press, 1974), p. 149. The date of 1963 is erroneously given for the adoption of the Constitution and By-Laws. The date was

1960. They were declared in force in 1961. (Italics added for emphasis.)

12. See note #3, chapter 1.

13. H. Richard Niebuhr, *The Kingdom of God in America* (New York: Harper & Bros., 1937), p. ix. (Italics added for emphasis.)

14. Sydney E. Ahlstrom, *A Religious History of the American People* (New Haven: Yale University Press, 1972), p. 116.

15. John Calvin, *Institutes of the Christian Religion* (Philadelphia: Presbyterian Board of Christian Education, 1930), Bk. III, 7, 1.

16. Cf. Perry Miller, *Errand into the Wilderness* (2d ed.; Cambridge: Harvard University Press, 1964), pp. 2-3.

17. Campbell and Fukuyama, op. cit., pp. 212-15.

18. Ibid., p. 214.

19. John Winthrop, "A Model of Christian Charity," quoted by H. Shelton Smith, Robert T. Handy, Lefferts A. Loetscher, *American Christianity*, Vol. I, 1607-1820 (New York: Charles Scribner's Sons, 1960), p. 101. (Spelling has been modernized but punctuation is unchanged.)

20. Leonard J. Trinterud, "Origins of Puritanism," *Church History*, XX, 1951. The difference to which Trinterud refers is exhibited in those who viewed the covenant as a social contract that could be voided if either party failed to fulfill its part. This led to revolt and separatism and to a view of the covenant as a protection of the individual and his/her rights rather than a protection for the community.

21. Niebuhr, *The Kingdom of God in America*, op. cit., p. 98.

22. Cf. 2 Corinthians 5:11—6:2.

23. Cf. John T. McNeill, *Unitive Protestantism* (Richmond: John Knox Press, 1964), especially chapters IV and V. McNeill, in a scholarly fashion, dispels many of the popular misconceptions about Protestantism as a divisive movement. It should be noted further that Martyr and á Lasco spent much time in England and were influential among the Puritans.

24. Ibid., p. 177.

25. *A History of the Evangelical and Reformed Church*, ed. David Dunn (Philadelphia: Christian Education Press, 1961), p. 14. (Italics added for emphasis.)

26. Bard Thompson and others, *Essays on the Heidelberg Catechism* (Philadelphia: United Church Press, 1963), p. 31.

27. Ibid., p. 35. (Italics added for emphasis.)

28. Carl E. Schneider, *The German Church on the American Frontier* (St. Louis: Eden Publishing House, 1939), p. 1. (Italics added for emphasis.) Used by permission of Eden Publishing House.

29. Cf. ibid., pp. 7-10.

30. Cf. ibid., pp. 10-14.

31. Ibid., p. 397. See also pp. 407-17.

32. Ibid., pp. 408-9.

33. Walter Brueggemann, *Ethos and Ecumenism, an Evangelical Blend* (St. Louis: Eden Publishing House, 1975), p. v. In conformity with my distinction between piety and pietism, I would prefer the former term instead of "an evangelical *pietism.*"

34. Charles Johnson, "Is Church Union Dead?" *A.D.*, March 1973, p. 47. (Italics added for emphasis.)

35. Albert Outler, "Ecumenism for Third-Generation Ecumenists," *Mid-Stream: An Ecumenical Journal,* October 1975, p. 530.

36. Willem A. Visser 't Hooft, Preface, in François Gerard, *The Future of the Church: The Theology of Renewal of Willem Adolf Visser 't Hooft* (Pittsburgh: Pickwick Press, 1974), p. ix. (Italics added for emphasis.)

37. Cf. Avery Dulles, S.J., *Models of the Church* (Garden City, N.Y.: Doubleday, 1974), p. 138.

38. Cf. McNeill and Nichols, op. cit., p. 177.

39. Quoted in ibid., p. 182. (Italics added for emphasis.)

40. I am much indebted to John T. McNeill and James H. Nichols for the discussion of the Evangelical Alliance.

41. I am grateful to the library and the archivist at Lancaster Theological Seminary for the privilege of working through a mass of uncataloged material left by Dr. Richards. From that I have gleaned this view of Richards' ecumenical concern.

42. Everett C. Parker, ed., *Crisis in the Church* (Philadelphia: United Church Press, 1968), pp. 5-6. (Italics added for emphasis.)

CHAPTER 6   FROM MOVEMENT TO DENOMINATION: THE CONGREGATIONAL CHRISTIAN STORY

1. H. Shelton Smith, Robert T. Handy, and Lefferts A. Loetscher, *American Christianity*, 1607-1820 (New York: Charles Scribner's Sons, 1960), I, 82. This two-volume work is a treasure of source material. See also Edmund S. Morgan, *Visible Saints: The History of a Puritan Idea* (New York: New York University Press, 1963); Perry Miller, *Orthodoxy in Massachusetts 1630-1650* (New York: Harper & Row, Harper Torchbook edition, 1970); Douglas Horton, *Congregationalism: A Study in Church Polity* (London: Independent Press, 1952).

2. Morgan, op. cit., pp. 13-14.

3. Ibid., p. 12.

4. Smith, Handy, Loetscher, op. cit., p. 84. (Italics added for emphasis.)

5. John T. McNeill, *The History and Character of Calvinism* (New York: Oxford University Press, 1954), p. 336.

6. Cf. Smith, Handy, Loetscher, op. cit., pp. 84-87.

7. Ibid., pp. 90-91.

8. See William T. Davis, ed., *Bradford's History of Plymouth Plantation* (New York, 1908).

9. See Smith, Handy, Loetscher, op. cit., pp. 99-102.

10. Quoted in ibid., p. 102.

11. Ibid., pp. 95-96.

12. Ibid., p. 92.

13. Morgan, op. cit., pp. 31-32.

14. Ibid., pp. 77-78.

15. Smith, Handy, Loetscher, op. cit., p. 84.

16. Cf. Miller, op. cit.

17. Cf. Williston Walker, *The Creeds and Platforms of Congregationalism* (New York: Charles Scribner's Sons, 1893).

18. Morgan, op. cit., pp. 80-88.

19. See Smith, Handy, Loetscher, op. cit., pp. 103-6.

20. Ibid., p. 112.

21. Cf. Morgan, op. cit., p. 102.

22. The complete text is reproduced in Smith, Handy, Loetscher, op. cit., pp. 129-40.

23. For original documents relating to these efforts, see ibid., pp. 197-229.

24. Sydney E. Ahlstrom, "The Saybrook Platform: A 250th Anniversary Retrospect," *Bulletin of the Congregational Library*, Part I, October 1959, Vol. 11, No. 1, Boston. (Part II, January 1960, Vol. 11, No. 2, should also be considered.)

25. Cf. Smith, Handy, Loetscher, op. cit., pp. 226-27, especially Articles II, V, VII.

26. Cf. Walker, op. cit., pp. 465-95, for a complete discussion. Also Smith, Handy, Loetscher, op. cit., pp. 374-92, for a discussion of the *Proposals* and Wise's response.

27. Cf. Henry May, *The Enlightenment in America* (New York: Oxford University Press, 1976).

28. Sydney E. Ahlstrom, *A Religious History of the American People* (New Haven: Yale University Press, 1972), p. 288.

29. Cf. Perry Miller, *Jonathan Edwards* (Cleveland: World Publishing Co., 1964).

30. Smith, Handy, Loetscher, op. cit., p. 315. (Italics added for emphasis.)

31. Quoted in Winthrop Hudson, *The Great Tradition of the American Churches* (New York: Harper & Bros., 1953; Harper Torchbook edition, 1963), p. 65.

32. Ahlstrom, *A Religious History*, op. cit., p. 458.

33. Cf. Samuel Pearson, "From Church to Denomination," *Church History*, Vol. XXXVIII, 1969, pp. 86-87.

34. Cf. Charles C. Merrill, *The State Conference* (Boston: Pilgrim Press, 1948), for the story of this development.

35. Gaius Glenn Atkins and Frederick L. Fagley, *History of American Congregationalism* (Boston: Pilgrim Press, 1942), p. 196.

36. Conrad Wright dates the liberal movement that produced Unitarianism from 1735 to 1805. See his *The Beginnings of Unitarianism in America* (Boston: Starr King Press, 1955), p. 3.

37. Atkins and Fagley, op. cit., pp. 131-32.

38. Cf. Walker, op. cit., pp. 530-31, for the full text of the *Plan of Union*.

39. For the full discussion see *Debates and Proceedings of the National Council*, Boston, Massachusetts, June 14-24, 1865, but also the helpful notes of Walker, op. cit., pp. 553-69.

40. Quoted in Walker, op. cit., p. 568. (Italics added for emphasis.)

41. Quoted in ibid., p. 573.

42. Quoted in ibid., p. 576.

43. Cf. Alice Felt Tyler, *Freedom's Ferment, Phases of American Social History from the Colonial Period to the Outbreak of the Civil War* (Minneapolis: University of Minnesota Press, 1944).

44. Cf. Martin E. Marty, *Righteous Empire: The Protestant Experience in America* (New York: Dial Press, 1970).

45. Dr. De Boer's dissertation on "The Role of Afro-Americans in the Origin and Work of the American Missionary Association: 1839-1877," was presented for her Ph.D. at Rutgers University, 1973, and was made available by courtesy of Wesley Hotchkiss, general secretary of the Division of Higher Education of the United Church Board for Homeland Ministries. I am much indebted to Dr. De Boer and also to Dr. Hotchkiss.

46. Ahlstrom, *A Religious History*, op. cit., p. 694.

47. Horace Bushnell, "Barbarism the First Danger," quoted in Robert T. Handy, *A Christian America* (New York: Oxford University Press, 1971), p. 27. An insightful interpretation of Bushnell is given by Barbara M. Cross, *Horace Bushnell: Minister to a Changing America* (Chicago: University of Chicago Press, 1958).

48. The *Minutes*, National Council of Congregational Churches, 1907, provide important perspectives on this development.

49. Atkins and Fagley, op. cit., p. 306, call attention to the fact that the term Congregational applied to those voluntary societies whose "constituency and control are substantially Congregational."

50. Ibid., p. 309.

51. Cf. ibid. for a fuller discussion of this. Most important, however, are the *Minutes* of the National Council for each of the biennial sessions. I found the *Report of the Committee of Nineteen* (1915) to be especially valuable. It is in the Congregational Library, Boston.

52. Atkins and Fagley, op. cit., p. 342.

53. George Eisenach, *A History of the German Congregational Churches in the United States* (Yankton, S.D.: Pioneer Press, 1938). This book, along with the records of the American Home Missionary Society in the Congregational Library in Boston, provides details of a fascinating story.

54. This department was later renamed the German Institute. In 1916 it was moved to Redfield, South Dakota and merged there with the theological department of Redfield College. In 1932 the General Conference closed Redfield and moved the School of Theology to Yankton College, Yankton, South Dakota. It is now part of United Theological Seminary of the Twin Cities.

55. William T. Scott, *A Brief History of the Christian Church*, Elon College, North Carolina, 1956, p. 3.

56. Ibid., p. 4. In 1975 D.T. Stokes and William T. Scott published *A History of the Christian Church in the South*, Elon College, North Carolina, a definitive history of the movement.

57. William T. Scott, unpublished paper entitled "Dedicated to Union," on file in the *Merger Materials*, Congregational Library, Boston. No date, but probably prepared in the early 1950s.

58. Cf. Smith, Handy, Loetscher, op. cit., pp. 465-69.

59. Scott, *A Brief History*, op. cit., p. 4.

60. Stokes and Scott, op. cit., pp. 71-72.

61. Ibid., p. 135.

62. Ibid., p. 145.

63. See chapter 5 for the discussion of this organization.

64. Stokes and Scott, op. cit., pp. 97-98.

65. Ibid., pp. 232-33.

66. Peter T. Forsyth, *The Church and the Sacraments* (London: Independent Press, 1953), pp. 68-69. (This book was prepared from Forsyth's 1917 "Lectures on the Church and the Sacraments.")

CHAPTER 7 FROM THE CONTINENT OF EUROPE:
THE EVANGELICAL AND REFORMED STORY

1. See James I. Good, *History of the Reformed Church in the United States, 1725-1792* (Reading, 1899); Joseph H.G. Dubbs, *The Reformed Church in Pennsylvania* (Lancaster, 1902). Good's work has often been discounted because of his anti-Mercersburg bias, but his factual account of early Reformed history is invaluable. I have drawn freely on these books.

2. The Reformed faith tradition was discussed at length in chapter 5.

3. Good, op. cit., pp. 65-66.

4. Ibid., p. 112.

5. James I. Good cites a "providential" coincidence in the fact that at the same time Boehm was seeking ordination from the Classis of Amsterdam, the

Palatinate Consistory at Heidelberg had officially requested the South Holland Synod to take the Pennsylvania German Reformed Church under its care. Op. cit., p. 135.

6. Good, op. cit., pp. 295-309. Good cites some confusion in Holland that resulted from the fact that both the Classis of Amsterdam of the North Holland Synod and the South Holland Synod were involved. Slow communication between these bodies was a handicap too.

7. *Kirchen-Ordnung of 1748*, translated by Henry T. Spangler, from the Archives at Lancaster Theological Seminary. (Italics added for emphasis.)

8. William Toth remarks: "Coetus took a positive approach to the problem by instituting the *censura morum*, a kind of moral self-examination among the ministers; by strictly requiring proper ordination, election, and installation steps in every case." "On the Frontiers of a New Land," *A History of the Evangelical and Reformed Church*, ed. David Dunn (Philadelphia: Christian Education Press, 1961), p. 41.

9. Philip Schaff, writing about this in the midnineteenth century, contended that these Germans "have not naturally the talent for organization, and, under the State-church system of their fatherland, did not learn how to take care of themselves." *America* (Cambridge: Harvard University Press, 1961), p. 145. From that perspective the accomplishments of the Coetus are all the more remarkable. It is important to note, however, that Schaff was referring to "organization," not to "order." In matters of "order" by Word, Sacrament, and discipline, these German Reformed people were well equipped and thus did lay a foundation for organization.

10. Good, op. cit., pp. 435-59. These charity schools produced some controversy since a few of the German people saw them as an effort of the Crown to anglicize them.

11. Ibid., p. 458.

12. Toth, op. cit., pp. 50-51.

13. Good, op. cit., p. 616.

14. Ibid., p. 664.

15. J.H. Dubbs, *Historic Manual of the Reformed Church in the United States* (Lancaster, 1885), pp. 253-57.

16. Kenneth Scott Latourette, *The Great Century in Europe and the United States of America, A.D. 1800—A.D. 1914*, Vol. IV in *A History of the Expansion of Christianity* (New York: Harper & Bros., 1941).

17. See Winthrop Hudson, *Religion in America* (2d ed.; New York: Scribner's, 1973), p. 131.

18. Dubbs, op. cit., p. 253.

19. David Dunn, ed., *A History of the Evangelical and Reformed Church*, op. cit., p. 60.

20. James I. Good, *History of the Reformed Church in the United States in the Nineteenth Century* (New York: Board of Publication of the Reformed Church in America, 1911), chapters I and II.

21. Quoted by Dunn, op. cit., p. 63. It is of interest that a primary concern voiced here is the welfare of "ministers" and the maintenance of a bond between them. In actuality, a classis in the Reformed system was as much a bond for the laity (in this case the elders) of the scattered churches as it was for the clergy.

22. Bard Thompson and others, *Essays on the Heidelberg Catechism* (Philadelphia: United Church Press, 1963), p. 58. See references of chapter V.

23. Cf. H. Shelton Smith, Robert T. Handy, and Lefferts A. Loetscher, *American Christianity*, 1820-1960 (New York: Charles Scribner's Sons, 1960), II, 66-74.

24. Ibid., p. 74.

25. See note #3, chapter 1.

26. Thompson and others, op. cit., p. 74.

27. See Claude Welch, *Protestant Thought in the Nineteenth Century*, 1799-1870 (New Haven: Yale University Press, 1972), I, 16. See also pp. 226-33.

28. Schaff, *America*, with Introduction by Perry Miller, op. cit.

29. Ibid., p. 95.

30. Ibid., p. 94.

31. Welch, op. cit., p. 228.

32. Discomfort with the "mourner's bench" and "new measures" tendencies in the Ohio Synod led in 1846 to an eight-year separation of the Columbiana Classis. It was known as the Herbruck Synod after Peter Herbruck, its chief spokesman. Josias Friedli says that this had a salutary effect on the Ohio Synod. See Dunn, op. cit., p. 123.

33. I am much indebted to Reinhard Ulrich for his exceptionally penetrating discussion of these issues in his unpublished doctoral dissertation: "The School of Prophets, a Study of the Cultural and Theological Patterns in the Establishment and Early Development of the German Reformed Mission House in Wisconsin," written under the Faculty of Graduate Studies of the Lutheran School of Theology, Chicago, 1962.

34. See also Reinhard Ulrich's four chapters in Eugene C. Jaberg, et al., *A History of Mission House-Lakeland* (Philadelphia: Christian Education Press, 1962).

35. Dunn, op. cit., pp. 107-8.

36. Carl E. Schneider, *The German Church on the American Frontier* (St. Louis: Eden Publishing House, 1939), p. v. Used by permission of Eden Publishing House.

37. Ibid., p. 38.

38. Ibid., pp. 85 ff. The Hartford group financed the effort out of concern about increasing Roman Catholic work among the Germans.

39. Ibid., pp. 99-100.

40. Ibid., p. 109.

41. Roger Shinn, *Unity and Diversity in the United Church of Christ* (Royal Oak, Mich.: Cathedral Publishers, 1972), p. 5.

42. John S. Whale, *The Protestant Tradition* (New York: Cambridge University Press, 1955), p. 113.

43. Theophil W. Menzel, "Frontier Beginnings," in Dunn, op. cit., p. 175.

44. See Walter Brueggemann, *Ethos and Ecumenism, an Evangelical Blend* (St. Louis: Eden Publishing House, 1975), p. 2.

45. Schneider, op. cit., p. 417.

46. Cf. Welch, op. cit., p. 232.

47. Ibid., p. 232.

48. Schneider, op. cit., p. 396.

49. *Acts and Proceedings*, General Synod of the Reformed Church in the U.S. 1911-1919. Archives, Lancaster Theological Seminary.

50. Carl E. Schneider, "Journey into Union," in Dunn, op. cit., p. 281.

51. See *The Messenger* issues of that period, especially of January 8, 1931, pp. 6-7.

52. See correspondence between L.W. Goebel and C.F. Locher in the Louis W. Goebel files, folder 48-1, cor. 81. Archives, Eden Theological Seminary Library.

53. *Acts and Proceedings*, Uniting Synod of the Evangelical and Reformed Church, June 1934.

54. "Comments on the Constitution and By-Laws of the Evangelical and Reformed Church," unpublished paper in the George W. Richards Collection, Archives, Lancaster Theological Seminary.

55. See letter dated July 3, 1932, Louis W. Goebel files, op. cit. (Italics added for emphasis.)

56. Carl E. Schneider, "The Genius of the Reformed Church in the United States" (a Genetic Appraisal of her Union with the Evangelical Synod of North America), *The Journal of Religion*, January 1935, p. 27. (Italics added for emphasis.) Used by permission.

57. Ibid., p. 34.

58. Cf. George W. Richards, "Calvinism in the Reformed Churches of Germany," *Reformed Church Review*, April 1909.

59. Thompson and others, op. cit., p. 44.

60. Answer to question 54, "What do you believe concerning 'the Holy Catholic Church'?" *The Heidelberg Catechism with Commentary* (400th Anniversary Edition; Philadelphia: United Church Press, 1962), p. 97.

61. George W. Richards, "The Evangelical and Reformed Church," *Advance*, September 1, 1942, pp. 400 ff. (Italics added for emphasis.)

62. Quoted by Schneider, in Dunn, op. cit., p. 295. (Italics added for emphasis.)

63. James E. Wagner, "The New Witness—1940 to 1959" in ibid., p. 297.

CHAPTER 8   ASSESSMENT AND FORECAST

1. John T. McNeill and James H. Nichols, *Ecumenical Testimony* (Philadelphia: Westminster Press, 1974), p. 11.

2. John Macquarrie, *Christian Unity and Christian Diversity* (Philadelphia: Westminster Press, 1975), p. 46.

3. Lukas Vischer in *Mid-Stream*, Spring 1967, p. 5.

4. Paul Tillich, *Systematic Theology* (Chicago: University of Chicago Press, 1963), III, 172-73.

5. Daniel Jenkins, *The Strangeness of the Church* (Garden City, N.Y.: Doubleday, 1955), p. 74.

6. Cf. Keith Bridston, *Church Politics* (New York: World Publishing Co., 1969), pp. 47-72, for a discussion of these concepts.

7. Jenkins, op. cit., p. 75.

8. *Minutes*, Ninth General Synod, 1973, p. 98.

CHAPTER 9   SHAPED AND BEING SHAPED

1. Minutes, Uniting General Synod, 62, 65, 78.

2. The UCC Constitution has never had a separate article on faith as did the Basis of Union. Its reference to the faith of the church is limited to Paragraph 2 of the Preamble. The original Statement of Faith is on pages 75–76 of the 1959 General Synod Minutes. It was modified by President Robert Moss in response to demands for more-inclusive language.

3. See Barbara Brown Zikmund, "But I Have Called You Friends: A Theology for the Laity in the United Church of Christ," Minutes, 1977 General Synod, 129–36.

4. OCLL *Church Leaders Bulletin*, no. 35, 1988.

5. Many Christians do not recognize that worship resources and Christian education curricula are based upon theological beliefs. One of the best discussions of this idea can be found on pages 20–23 of Arthur G. Clyde, "The Language of *The New Century Hymnal*," in *The New Century Hymnal Companion* (Cleveland, Ohio: The Pilgrim Press, 1998).

6. Chapter 2 of Louis H. Gunnemann, *United and Uniting* (New York: United Church Press, 1987), provides excellent background for this discussion. He describes the ecumenical vision of both the Congregational and Christian Churches and the Evangelical and Reformed Church that led them to unite with each other and look forward to further mergers.

7. Ibid., 160.

8. Minutes, 1979 General Synod, 55.

9. The entire report of the steering committee is worth reading. It is in the Minutes, 1985 General Synod, 165–73. This quote is found on page 167f.

10. Minutes, 1973 General Synod, 60.

11. Details about this history can be found in *United and Uniting*, 59–84. The resolution authorizing the covenant is in the 1981 Synod Minutes, 61f.

12. Ibid. This history is the subject of chapter 5, 85–109.

13. Ibid. Again, this part of the story is told in chapter 6, 110–32.

14. See Minutes, 1995 General Synod, 140–46, for "UCC Response to Churches in Covenant Communion."

15. See Minutes, 1997 General Synod, 14, for the full text. The last of the parties to full communion, the Evangelical Lutheran Church in America, approved the resolution in June 1998.

16. Minutes, Uniting General Synod, Appendix 22, 129, 131.

17. Both papers are reproduced in "Restructure in the UCC: A Report to the (Twenty-First) General Synod," E-1 to E-4 and F-1 to F-7. The full report of the committee to the 1985 Twentieth General Synod is found on pages 118–35 of that synod's minutes.

18. Minutes, Uniting General Synod, Appendix 3, 63.

19. Ibid., 79.

20. Report on Restructure to the Twenty-First General Synod, E-4.

21. Note the background paper, "A Mission Framework for the General Synod Committee on Structure," in the committee's report to the 1997 General Synod, E-1 to E-4.

22. The full text of the UCC Statement on Mission is found in Minutes, 1987 General Synod, 12. There are two other formal UCC Mission Statements: the Mission Statement of the 1969 Committee on Structure found in the Minutes of the 1969 Synod and the Mission Statement on Health and Welfare contained in the Report of the Advisory Commission on Health and Welfare to the 1985 General Synod (see page 103 of the 1985 Minutes).

23. John von Rohr, *The Shaping of American Congregationalism, 1620–1957* (Cleveland, Ohio: The Pilgrim Press, 1992), 307–8.

24. See Minutes, Uniting General Synod, Appendix 10, 82.

25. The full revised text of "The Call to Christian Action in Society" is found in Minutes, 1959 General Synod, Appendix 13a, 171–75.

26. Minutes, 1963 General Synod, 135.

27. See Minutes, 1993 General Synod, 38–42.

28. See Minutes, 1977 General Synod, 125.

·

BIBLIOGRAPHICAL NOTE

Although the reference notes identify many of the source materials for the first four chapters, some indication of the categories and their location should be helpful to those who may wish to pursue a particular facet of the story of the United Church.

At Lancaster Theological Seminary, Lancaster, Pennsylvania, the archives of the Evangelical and Reformed Historical Society hold the official files of the General Council (E&R), including the Minutes of the Committee on Closer Relations with Other Churches and the documents of the Reformed Church in the United States. The official United Church of Christ archives are also located there.

The Library at Eden Theological Seminary houses a large collection of materials pertaining to the entire union process, including the correspondence files of Dr. Louis W. Goebel. The Evangelical Synod archives are located there, as well as the James I. Good collection in the history of the Reformed Church in the United States.

The Congregational Library in Boston houses a vast collection of records and papers pertaining to the union, including all the significant anti-merger materials. The official files of the General Council of the Congregational Christian Churches are housed there. These include the important records of the Commission on Interchurch Relations and Christian Unity. The archives of the General Convention of the Christian Church are located at Elon College, North Carolina.

As noted elsewhere, the Library of the World Council of Churches in Geneva, Switzerland is the depository of a large body of materials collected by Hanns Peter Keiling.

The papers of Truman B. Douglass and Ben Mohr Herbster are cataloged in a special collection at the George Arents Research Library of Syracuse University, Syracuse, New York.

A major source of information is located in journal articles: *Advance* (CC), *The Messenger* (E&R), and the *United Church Herald* (UCC). Throughout the period leading to the union, from 1937 to 1957, and through the formative years of the United Church, many articles appeared in *The Christian Century*, an interdenominational journal.

Researchers will find four doctoral dissertations to be especially helpful. Two pertain to the union process. Reference has been made to Hanns Peter Keiling's *Die Entstehung der "United Church of Christ" (USA)*, with the subtitle: *Fallstudie einer Kirchenunion unter Berücksichtigung des Problems der Ortsgemeinde*, published by Lettner-Verlag of Berlin in 1969. Keiling's *The Formation of the United Church of Christ (USA): A Bibliography* was published by the Clifford E. Barbour Library of Pittsburgh Theological Seminary. Alan Bowe Peabody's "A Study of the Controversy in Congregationalism Over Merger with the Evangelical and Reformed Church," written for the Graduate School of Syracuse University in 1964, is available through University Microfilms, Inc., Ann Arbor, Michigan.

The other two important dissertations were noted in the text and are not directly related to the union. Clara Merritt De Boer's dissertation on "The Role of Afro-Americans in the Origin and Work of the American Missionary Association: 1839-1877" was written for the Graduate School of Rutgers University in 1973. A copy is also available through the Board for Homeland Ministries. Reinhard Ulrich has written the only known study of the German Reformed Church in the Midwest in his dissertation, "The School of the Prophets, A Study of the Cultural and Theological Patterns in the Establishment and Early Development of the German Reformed Mission House in Wisconsin." This was written for the Faculty of Graduate Studies of the Lutheran School of Theology in Chicago, 1962. It is also available from the library at Lancaster Theological Seminary.

INDEX

273

German immigration, 123, 127, 167-68, 175, 181-82
German piety, 178
German synods, 174-83
German theology, 179-80
German-Russians, 161
Gibbons, Paul E., 86
Gibbons, Ray, 15
Gibson, George, 21
Gladden, Washington, 158
Goebel, Louis W., 20-21, 29, 31-32, 34-35, 41, 46, 54, 192, 195
Graham, Billy, 14
Grauer, Gerhard W., 66, 69
Gray, Arthur D., 86
Great Awakening, First, 144, 147, 149, 174, 177
Great Awakening, Second, 121, 129, 150-51, 162-63, 174, 177
Grinnell General Council, 30
Guldin, Samuel, 170
Guptill, Nathanael M., 72
Gustafson, James M., 57

Haggard, Rice, 163
Half-Way Covenant, 143-44
Hammer, Paul L., 11
Harvard, 153, 158
Hastings, George B., 54
Heidelberg Catechism, 125-26, 169-70, 177, 179, 181-82, 193
Heimert, Alan, 118, 148
Herald, United Church, 59-60, 87, 104, 109
Herald of Gospel Liberty, 163
Herbster, Ben Mohr, 74, 77-78, 84-85
Heyer, Philip, 186
Hispanic Caucus, 101
Holland, 139-41, 171
Home Missions, Board for (CC), 54, 64, 160
Homeland Ministries, Board for, 54, 75, 84, 88, 90, 93, 96, 101, 157, 202
Homrighausen, Elmer, 20
Horton, Douglas, 20-21, 26-27, 29, 32, 34, 40-41, 43, 46, 49-50, 64, 83, 113-14
Hoskins, Fred, 19, 54, 63, 74
Hotchkiss, Wesley A., 11
Hultgren, Dayton, 10
Hungarian Reformed Church, 183

Hymnal Committee, 84
Hymnal of the United Church of Christ, The, 107

Identity (UCC), 60, 74, 84, 102-5
Inclusive language, 100-101
Independents, 138
Indian-Americans, 97
Indiana-Kentucky Conference, 10
Instrumentalities, 77-80, 91-93, 95, 107, 202
Interchurch Relations and Christian Unity, Commission on, 21, 25, 30-31
International Council of Congregational Churches, 83
International Missionary Council, 134
Irion, Andreas, 188
Issue Exploration Groups, 96

Jacob, Henry, 139, 141
Japanese-American Congregational Church, 101
Jenkins, Daniel, 199
Jewish question, 24
Johnson, Charles, 130
Joint Committee on Union, 21-22, 24-28
Jones, Abner, 162-63

Keck, F.A., 54
Keiling, Hanns Peter, 9-10
Kent State University, 94
Kirchen-Ordnung of 1748, 171
Kirchenverein, 126-29, 132, 186-89, 191
Korean War, 14

Lancaster Theological Seminary, 176
Language question, 175
Lay Life and Work, Council for, 75-76, 96, 98
Laymen's Fellowship (UCC), 61
Leadership Development, 96
League to Uphold Congregational Principles, 30
Lee, Robert, 113
Leyden, 139-40
Liberal evangelicalism, 23
Liberalism, 23
Life and Work
 Oxford Conference, 134
 Stockholm Conference, 134

Plymouth Colony, 22, 139-41
Plymouth Rock, 140, 168
Polity, 24, 33, 65
Presbyterian Life, 109
Presbyterianizing, 148
Presbyterians, 107, 116, 138, 146, 150, 152, 154, 190
Press, Samuel, D., 20-21, 190
Priesthood of all believers, 40
Protestant principle, 18
Puritan, 118-20, 125, 137
  Bay Puritans, 141-43
  English, 118-19
  faith, 118, 142-43
  movement, 118-19, 123, 126, 137-43
  tradition, 131

Racial
  crisis, 15, 78-79, 82
  discrimination, 78
  pluralism, 17
Racial Justice, Commission for, 82
Racial Justice Now, 78, 86
Randall, A.E., 25
Rauschenbusch, Walter, 158
Realignment of Conference and Synodical Boundaries, 76
Reformed
  churches 124-25, 128-29, 132, 173
  ecclesiology, 91, 191
  faith, 121, 124, 149, 195
  movement, 122
  tradition, 66, 118, 120, 122, 148, 155, 171, 191
Reformed Church in the United States, 20, 22
Reformed people
  Dutch, 172
  German, 22, 123-24, 167-68, 184
  Hungarian, 167
  Swiss, 124, 131, 138, 167-68
Reforming synod, 143
Religious ethos and style, 22-23
Religious revival, 14
Republican Methodists, 162
Rest, William L., 71, 89
Revivalism (see *Great Awakening*), 144, 178
Rhineland
  area, 125, 127
  reformers, 120, 124, 126

Richards, George W., 20-21, 25-27, 33, 35, 133, 190-92, 194-95
Rieger, Joseph, 185
Riess, Johann, 186
Robinson, John, 139
Rural-urban distribution, 23

St. Louis, 21
Saybrook
  Platform, 144-46, 148-49, 155
  Synod, 144, 146
Scandinavian immigration, 158
Schaff, Philip, 124, 132, 179-80, 188, 191, 193, 198
Schlatter, Michael, 171, 173
Schleiermacher, Friedrich, 128, 184
Schmid, Friedrich, 185
Schmucker, Samuel, 185
Schneider, Carl E., 44, 127-28, 183-84, 186, 188, 192-93
Schomer, Howard F., 68
Scots-Irish, 146
Scott, William T., 163-64
Scrooby, 139
Secularization, 16-17
Seminary issue, 175
Services of the Church, 107
Services of Word and Sacrament, 107
Sheares, Reuben A., 11
Shinn, Roger L., 111
Slavery, 132, 156-57, 164
Smith, H. Shelton, 137, 140
Social Action, 78
  Center for, 99
  Council for Christian, 54, 99
Social Gospel, 158
Solicitation, Collection and Disbursement of Funds, Committee on Methods of, 54, 75
South Africa, 82, 97
Spener, Philipp, 125
Spike, Robert W., 63, 65
Spragg, Howard E., 11
Statement of Faith, 52, 63, 68-69
  Commission to Prepare, 54, 69
Stewardship Council, 75-76, 104
Stoddard, Solomon, 144, 147
Stone, Barton W., 162-63
Stowe, David M., 11
Strong, Josiah, 158
Structure, 15

Structure, Committee on, 79-81, 89, 98, 200
Stuart, Moses, 154
Synods (E&R), 28, 30, 32

Taylor, Graham, 158
Telegram, 21
Templeman, Conrad, 170
Thatcher, Samuel, 154
Theological Commission, 98
Theological Education, Committee on, 98
Theological tradition, 23
Thompson, Bard, 126, 177, 193
Thompson, William M., 10
Thomson, David, 173
Thurneysen, Eduard, 20
Tillich, Paul, 198-99
Toth, William, 125-26
Trinterud, L.J., 120
Tripp, Thomas A., 23
Turbulent Sixties, 15

Union
    affinity for, 114, 116-17, 123, 127
    Conference on, 20, 190
    organic, 20, 28, 33, 133, 190
Unitarian, 153-54
Unite, will to, 27, 108, 116
United Brethren, 173, 177, 190
United Church in America, The, 26
United Church Ministers for Racial and Social Justice, 86, 88, 96
United Church of Christ, birth of, 13
United Churchmen for Change, 86, 88
United Evangelical Church, 128
United Presbyterian Church, 109
United Theological Seminary of the Twin Cities, 61
Uniting General Synod, 13-14, 51-56
Unity, Christian, 13-14, 16, 25, 108, 114, 129-36, 161, 163, 165-66, 189, 194-95, 197
    commitment to, 68, 72
Urbanization, 16
Urbanization Emphasis, 78, 82
Ursinus, Zacharias, 126

Van Vlecq, Paul, 170
Vatican Council II, 83, 131

Vaughn, Myra, 11
Vietnam, 82, 94
Vischer, Lukas, 198
Visser 't Hooft, Willem A., 131
Voluntary association, 16, 19
Voluntary societies, 132

Wagner, Jacob B., 95
Wagner, James E., 19, 33, 46-47, 49, 51, 54, 61, 74-75, 195
Walker, Raymond, 50
Wall, George W., 185-86
Ware, Henry, 154
Webber, Donald W., 79
Webster Groves, 21
Whiterabbit, Mitchell, 101
Wilder, Amos N., 25
Williams, J. Paul, 68
Winebrenner, John, 177
Winter, Gibson, 80, 103
Winthrop, John, 119, 140
Wise, John, 146-47
Women
    caucus, 100
    movement, 108
    Revolution, 100
    rights, 100
    status of in church and society, 97
    Task Force on, 100
Women's Fellowship (CC), 60-61
Women's Guild (E&R), 61
Woods, Leonard, 153-54
World Alliance of Reformed Churches, 83
World Council of Churches, 20, 83, 134
World Ministries, Board for, 54, 75, 84, 90, 201
World War II, 14, 24, 113
Worship, 106-7
    Commission on, 84, 106

Yale, 151, 158
Yankton College, School of Theology of, 61
Youth, 88, 93-94, 100
    caucus, 94
    Fellowship (E&R), 60

Zwingli, Ulrich, 124, 138
Zwinglian, 16, 124-26

277